DESIGN WITH CULTURE

DESIGN WITH CULTURE

Claiming America's Landscape Heritage

EDITED BY CHARLES A. BIRNBAUM *and* MARY V. HUGHES

A project supported by the
Cultural Landscape Foundation and the
National Park Service Historic Landscape Initiative

UNIVERSITY OF VIRGINIA PRESS
Charlottesville and London

UNIVERSITY OF VIRGINIA PRESS

Printed in the United States of America on acid-free paper

First published 2005

9 8 7 6 5 4 3 2 1

LIBRARY OF CONGRESS CATALOGING-IN-PUBLICATION DATA

Design with culture : claiming America's landscape heritage / edited by Charles A. Birnbaum and Mary V. Hughes.

p. cm.

"A project of the Cultural Landscape Foundation and the National Park Service Historic Landscape Initiative."

Eight of the papers were originally presented at a conference held in the Bronx, New York, on April 17 1999.

Includes bibliographical references and index.

ISBN 0-8139-2329-8 (cloth : alk. paper) – ISBN 0-8139-2330-1 (pbk. : alk. paper)

1. Landscape architecture–Conservation and restoration–United States–Congresses. 2. Historic sites–Conservation and restoration–United States–Congresses. 3. Landscape protection–United States–Congresses. I. Birnbaum, Charles A. II. Hughes, Mary V., 1952–

SB472.8.D47 2005

712′.0973–dc22 2004017412

Contents

Acknowledgments

This publication grew out of the Wave Hill conference that was held in the Bronx, New York, on April 17, 1999. Titled "If Only We Knew: Landscape Preservation in Context 1890–1950," the conference was sponsored by the National Park Service Historic Landscape Initiative, the CATALOG of Landscape Records in the United States at Wave Hill, the Cultural Landscape Foundation (CLF), and the Garden Club of America.

The symposium aimed to demonstrate that respect for our nation's landscape heritage is not a new concept. It was an integral part of the design and planning process implemented by American landscape practitioners early in the last century. In keeping with past symposia organized by the National Park Service, the CATALOG, and the CLF, this conference was designed to investigate previously unexplored aspects of American landscape history as they relate to making informed design and management decisions today.

Many individuals contributed to the conference and this publication. First, we are most grateful to Catha Grace Rambusch and Chris Panos at the CATALOG of Landscape Records in the United States at Wave Hill. This was the fifth NPS–Wave Hill collaboration, and both Catha and Chris, as always, provided organizational wizardry and business acumen. At the National Park Service, thanks go to Laurie Klinkel and Nancy Slade, who both provided valuable assistance, and to Bryan Mitchell and Sharon Park, who supported the symposium and this publication.

All eight of the papers presented at the Wave Hill conference are included herein. The editors are grateful that all the authors have been willing to respond to several rounds of peer reviews from both the editors and the University of Virginia Press outside reviewers. We are also grateful to David Streatfield, who has contributed an additional essay, "'Californio' Culture and Landscapes, 1894–1942: Entwining Myth and Romance with Preservation," thus broadening the scope of the volume to include the West Coast.

We want to thank the Graham Foundation for the Advanced Studies in the Fine Arts, which has generously provided the financial support to make this publication possible. Also we appreciate the efforts of the staff at the University of Virginia Press, who worked to make the project successful, especially our "frontline" editors, Boyd Zenner and Mark Mones, for their consummate professionalism and infinite patience throughout the manuscript preparation process. For the illustrations in the volume, we have relied on the knowledge and resourcefulness of many curators and librarians. In particular, we wish to express our gratitude to Pamela Seager at Rancho Los Alamitos; Marianne Martin at Colonial Williamsburg; Mary Daniels at the Frances Loeb Library, Harvard University; and Michele Clark at Frederick Law Olmsted National Historic Site for their assistance above and beyond the call of duty.

Finally we acknowledge the support of the Cultural Landscape Foundation, whose board members have sustained us through the long process of making this book with their enthusiasm and belief in the need to tell the story of our predecessors, who blazed the trail we follow today as modern-day advocates for preserving our nation's landscape heritage.

Introduction

Landscape Preservation in Context, 1890–1950

CHARLES A. BIRNBAUM AND MARY V. HUGHES

It can be said that history, like beauty, lies in the eye of the beholder, as preservation decisions reflect the values of the preservationist as much as the merits of that which is preserved. The eight essays in this volume illustrate how pioneering landscape architects, individual activists, and emerging national organizations considered historic landscape values in their planning and design projects during the years 1890–1950, offering a revisionist interpretation of this early work. Often decried as nostalgic and inauthentic when judged by contemporary standards, the work of early preservationists may instead be understood as a reflection of the cultural context within which they were created.

This early preservation work can also be seen as the precursor to issues and methodologies that have been rediscovered only in the last two decades. In revisiting the planning studies, executed works, and critical writings of this period, we can recognize an approach that foreshadows the preservation planning recommendations for documentation and treatment outlined over a half century later in National Park Service (NPS) cultural resources publications.[1] Instead of a steadily building momentum, interest in preservation atrophied during the era of modernist design in midcentury. When reinvigorated in the 1980s, landscape preservation became a specialized field, divorced from mainstream design professions. These examples offer a useful model of a holistic stewardship ethic that embraced the conservation of cultural, natural, and scenic resources, and demonstrate that historic preservation is a process that involves an imaginative *transformation* as much as a *conservation* of material culture.

ORIGINS OF THE LANDSCAPE PRESERVATION MOVEMENT

Harvard's program in landscape architecture, one of the first in the nation, promoted a generalist practice that embraced preservation issues along with other aspects of the new field, such as city planning and resource conservation. Referring to an epithet applied to one of Harvard's first professors of landscape architecture, Benjamin Marston Watson, Melanie Simo writes: "'An expert, yet not a specialist.' These words could describe a whole group of individuals who influenced the development of Harvard's program in landscape architecture at the turn of the twentieth century."[2] The Harvard faculty included former student Frederick Law Olmsted Jr. (1870–1957), and among its graduates (and often future faculty) were Charles W. Eliot II, John Nolen, Arthur Shurcliff, Morley Jeffers Williams, Percival Gallagher, James Frederick Dawson, Norman Newton, and Alden Hopkins. As a result of Harvard's landscape architecture program and the presence of several area firms (including the Olmsted firm and the offices of Warren Manning and John Nolen), the region became a focal point for professional practice that embodied a nature-culture stewardship ethic.

If Harvard is to be considered the geographical "home" to the early landscape preservation movement, it could be argued that Boston landscape architect Charles Eliot (1859–97) was the movement's "father." Eliot's writings in *Garden and Forest* magazine mirrored the eclectic interests of its publisher, Charles Sprague Sargent, and addressed such topics as horticulture, forestry, landscape design, landscape history, landscape management, professional practice, ethics, and the preservation of landscapes of scenic, natural, and historical significance. A representative list of his articles might include "The Sequoia Forests of the Sierra Nevada," "The Battle-ground in Prospect Park," "The Preservation of Washington's Birthplace," "A Great Battle Park" (about the field of Chickamauga), and "Bartram's Garden Today" (about the preservation of John Bartram's garden).

"View of notch, after opening," an illustration from Charles Eliot, Landscape Architect, *1901, drawn by Arthur Shurcliff. Note Shurcliff's characteristic shorthand "A^2S" in bottom right-hand corner.*

In 1893, Eliot joined forces with Frederick Law Olmsted Sr. and John Charles Olmsted to create the firm of Olmsted, Olmsted and Eliot. From then until his death four years later, his primary focus was the creation of a metropolitan park system for Boston and Cambridge. Perhaps his greatest and most lasting contribution, however, was the 1897 treatise *Vegetation and Scenery in the Metropolitan Reservations of Boston.* In this study, Eliot applied the theories he had articulated in *Garden and Forest* over the preceding seven years. The project's goal, he wrote, was to "invest public money in the purchase of the several metropolitan reservations to secure for the enjoyment of present and future generations such interesting and beautiful scenery as the lands acquired can supply." This work was, in essence, a laboratory that led to the development of an American landscape preservation ethic, and it is easy to imagine the influence it must have had on the firm's junior practitioners, such as thirty-seven-year-old Warren Manning and twenty-seven-year-old Arthur Shurcliff.

Twenty-five years later, these two would produce the landscape preservation benchmarks that guided the work of the next generation: Manning's *National Plan Study Brief* (1923) and Shurcliff's landscape restoration at

Colonial Williamsburg. Eliot's methodology can also be seen as an influence on the *California State Park Survey* undertaken by Frederick Law Olmsted Jr. in 1929. Later in this volume, Cynthia Zaitzevsky explores the broader impact of the Olmsted firm's planning studies on the field of historic preservation.

Eliot's 1897 obituary in *Garden and Forest* observed that his "greatest public service, was the organization of the Board of Trustees for the preservation of beautiful and historic places in Massachusetts. If Mr. Eliot did not originate this idea, he was, at least, the most active promoter of the scheme which is bearing good fruit not only in Massachusetts, but has been adopted in other States, and promises to save from desecration and defacement many spots in different parts of the country which deserve protection for their beauty or patriotic association."[3] Eliot biographer Keith Morgan suggests that his work "became a model for subsequent efforts such as the National Trust in Great Britain, and ultimately, the National Trust in the United States."[4]

Fueled by patriotic fervor and a nostalgia for simpler times, the preservation ethic of these early practitioners ran parallel to other cultural trends of the period, such as the Colonial Revival and Arts and Crafts movements. The former, in particular, gained momentum during the nation's anniversary celebration of the Philadelphia Centennial Exposition of 1876, which spawned numerous preservation efforts across the country, including the founding of the Association for the Preservation of Virginia Antiquities (APVA) in 1880.[5] These early examples of "proto-preservationism" are covered in essays by Phyllis Andersen on Charles Sprague Sargent's early work in the Mount Vernon landscape and by Elizabeth Hope Cushing in her evocative portrait of the cultural influences affecting the formative years of Arthur Shurcliff. David Streatfield broadens the geographic range of the discussion with his essay, "'Californio' Culture and Landscapes, 1894–1942." Catherine Howett reminds us as well of the contributions of active citizen groups, particularly women's garden clubs in the South.

The volume goes on to cover the full flowering of the landscape preservation movement in the 1920s and 1930s when the restoration of Colonial Williamsburg drew national attention to preservation issues and set a high aesthetic standard for such work around the country. As consulting land-

W. A. R. Goodwin, Robert Trimble, John D. Rockefeller Jr., and Arthur Shurcliff (left to right) reviewing plans at the Palace Green, Williamsburg, c. 1928. Background shows Matthew Whaley School, which was later replaced in this location by the reconstructed Governor's Palace. (Courtesy of Colonial Williamsburg Foundation)

scape architect to Colonial Williamsburg, Arthur Shurcliff (1870–1957) pioneered a methodology for documenting and treating historic landscapes that proved highly influential nationwide.

Lacking specific documentation for the colonial era gardens associated with the restored and reconstructed buildings, Shurcliff spent considerable time documenting surviving Virginia gardens from this period as well as their English precedents. He produced detailed measured drawings of extant garden features at forty-three sites, including Gunston Hall, Shirley Plantation, and Westover. These garden plans then served as the research basis and design precedent for the features and patterns of gardens he created in Williamsburg.[6] In 1929, with the work at Williamsburg already underway, he described his approach in an article illustrated with a series of measured plans: "In old work under restoration the free lance method leads to designs which are violently repugnant to everyone who has ever really studied old places and has learned to appreciate their individual charm and to understand the elements of planning upon which their layouts were

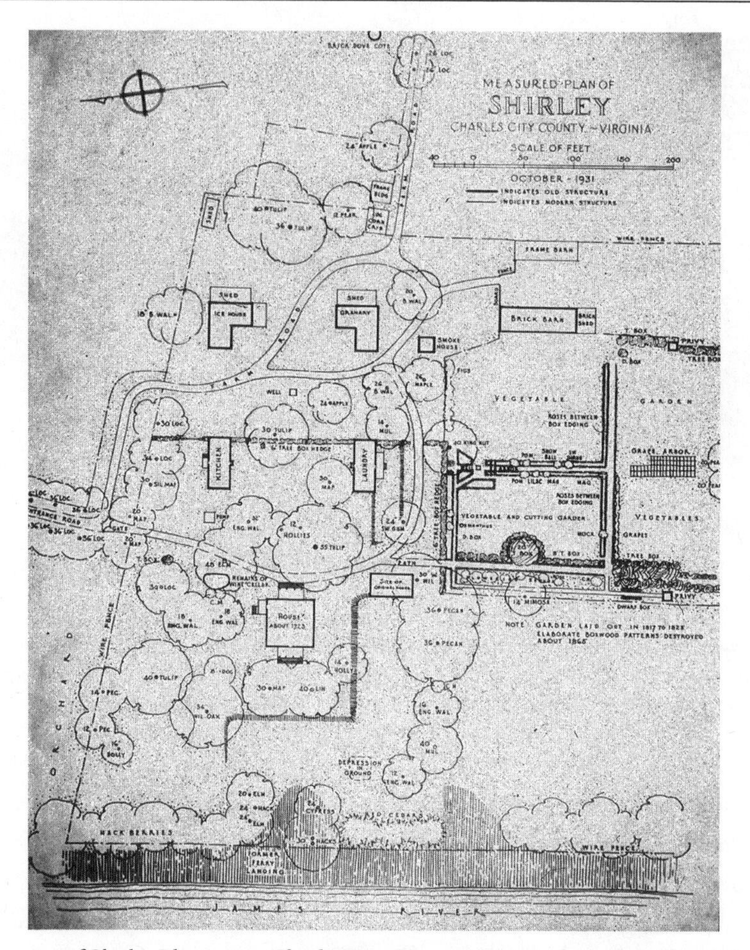

Drawing of Shirley Plantation, Charles City County, Virginia, by Arthur Shurcliff, c. 1930. (Courtesy of Colonial Williamsburg Foundation)

based. On the other hand, an adherence to these traditions in the case of new work in the South is not essential. In fact, a departure has at least one great advantage,—that the new work does not cumber the countryside with hackneyed endless repetition. The old work then stands unrivalled in its own field of historic beauty."[7]

The historical accuracy of these gardens, however, was hotly debated even by Shurcliff's contemporaries. Charles Hosmer cites numerous examples of these discussions, none more heated than at the Governor's Palace, where Shurcliff proposed creating a maze based on period practice in England, despite the fact that there was no evidence that any such feature had existed in the gardens of Virginia's governors. Both architect William Perry and staff historian Harold R. Shurtleff protested the use of such a conjectural feature, but in the end what Hosmer calls "the more or less poetic concepts proposed by the landscape architects" prevailed over the more strict application of known facts.[8] Thomas Beaman's essay explores a similar debate over the work of Morley Jeffers Williams (1886–1977), a landscape architect who used archaeological investigations as a tool to reveal the hidden history of site features.

At the same time, the War Department turned over its eastern memorials and battlefields to the NPS in 1933, thereby directing the attention of this agency toward landscape preservation alongside its conservation and scenic interests. The career of Thomas Vint (1894–1967), as described by Ethan Carr, chronicles the introduction of a preservation ethic into national park master plans. The movement matured and came of age in the New Deal, with the integration of vernacular Shenandoah Valley landscapes into

Shirley Plantation outbuildings. (Courtesy of Smithsonian Institution, Archives of American Gardens)

the design aesthetic of the Blue Ridge Parkway and President Roosevelt's own interest in the rehabilitation of the historic White House grounds. In his essay on Stanley W. Abbott (1908–75), Ian Firth discusses Abbott's role in broadening the Park Service's interest in historic landscapes to include the rural traditions of Scots-Irish settlement in the Shenandoah Valley. Meanwhile, in the nation's capital, President Roosevelt himself was taking a personal interest in the preservation of the White House grounds, as described in Cynthia Zaitzevsky's essay on Frederick Law Olmsted Jr.

In 1950, Stanley W. Abbott, then serving as a regional landscape architect for the NPS, published the article "Historic Preservation: Perpetuation of Scenes Where History Becomes Real," in which he summarized the national interest in historic preservation: "Indeed, the business of caring for places of history is a fascinating business, and, despite nature and human nature, a going business. Nowhere in the world, probably at no time in the world, have a people so young wanted things to hold onto more than we; nor has any people been prouder with better reason of a new tradition. It is worth a great deal to this nation if only a few can visit these places where history becomes real, and there catch something of the past which might otherwise go unfinished or even undiscovered."[9]

Even as Abbott's words predict the enduring appeal of preserving the nation's past, by 1950 enthusiasm for landscape preservation was, in fact, abating. This volume concludes with the advent of modernism on the design consciousness of America. If Harvard University's graduate program in landscape architecture played a leadership role in fostering the holistic approach to design and preservation fields, it also played a pivotal role in opening the schism between the two. In 1936 Joseph Hudnut became dean of the Graduate School of Design (GSD), the same year that Walter Gropius came to serve as professor of architecture. Jill Pearlman, in her recent paper on Hudnut, describes the dean's role in the purging of history books from the school's library collection.[10] Melanie Simo quotes the anti-historicist views of Dan Kiley, then a student in landscape architecture at the GSD: "One thing that set everyone back was that the history of landscape architecture course was so dull and so bad that we just hated anything to do with the past."[11] During the same time period, Kiley, along with fellow Harvard students Garrett Eckbo and James Rose, wrote three groundbreaking articles in the *Architectural Record* promoting a new approach to landscape design.[12] These articles as well as the publication of Christopher Tunnard's influential book *Gardens in the Modern Landscape* (1938) set a new course for the profession that divorced design from history.[13] According to historian John Dixon Hunt, this transformation was "a ludicrously cavalier treatment of history,"[14] but it became the standard view in many landscape architecture programs around the nation, which reduced the emphasis on the study of history in their curricula.

CONTEMPORARY PERSPECTIVE

From the perspective of the early twenty-first century, what do we see that interests us in the work of these early practitioners? The past two decades have seen renewed emphasis on historic landscape preservation, spearheaded by the NPS, which has incorporated historic landscapes into NPS cultural resources management policies as well as its publications for the general public, including the *Secretary of Interior Standards with Guidelines for the Treatment of Cultural Landscapes,* and a number of National Register bulletins on topics ranging from rural historic districts to battlefields and cemeteries. Landscape archaeology, too, has come of age, permitting a new level of accuracy in understanding the evolution of landscapes over time based on technologies for interpreting biotic remains as well as structural features, a boon Morley Williams could only have dreamed possible a half century earlier. Amid all this new technical expertise, historical information, and renewed professionalism in the landscape preservation field, are there any lessons to be learned from looking back at the work of our predecessors in the field, who labored without benefit of an existing road map?

First we can detect that this early work foreshadows to a surprising degree the preservation planning process recommended by professional standards today. We note early models of research and documentation such as those found in the ten garden books written between 1910 and 1921 by Grace Tabor (1873–1973), one of the first women to identify herself professionally as a landscape architect.[15] In 1913 she published *Old-Fashioned Gardening: A History and a Reconstruction.* Tabor was the first to recognize that

Grace Tabor, from Country Life in America, *March 1919.*

all old-fashioned gardens are not beautiful. She suggested that "by reason of their antiquity we have accepted their beauty as a matter of course."[16] Tabor goes on to recommend that these landscapes "be more rationally interpreted in the future." Although the book's plans are schematic and their rendering technique primitive, they are drawn to scale and accurately convey the spatial organization and land patterns of an assortment of garden types, such as "Spanish Gardens of the Semi Tropics," "New Amsterdam Housewives Gardens," and "Presidents' Gardens."

Concurrent with Tabor's publication, the American Academy in Rome began a fellowship program in landscape architecture in 1915, largely because of the efforts of landscape architects Ferruccio Vitale and Frederick Law Olmsted Jr.[17] Among the most influential products of the academy were the measured plans drawn by fellows and initially published in 1917 as the "first fruits" of the fellowship. Representative projects during these early years included the beautifully rendered, measured drawings and planting plans of Villa Torlonia at Frascati and the Villa Gamberaia at Settignano by Edward Lawson and the sections and plans of Villa Capponi at Arcetri, measured and drawn by Richard K. Webel.[18] The drawings of academy fellows were published over a twenty-year period in *Landscape Architecture* magazine, inspiring an interest in studying and recording the past.

In 1930, documentation of Horace's Sabine Villa moved beyond inventory and recordation to analysis and evaluation. Landscape architect Thomas D. Price worked closely with an Italian colleague to supervise the work of eleven men who discovered through archaeological investigation that "the restored wall in the northwest corner of the garden is not in accor-

Thomas D. Price, from "A Restoration of Horace's Sabine Villa," in Memoirs of the American Academy in Rome, *1932. (Courtesy of Charles A. Birnbaum)*

dance with the original layout." As a result of these findings, Price generated "an accurate pictorial representation of the villa in its original state." The report goes on to note that "the drawings are based on authentic evidence secured at the site, and, where the authentic evidence proved insufficient, imaginary elements derived from other contemporary sources have been employed."[19]

In 1932–33, Earle Draper (1893–1994), another academy fellow, returned home to publish "Southern Plantations," a two-part article in *Landscape Architecture.* Draper's comprehensive articles, which included a plan drawing of Middleton Place outside of Charleston, go beyond the conventional inventory of plants and other landscape features to suggest the presence of lost or remnant features—an early effort of historical site analysis for a landscape architect. For example, his plan of Middleton Place, and the plan and section for the Terraces that followed, document lost landscape features such as the "negro quarters" or the remnants of what was "originally a circular carriage turn bordered with cedars in front of the house." He observed that "the interest in the historic phase of southern gardens—or, if you will, archaeological research—within this last decade has had the effect not only of preserving old plantations for posterity but also of building up a sentiment of respect for tradition and for the successful efforts of the early pioneers along garden lines that is making the old-time garden atmosphere breathe again in modern gardens."[20]

The Historic American Buildings Survey (HABS), another New Deal program, began producing measured drawings of historic properties in Massachusetts in 1933. The landscape documentation initiative began in May 1935 when additional funding was secured for "the purpose of measuring historic and colonial gardens."[21] The field reconnaissance was undertaken by seven landscape architects, one civil engineer, and one surveyor.[22] These measured plans included standard landscape features—boundaries, structures, topography, vegetation (including caliper, genus, and species), circulation, furnishings, and so forth—but the work also contained early examples of chronological analysis. For example, old foundations or remnant structures, roads, paths, and furnishings were all noted, and the rendering techniques differentiated older landscape features from more modern ones. This practice can be seen as a precursor to the practice of recording the layers of a property's evolution in a series of period plans, as is common practice today.

The seven-sheet set of measured drawings for the John N. Cushing Place in Newburyport, Massachusetts, for example, contains a plethora of annotations. It records that "the property has been in the Cushing family since 1818. In 1905 the north section of the property was laid out as a flower bed and vegetable garden." Even small-scale furnishings such as edging and fencing materials are documented in photographs, plans, and detailed annotations. On one plan the following notes may be found: "the brick and rail edging around the flower beds in the garden were formerly box," or, on another, "the iron fence was erected about 1890 and it replaces a wood rail fence."

Another influential work that brought a higher level of analysis to historical documentation was *The Trees at Mount Vernon,* Charles Sprague Sargent's 1926 report to the Mount Vernon Ladies' Association, the subject of Phyllis Andersen's essay in this volume. As with the HABS work, Sargent

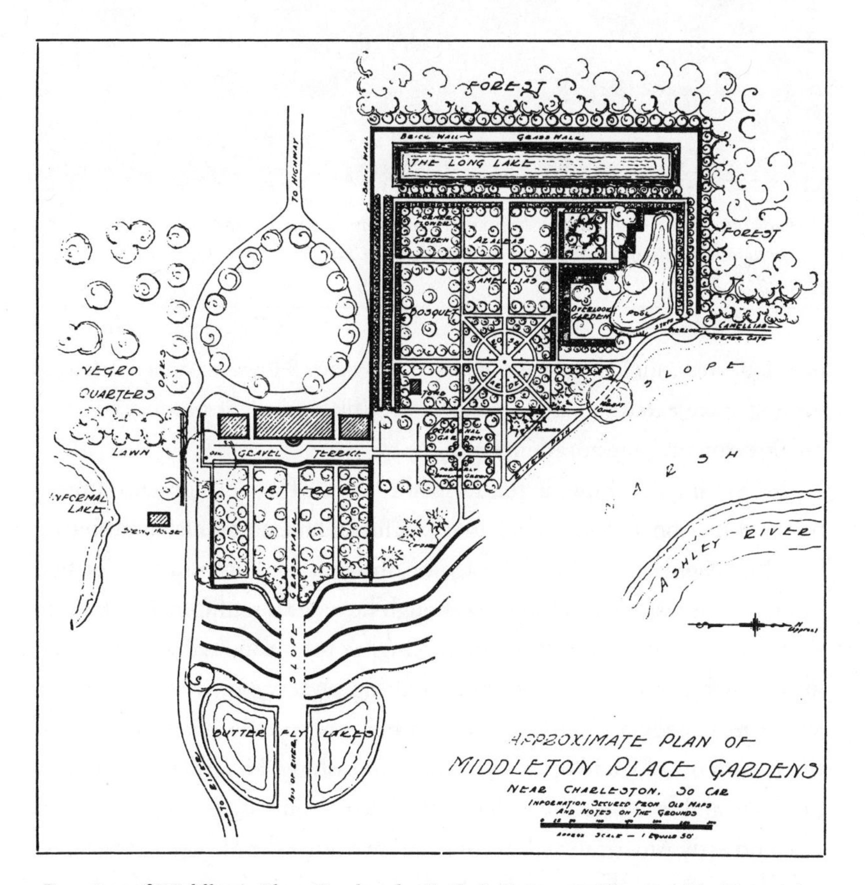

Drawing of Middleton Place Gardens by Earle S. Draper as illustrated in his article "Southern Plantations," which appeared in Landscape Architecture, *1932. (Courtesy of National Park Service,* Pioneers of Landscape Design *files)*

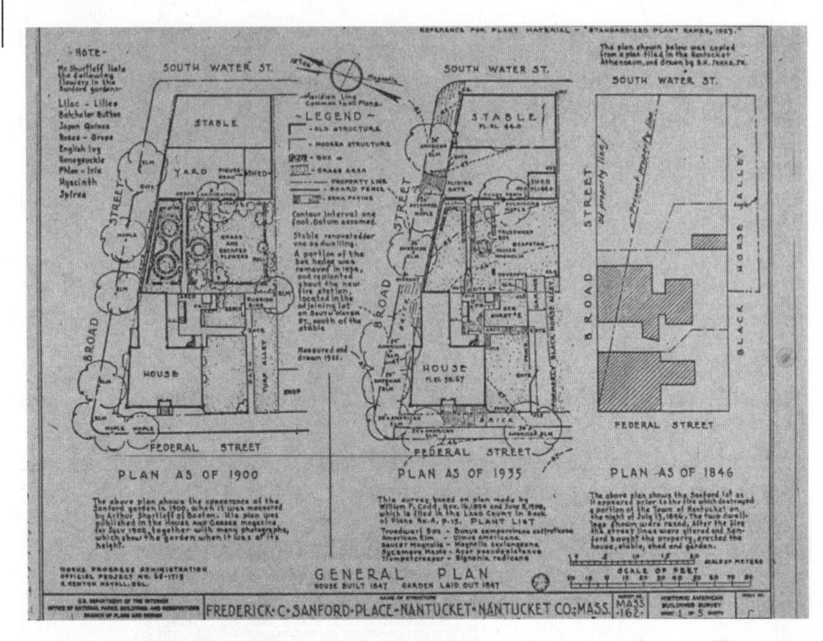

Period plans of the Frederick C. Sanford Place, Nantucket, Massachusetts, illustrating chronological analysis, from the Historic American Landscape and Garden Project, 1935–38. (Courtesy of the National Archives)

noted all trees, including their genus and species. However, this work goes beyond mere careful analysis, resulting in the equivalent of what we now call "treatment," a restoration plan.

One final example is found in the work of a more obscure practitioner, Emerson Knight (1882–1960). Knight had no formal training; in fact, his schooling ended at the age of thirteen. Knight's practice focused primarily on residential designs, although he had assisted Olmsted Jr. with his 1929 *California State Park Survey.* Knight's 1937 plan for Monterey, California, is his most ambitious and enduring preservation effort. The plan aimed to remedy a situation in which new construction was not sympathetic with the old, and open space was diminishing. He sought to stabilize, preserve, and interpret the waterfront city's rich mosaic of Spanish, Mexican, and early American architecture and recapture the early plazas that had been lost, or their charm eroded, by "modern utility structures."[23]

Knight's groundbreaking report focuses on the city in relation to its bay and proposes an "adaptation [of the bay] for human use and enjoyment."[24] He suggests that this project work, what we now call rehabilitation treatment, should be "so unobtrusive as to heighten the feeling and appreciation for all latent beauty." Knight went on to define what might be called today an interpretive trail. This "ring route," he suggested, should "link together most of the historic houses and make broad suggestions for street tree and vacant lot planting." He also unites this circulation system with the new treatment along the beach promenade. The result is a plan that reunites the bay and the city's historic fabric.

LESSONS LEARNED

Although their work in many ways mirrors contemporary practices, these men and women tended to view historic preservation in context with a broader stewardship ethic that included conservation of natural and scenic resources, avoiding the nature/culture clash that clouds so many discussions today. Integrated within the general design practice of landscape architecture, the preservation field was also seen as an interdisciplinary enterprise involving historical research, archaeology, horticulture, landscape management, and city planning. In this broad realm, there was a role for both professionals and amateurs, men and women alike, in an era when other areas of endeavor were not so inclusive. While these professionals have left a legacy of influential reports, exquisite technical drawings, and significant built works, the importance of the amateur enthusiasts in the preservation movement has been undervalued. These individuals, many of them women, articulated a sense of purpose so passionate and compelling that it drew energy and resources to the new cause of landscape preservation.

Perhaps this fervor is troubling to us today in light of the seemingly more dispassionate, professional discourse of our policy debates. The rhetoric sounds naive and politically incorrect, arguing for a "great man" theory of history that was largely debunked by social historians in the 1970s. Overall, the most frequent criticism lodged against the work of these early practitioners is that they represent an inauthentic, sanitized view of America's historic gardens and landscapes. Our advanced technologies, policies, and guidelines may have lulled us into believing we *can* objectively know and re-create an authentic image of the past. However, as David Lowenthal cautions, "We do require reminders of our heritage in our memory, our literature, and our landscapes. But advocates of preservation who abjure us to save unaltered as much as we can fight a losing battle, for even to appreciate the past is to transform it. Every trace of the past is a testament not only to its initiators but to its inheritors, not only to the spirit of the past, but to the perspectives of the present."[25]

For the past is always seen through the lens of the present. The essays that follow chronicle not only the work of these early designers and preservationists but the values, concerns, and beliefs that inspired them. With this understanding, perhaps we will consider with renewed appreciation the accomplishments of our forerunners in the landscape design and preservation fields, seeing in their work the certain imprint of their own time and cultural milieu. This awareness, in turn, may lead to recognition of these efforts as significant historical milestones and artifacts worthy of preservation in their own right.

NOTES

1. See the following National Park Service publications: Charles A. Birnbaum, *Protecting Cultural Landscapes,* Preservation Brief no. 36, 1994, and *The Secretary of the Interior's Standards for the Treatment of Historic Properties with Guidelines for the Treatment of Cultural Landscapes,* 1996.
2. Melanie L. Simo, *The Coalescing of Different Forces and Ideas: A History of Landscape Architecture at Harvard, 1900–1999* (Cambridge, MA: Harvard University Graduate School of Design, 2000), 2.
3. Charles Eliot obituary, *Garden and Forest,* no. 475 (1897), 130.
4. Keith Morgan, "Charles Eliot," in *Pioneers of American Landscape Design,* ed. Charles A. Birnbaum and Robin Karson (New York: McGraw-Hill, 2000), 107–9.
5. For a multifaceted discussion of the Colonial Revival movement, see *The Colonial Revival in America,* a collection of essays edited by Alan Axelrod (New York: W. W. Norton, 1985).
6. For a discussion of Shurcliff's documentation efforts and working methodology, see Kent Brinkley, "Interpreting Colonial Revival Gardens in Changing Times," in *Breaking Ground: Examining the Vision and Practice of Historic Landscape Restoration,* proceedings of the 11th Conference on Restoring Southern Gardens and Landscapes (Winston-Salem, NC: Old Salem, 1999): 62–82.

7. Arthur A. Shurtleff, "The Design of Colonial Places in Virginia," *Landscape Architecture* 19, no. 3 (April 1929): 163–69.

8. Charles B. Hosmer, "The Colonial Revival in the Public Eye: Williamsburg and Early Garden Restoration," in *The Colonial Revival in America,* ed. Alan Axelrod (New York: W. W. Norton, 1985), 59.

9. Stanley W. Abbott, "Historic Preservation: Perpetuation of Scenes Where History Becomes Real," *Landscape Architecture* 40, no. 4 (July 1950): 153–57.

10. Jill Pearlman, "Joseph Hudnut's Other Modernism at the 'Harvard Bauhaus,'" *Journal of the Society of Architectural Historians* 56, no. 4 (December 1997): 452–77.

11. Simo, *Coalescing of Different Forces,* 31.

12. The three articles by Dan Kiley, Garrett Eckbo, and James Rose published in the *Architectural Record* were "Landscape Design in the Urban Environment" (May 1939), "Landscape Design in the Rural Environment" (August 1939), and "Landscape Design in the Primeval Environment" (February 1940).

13. Lawrence Halprin, personal interview by Charles A. Birnbaum, June 2003. Halprin noted that while he was a student at Harvard in 1943–44, Tunnard was a "monumental" influence whereas the numerous *Pencil Point* articles by Kiley, Rose, and Eckbo were little known.

14. John Dixon Hunt, "The Dialogue of Modern Landscape Architecture with Its Past," in *Modern Landscape Architecture: A Critical Review,* ed. Marc Treib (Cambridge, MA: MIT Press, 1993), 134–43.

15. Virginia Lopez Begg, "Grace Tabor," in Birnbaum and Karson, *Pioneers,* 388–89.

16. Grace Tabor, *Old-Fashioned Gardening: A History and a Reconstruction* (New York: McBride, Nast, 1913), 161.

17. Norman T. Newton, "The American Academy in Rome," chap. 27 in *Design on the Land: The Development of Landscape Architecture* (Cambridge, MA: Belknap Press of Harvard University Press, 1971), 393–99.

18. For example, see Edward Lawson, "Villa Gamberaia," *Landscape Architecture* 8, no. 1 (October 1917): 76–83; "The Cascade in Villa Torlonia at Frascati," *Landscape Architecture* 11, no. 4 (July 1921): 186–89; "Bosco Parrasio, Rome," *Landscape Architecture* 19, no. 3 (April 1929). These articles were by or about the travels of the American Academy's first fellow in landscape architecture, Edward G. Lawson. They were illustrated with measured plans and photos from his travels.

19. Thomas D. Price, "A Restoration of Horace's Sabine Villa," American Academy in Rome (report, March 9, 1932), 12. Reprinted in *Memoirs of the American Academy in Rome,* vol. 10 (Rome: American Academy in Rome, 1932): 135–42.

20. Earle S. Draper, "Southern Plantations," *Landscape Architecture* 23, no. 1 (October 1932): 1–14, and no. 2 (January 1933): 3–4. Of interest is the note at the beginning of the first article that states: "the editors are glad to present this article by an author who has been gathering data over a period of seventeen years of residence in the South and of acquaintance with its traditions."

21. Ibid., 1:3.

22. There has been no research to date on these project landscape architects. The names of the delineators that appear on these plans include R. Newton Mayall, Alfred Cavileer Jr., G. Parker Oviatt, Louise Rowell, Raymond van Schaack, Margaret Webster, and Ruth W. Williams.

23. Emerson Knight, *Preliminary Report Concerning the Master Plan for Historic Monterey, California Project for Protection and Treatment of the Beach,* National Park Service Region IV, Los Angeles, February 11, 1938, Emerson Knight Collection, Correspondence and Reports, 1936–38, box 1, folder 1, Environmental Design Archives, University of California, Berkeley, submitted by the Planning Commission in Collaboration with Emerson Knight, city planning adviser, May 24, 1939, 20–21.

24. Ibid.

25. David Lowenthal, "Age and Artifact: Dilemmas of Appreciation," in *The Interpretation of Ordinary Landscapes,* ed. D. W. Meinig (Oxford: Oxford University Press, 1979), 125.

Grounding Memory and Identity

Pioneering Garden Club Projects Documenting Historic Landscape Traditions of the American South

CATHERINE HOWETT

Within the correspondence of the family of the Reverend Dr. Charles Colcock Jones of Liberty County, Georgia, there is a letter of March 1858 sent by Mrs. Mary Jones from her plantation home Montevideo to her oldest son, living in Savannah. She thanks Charles Jr. for having forwarded to her a package containing portraits of George Washington entrusted to him by her friend Mrs. Grant. "I am trying to dispose of them for the Mount Vernon cause," his mother writes, going on to express some vexation at the difficulties she had encountered: "It is really surprising how little sympathy *we* (I mean the *ladies*) meet with in this cause. People seem to have money for every other call."[1]

The letter was written just three days after the passage of a bill in the Virginia legislature authorizing bonds to be issued for the purchase of Washington's plantation estate on behalf of the Mount Vernon Ladies' Association of the Union, whose members had agreed to reimburse the state for the full amount just as soon as the money was raised, thus leaving the work of rescuing the historic Potomac River property from impending development squarely "in the laps of the women of the nation."[2]

This daunting project (the selling price of two hundred thousand dollars exacted by the general's heir was widely thought to be exorbitant) had actually been set in motion four years earlier with an appeal published in a

Charleston, South Carolina, newspaper and addressed to the "Ladies of the South," urging them to take upon themselves the cause of rescuing Mount Vernon—that place of "sacred associations"—from the shameful indifference of the nation and from the hands of venal speculators. The anonymous author of this spirited challenge was Ann Pamela Cunningham, a physically frail but intellectually vigorous and personally indefatigable thirty-seven-year-old unmarried daughter of a wealthy up-country planter. She appears to have been in every respect a woman of her time, place, and class—refined, self-effacing, pious. But within the privileged world of her upbringing, women as well as men were formed by a classical Greek and Roman understanding of patriotism—love of country—as an extension of filial piety and hence a moral virtue. Learning of the ruinous condition of the relict homeplace of this country's *pater patriae* (described, apparently, in a letter from her mother) had thus profoundly offended Miss Cunningham's religious sensibility, which accounts for the tone of righteous outrage by which she rallied the sisterhood of southern women—women like Mrs. Grant and Mrs. Mary Jones in Georgia, ashamed that their men did nothing for a cause that they took to be a moral imperative.

Once northern newspapers decided that her letters were interesting enough to reprint, the crusade became national, and Ann Pamela Cunningham soon found her familiar life swept away by a tide of events that required her to function in ways more typical of an executive woman of today than a maiden lady of the antebellum South—first organizing and then administering a complex business enterprise, traveling constantly, making public presentations, courting private support, lobbying governmental bodies, seizing opportunities for press coverage.

For Cunningham, as for some others among the women activists of the nineteenth century, missionary zeal in what was universally perceived to be a noble cause offered a surprising liberation from societal constraints that would otherwise have kept them at home attending to things domestic. A contemporary feminist scholar has described the widespread belief that women were better suited by nature to assume responsibility for the establishment and protection of moral standards within society as the single "loophole," in the period prior to the Civil War, that might be used to justify a woman's moving into a public sphere of action that otherwise was reserved exclusively for men.[3]

Moreover, in an age when the tender and scrupulous care of home, husband, and children was presumed to be the only proper outlet for a woman's natural predisposition to virtue and moral sensitivity, single women—expected to remain at home with their families—suffered a particular onus. Imagine, then, what it must have been like for Ann Pamela Cunningham to take up the mission that would be her life, to lead her troop of saints, as it were, into the battle to save Mount Vernon. She wrote a charter for the new association, chose the title "regent" for the leadership position she would occupy, appointed "vice-regents" in each state that seemed likely to yield contributions, who in turn appointed "lady managers" to enlist additional help and support at the grass-roots level. William Murtagh has underscored the originality and lasting importance of this organizational structure, which "not only documents the leadership of women in preservation, but, like the effort at Williamsburg almost three-quarters of a century earlier . . . became an instant informational resource and blueprint for other potential preservationists to emulate."[4]

It took just five years for the Ladies' Association to secure their rights to Mount Vernon, but the years that followed—commencing with the outbreak of hostilities that threatened to destroy the very Union celebrated in the name of their organization—presented challenges of management even more formidable than the original fundraising campaign. The war years took a severe toll on the condition of the property and the financial resources of the association, yet Ann Pamela Cunningham resisted adamantly a postwar effort by those within her own ranks to have the federal government take over responsibility for Mount Vernon. Instead she lobbied Congress for a substantial sum to repair the mansion and its grounds. Once the grant was provided, she offered to move into the house, adding to her role as regent a custodial function, managing both the ongoing restoration and the expenditures required, until her retirement in 1874.[5] Long before that parting, or her death less than a year later, she was acclaimed as an American heroine for her work in conceiving and overseeing the first successful national campaign for the preservation of a historic property.

Not least among the consequences of the spectacular success enjoyed by the Mount Vernon Ladies' Association of the Union was the example it provided of a national organization of women engaged in a worthwhile public cause without jeopardy to their respectability, to their status as "ladies." Americans had, of course, at first borrowed their notions of what constituted ladyhood from European aristocratic traditions in which that status was reserved for women of distinguished lineage, wealth, refinement, and leisure. Well through the opening decades of the nineteenth century, American women of Ann Pamela Cunningham's class, North or South, were expected to embody that same ideal of womanhood.

As the nineteenth century progressed, however, the technological progress, urbanization, and increased employment opportunities outside the home that offered greater mobility and freedom to working-class women also expanded the size and wealth of this country's middle class. For men of this class, having a wife who devoted herself exclusively to homemaking, child care, and the moral guardianship of the home was an important indication of achievement. No matter how hard such women might actually be working within their households, they were presumed to possess the attribute of "leisure" essential to their status as ladies because their unpaid work was simply the most fitting possible expression of their natural feminine domesticity, as well as their constitutional incapacity for the sorts of work to which men were suited.[6] This is the context within which the experience of the ladies involved in the rescue of Mount Vernon takes on special significance, both for the history of the women's movement and for the history of preservation—and particularly *landscape* preservation in this country. The Mount Vernon model fostered the expectation among Americans that as the movement to preserve historic places expanded, "women would assume a dominant role in the acquisition and management of such properties."[7]

Certainly the struggle to achieve voting rights in the period from about 1848 to 1920 must have raised troubling questions, even in the minds of women scandalized by the bold political defiance of the suffragists, about the restrictions society imposed on their sex. Moreover, the limited acceptance of women's involvement in the public realm through organizations aimed at the moral reform of society, such as the Women's Christian Temperance Union, had allowed many women to experience the kind of heady satisfaction that can come with testing one's powers of intelligence, will, and capacity for hard work outside of a domestic environment.

Recent scholarship has suggested that the militant feminism of the suffragists has overshadowed another, no less productive and significant movement for change that galvanized women who wanted more opportunities and greater freedom without putting at risk the serene security of their domestic lives and the happiness of their families. These were conservative, cautious, but equally determined "domestic feminists," and the primary instrument of their own, almost unnoticed liberation at the end of the nineteenth century and later would be the proliferation of women's clubs devoted to worthwhile social and cultural agendas.[8]

Describing the cultural clubs for women focused on the study of literature, history, and the arts, historian Karen Blair has observed that these groups, meeting together regularly and usually in the members' homes, developed close bonds of friendship while nurturing one another's social and intellectual development and reaching out to their communities through activities directed at civic improvement.[9] Speaking of the clubwomen whose particular interest was in the conservation movement that gathered force as an outgrowth of early-twentieth-century progressivism, Carolyn Merchant has written:

> Nowhere has women's self-conscious role as protectors of the environment been better exemplified. . . . Although that role has been rendered all but invisible by conservation historians, women transformed the crusade from an elite male enterprise into a widely based movement. In so doing, they not only brought hundreds of local natural areas under legal protection, but also promoted legislation aimed at halting pollution, reforesting watersheds, and preserving endangered species. Yet this enterprise ultimately rested on the self-interested preservation of their own middle-class life styles and was legitimated by the separate male/female spheres ideology of the nineteenth century aimed at conserving "true womanhood," the home, and the child.[10]

Similarly, the women's garden club movement of the same period has been largely ignored by historians in spite of a remarkable record of achievement, particularly with respect to its contributions to the preservation of historic American landscapes. The widespread failure to acknowledge the importance of such pioneering efforts in landscape inventory and documentation as, for example, the publication by the Garden Club of America in 1933–35 of the two volumes of *Gardens of Colony and State*[11] should challenge preservation scholarship not just to redress inequities in the historic record, but to account for them. Why have the landscape preservation projects undertaken by these women's groups been so consistently overlooked within canonical accounts of American preservation's coming-of-age with respect to standards for the protection and interpretation of historic landscapes?

This question has neither a simple nor single answer. In seeking explanations for the indifference of historians it may be useful, however, to move from the general problem of adequate recognition of the part that women's organizations have played in the preservation movement to an examination of a smaller set, namely, the experience of southern women in garden club projects related to historic landscape preservation. In this case, a specific cluster of factors may serve to illuminate some of the larger reasons for the failure to give the work of women's organizations its legitimate place in preservation history. Southern women active in garden club preservation projects were, after all, the most immediate inheritors of the legacy of the Ladies' Association crusade on behalf of Mount Vernon. This was not only the earliest example of the leadership role that the South has played in American preservation but also dramatic evidence of southern women taking the first major initiative in what quickly became a national cause. How did the next few generations of their daughters and granddaughters find opportunities to carry on the work of historic landscape preservation, and what meanings and values did that work embody for them?

Even if they might have been inspired by the story of Ann Pamela Cunningham's heroic rescue of Mount Vernon, most of them, married and with children, were unwilling or unable to follow her model of total surrender of one's ordinary life on behalf of a public cause. Moreover, it was important to them, as it had been to her, not to act in ways that threatened their status as ladies, since that appellation embodied so many values related to women's historic role as selfless nurturer and guardian of social stability that they still personally espoused. Indeed, it might be argued that what historians have dubbed the "cavalier" traditions of the American South made it more important for southern women to play out the role of lady than for women living in any other region of America.[12]

Nevertheless, these women, as was true for their peers elsewhere in the country, were not content to remain relegated entirely to domestic affairs and enjoyed opportunities to work energetically with one another on behalf of the commonweal.[13] Furthermore, just as Carolyn Merchant identified "women's self-conscious role as protectors of the environment" with their significant involvement in the conservation movement, a set of values important to southern women and related to these environmental concerns found expression first in the garden club movement, which traces its historic beginnings to the foundation of the Ladies Garden Club of Athens, Georgia, in 1891, followed soon after by that movement's commitment to the cause of historic landscape preservation.

One need hardly demonstrate that a mythology linking the feminine with the garden is as old as civilization. In nineteenth-century America, botanizing, horticulture, and flower painting were, like music and needlecrafts, more central to the education of a young lady than the more rigorous academic curriculum that formed the core of her brothers' schooling. This connection between refined women and the arts of the garden laid the groundwork, in fact, for what soon became a liberating involvement of increasing numbers of women as authors whose articles and books contributed to the burgeoning body of American garden writing from the beginning of the twentieth century onward. In an essay exploring this phenomenon, Diane Harris has shown the extent to which many of these women garden writers acted as proto-feminists, not just in occasionally addressing political issues as their male counterparts did, but through less overt but consistent advocacy of greater female self-esteem, independence, and social empowerment.[14]

Small wonder, then, that a group of twelve late-nineteenth-century southern ladies, sensing that such pursuits were as natural an extension of their feminine preoccupations as church work, conceived the idea of the garden club, anticipating the pleasure of an escape from domestic routine for a regular afternoon of conversation and gardening education. It is also worth noting that Athens was a university town, and the women who gathered for that first meeting in Mrs. E. K. Lumpkin's fine house on Prince Avenue represented the southern equivalent of those women across America at the end of the nineteenth century for whom the transition to a more urban lifestyle had significantly reduced the burden of domestic work. As one historian of female education noted in 1911: "The result is not to free her from responsibility; on the contrary, there arises here a new duty for women, that of intelligently and effectively cooperating with the other members of the community. . . . The home does not stop at the street door; it is as wide as the world into which the individual steps forth. The determination of the character of that world and the preservation of those interests which she has safeguarded in the home, constitute the real duty resting upon women."[15]

Although life even in most cities and towns of the South remained more closely tied to a rural culture than would have been true in urban areas of the North throughout the first half of the twentieth century, this sense of the women's club as a serious undertaking with a mission to make the community and the world a better place informed the garden club movement in the South from the start. One sees it reflected even in the foundation of the club in Athens, whose members framed their constitution and bylaws as a legal document, elected officers, and conducted their meetings according to parliamentary procedure. Flower and vegetable shows held as early as the second year were judged according to regulations scarcely differing from those of today.[16]

Almost from its beginnings, too, members of the Athens Garden Club looked for opportunities to support departments of the University of Georgia whose programs related to their own interests. Hubert Bond Owens, who founded the program in landscape architecture at the university in 1928, reminisced in a memoir about class trips during his undergraduate days when horticulture faculty regularly brought students to the gardens of Mrs. Lumpkin and others of the garden clubwomen for field study. Throughout his later professional life, Owens worked very closely with garden clubs at both state and national levels, providing educational programs through which members could earn garden club accreditation in specific areas of practice, including historic preservation. In turn, he received invaluable support from the clubs for scholarships and other needs of the academic program he chaired for a half-century. He remarked of his experience of these women:

> As I came to know the leaders of the garden clubs, I realized that most of them were college graduates with experience in flower and vegetable gardening. Some of them had the advantage of wide travel experience at home and abroad. I soon saw that they seemed instinctively to know the significance of my educational mission and what the training of our native youth in this little known profession could mean to Georgia and the southeastern region. In fact, most garden club leaders had a better conception of the possibilities for a Landscape Architecture program than some of the key administrative officials with whom I had to deal.[17]

"They seemed to know instinctively"—the language clearly expresses that well-entrenched societal conviction that women intuitively understood the importance of certain human, cultural, or environmental domains to which male-dominated governmental institutions and profit-driven private enterprise too often proved indifferent or hostile. But that view clearly resonated with the women of the garden club movement themselves, who became important players in village, city, and highway beautification projects that channeled progressivism's planning and design theories into local action and improvement projects. The Garden Club of Georgia, for example, had board members assigned to highway beautification and roadside improvement from 1928, the first year of its foundation. The National Council of State Garden Clubs was founded a year later and was invited, early in the 1930s, to participate in federal programs aimed at educating the public, including political leaders, to the need for careful professional planning of highways and roadside development.[18]

But perhaps nothing is more revealing of that peculiar combination of conservative values with liberal and progressive attitudes toward the involvement of women in active—and, on occasion, militant—political advocacy on behalf of what were perceived to be important social goods than the leadership role assumed by garden club women, and particularly southern clubs, in projects to protect, rescue, or restore historic landscapes. The fundamentally conservative nature of all such efforts to rescue physical remnants of earlier times and patterns of communal life should not blind us to the equally compelling evidence that the "ladies" of the garden club movement discovered in their preservation projects a scale and scope of work that, in its financial and organizational dimensions, required them to move far beyond their familiar domestic and societal domains of action—worlds away from garden making, horticulture, and flower arranging.

The evolution of projects related to research, documentation, and treatment of historic landscapes initiated and supported by the Garden Club of Virginia during the period 1920 through 1950 may provide the most dramatic illustration of an organization of women who, while modestly describing themselves as amateurs, set in motion a series of projects that taken together form a corpus of work exemplary for its ambition, originality, and consistently high standards. A small group of local Virginia clubs worked together to create a state garden club in 1920. Just a few years later, the fledgling Garden Club of Virginia began to explore the possibility of helping to restore the grounds of Kenmore, a Fredericksburg, Virginia, property that had belonged to George Washington's only sister and her husband. The Garden Club's Restoration Committee recommended as a first step what subsequently became an ongoing commitment to obtaining the best possible professional advice for the development of historic landscape plans. For the original Kenmore project, the Garden Club of Virginia commissioned as consultants both the president of the American Society of Landscape Architects, who was then James Greenleaf, and Richmond landscape architect Charles Gillette.

When the Kenmore Association was unable to fund implementation of the Gillette plan as had been anticipated, the Garden Club of Virginia decided to see the work through to completion at their own expense. Moreover, club members seized upon an idea for raising the money necessary to execute the landscape plans of Kenmore and the Lee family plantation at Stratford Hall, a bold, ambitious design that became their second hugely successful project: in 1929 the club sponsored the first "Historic Garden

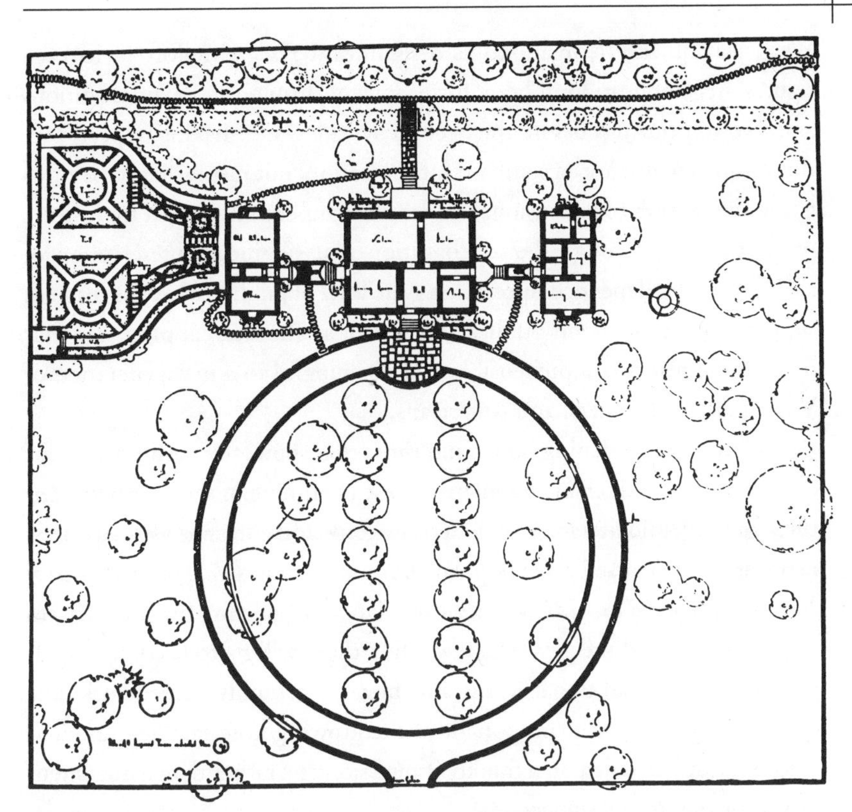

Plan drawing of proposal for development of the landscape at Kenmore by Charles F. Gillette, ca. 1924–25. (Courtesy of the Garden Club of Virginia and the James River Garden Club)

Week," a statewide pilgrimage that offered the paying public an opportunity to tour private homes and gardens opened for a week in April. This annual event, which now attracts more than forty thousand historic garden enthusiasts from around the nation and the world, has since its inception provided a self-perpetuating source of revenues used to fund landscape and garden projects at more than thirty-five historic properties. Landscape architect and historian Rudy J. Favretti has pointed to the Garden Club of Virginia's record of landscape restoration activity as, in fact, "unique in the nation. No other volunteer organization has consistently raised funds for a span of more than sixty years to restore so many important landscapes."[19]

The earliest guidebook that club members compiled to acquaint visitors with a brief history of properties on the tours visited during Garden

Week was quickly reorganized as a significant research effort in its own right. After publication in book form, it went through three more editions and twelve printings before the Second World War.[20] In this respect, too, the Virginia women set a standard for the nation, not just through their ongoing subvention of professional landscape plans commissioned for historic properties, but through their recognition that significant preservation of such properties depended upon raising the level of public awareness through support for research and publication as well as educational programs that made these places comprehensible and meaningful to a new generation of Virginians, southerners, and Americans.

Although gardening books and those that showcased fashionable gardens enjoyed considerable popularity at the beginning of the twentieth century, an academic literature of American garden history was virtually nonexistent. Alice Morse Earle's popular 1901 publication *Old Time Gardens: A Book of the Sweet o' the Year,* with its insouciant rhapsodizing about the charm of old gardens and the pleasures rewarding those willing to become knowledgeable about traditional forms and flowers, certainly helped to kindle interest in gardens as a component of the growing nostalgia for America's colonial past but relied on a frankly impressionistic rather than a documentary approach to the subject.

That distinction really does not apply to the 1923 publication of the James River Garden Club, *Historic Gardens of Virginia,* edited by Edith Tunis Sale, a work that turned out to be the first of a landmark sequence of books produced under the auspices of American garden clubs in the period of the 1920s and 1930s. Research on the forty-five gardens included in this volume was coordinated among club members, while the plans, most of which appear to have been based on existing architectural or landscape surveys, were in all but four instances drawn or redrawn by Lila Williams. The editor expressed pride that "a large part of this material has never before been made public," at the same time that she was at pains to disclaim any "literary merit," most of the work being, in her words, "altogether the work of amateurs."[21]

The almost painfully deprecatory tone of these remarks belies the quality and importance of what the women of the James River Garden Club had actually accomplished, viewed from the perspective of American garden history over the course of the more than three-quarters of a century that separates their pioneering work from the present day. They were indeed amateurs, not trained surveyors, historians, or archaeologists, but the level of care expended on thoroughness and accuracy in both text and illustrations compares favorably with most of what was being done by professionals in the early 1920s. One such professional was undoubtedly the anonymous author of a review appearing in *Landscape Architecture* magazine, who, shortly after its publication, took the book to task for having consistently omitted north arrows and indications of scale, venturing further that the landscape plans appeared to his eye to have been excessively regularized, "giving an effect of stiff formality which . . . [was] seldom characteristic of these gardens, either now or in the past"[22] This criticism represented a serious misapprehension of historic southern design traditions that may have been occasioned by the reviewer's familiarity with existing gardens where the underlying geometry had been softened by the growth of vegetation or changes made over time to the original layout.

It is also worth noting that *Historic Gardens of Virginia* significantly predates even the Colonial Williamsburg Restoration, which in recent years has been subjected to much harsher criticism for distortions and outright failures of philosophy, historicity, and methodology in its architectural, as well as its garden and landscape, projects. For that matter, Williamsburg had no historian on staff as late as 1935, when their director of research expressed the conviction that there were at least eight landscape projects completed or underway under landscape architect Arthur Shurcliff's direction that he considered "frankly unauthentic or of dubious authenticity."[23]

In a sense, the work accomplished by the women of the James River Garden Club was as important a precedent for the history of American landscape preservation as the achievement of the Mount Vernon Ladies' Association of the Union, because it, too, established an influential model that encouraged garden club women in the South to undertake research and publication of historic landscape and garden surveys within their own states: after *Historic Gardens of Virginia* in 1923, the Garden Club of Virginia's *Homes and Gardens of Old Virginia* in 1930; the Peachtree Garden Club of Georgia's *Garden History of Georgia, 1733–1933;* in 1934, the second volume of the Garden Club of America's *Gardens of Colony and State,* which included surveys contributed by clubs in eleven southern states; the Garden

Study Club of Nashville's *History of Homes and Gardens of Tennessee* in 1936; the second, 1939 edition of E. T. H. Shaffer's *Carolina Gardens,* which had garden club support; and the Garden Club of North Carolina's *Old Homes and Gardens of North Carolina,* also in 1939. Garden historian Davyd Foard Hood has proposed that "as a group these books have no parallel in American garden history, and . . . stand as an unrivaled accomplishment by Southern gardeners and garden writers."[24]

Contemporary landscape historians and preservationists owe a debt of gratitude to these dedicated garden club women, who endeavored not just to rescue evocative physical remnants of gardens and landscapes created by earlier generations of the communities in which they felt themselves to be affectively grounded, but—perhaps even more importantly—to gather as much evidence of past people, times, and places as a careful search of public archives and private collections and interviews with reliable authorities could garner.

The historic mid-nineteenth-century photographs reproduced in *Gardens of Colony and State,* for example, provide invaluable documentation of such critically important historic features as the row of tabby slave quarters with paling-fenced yards at Hermitage Plantation outside Savannah, or the large formal gardens and aviary at Seabrook Plantation on Edisto Island, South Carolina, taken at the time of its occupation by Federal troops during the Civil War. At this distance in time, of course, many of the contemporary photographs taken of extant sites for this and other garden club publications have also become irreplaceable components of the historic record.

So, too, are the plans and drawings of garden layouts either made by members themselves or commissioned for these projects, of which Lila Williams's finely rendered plan of the formal garden at Bremo Recess, typical of the illustrations she produced for *Historic Gardens of Virginia,* is a useful example. Bremo Recess is part of what is now the Bremo Historic District, a remarkable plantation and landscape complex in the valley of the upper James River, developed in the nineteenth century as the home of the Virginia family of General John Hartwell Cocke. Over the years, the form of the one-acre formal garden at Recess had become almost unreadable, making the existence of the Williams plan published in 1923 obviously important. The accompanying text, contributed by club member Fannie

Historic photograph of the slave quarters at Hermitage Plantation, near Savannah, Georgia, reproduced in Gardens of Colony and State. *(Courtesy of the Garden Club of America)*

Campbell from vivid memories of visits to this garden from the time of her girlhood, recounted: "There are vines and rosebushes left in this garden that were loved and cherished by the wife of General Cocke. One in particular, that flourishes today and has given delight to many of her descendents, is called the musk cluster. This has the most unique and exquisite odor imaginable."[25]

This information provided the clue that enabled Peggy Cornett, director of the Center for Historic Plants at Monticello, to find this antique rose (*Rosa moschata Plena*) still growing in the garden at Bremo Recess, still "loved and cherished" by the present owners, descendents of General Cocke, who graciously provided cuttings for propagation at the center. But how old could the rose at Recess—obviously thought by Fannie Campbell to be very old indeed—actually be? Cornett decided to look into the Cocke family papers in the collections of the University of Virginia; her diligence was rewarded with discovery of a letter, dated September 4, 1815, sent to General

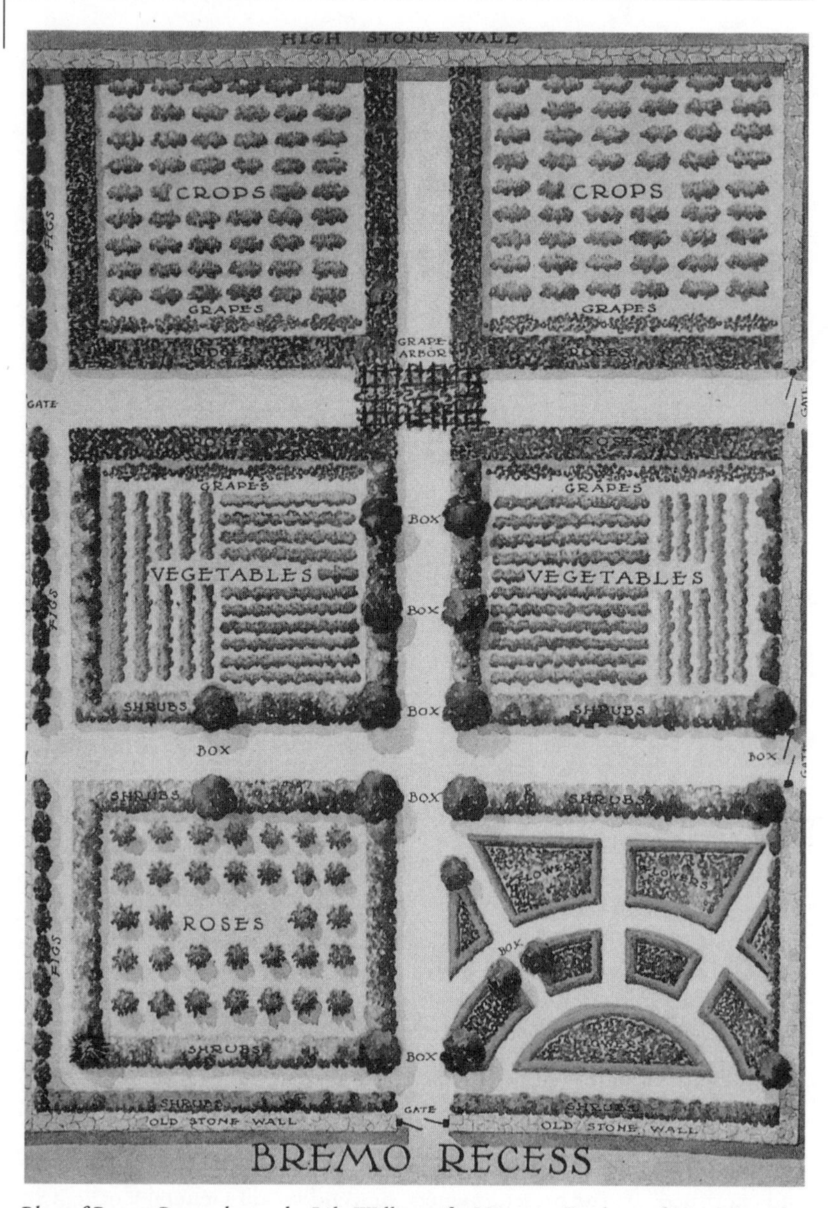

Plan of Bremo Recess drawn by Lila Williams for Historic Gardens of Virginia, *ed. Edith Dabney Sale (Richmond: James River Garden Club, 1923). (Courtesy of the Garden Club of Virginia and the James River Garden Club)*

Plan of the terraced hilltop site of Barnsley Gardens, Bartow County, Georgia, drawn by Thornton Marye for Garden History of Georgia, *1733–1933, ed. Hattie C. Rainwater (Atlanta: Peachtree Garden Club, 1933). (Courtesy of the Peachtree Garden Club, Atlanta, and the Garden Club of Georgia, Inc.)*

Cocke by Benjamin Prince of the renowned Prince Nurseries in Long Island, New York, in connection with an order to be sent to Bremo in November: "I have a great number of very handsome Roses. . . . The white musk or cluster rose is very ornamental. It flowers in clusters of Roses all the Fall (till Winter)."[26] With a sales receipt in hand to verify shipment of the rose, the likelihood is now strong that Bremo's musk cluster is the "oldest documented musk rose in America."[27] Fannie Campbell and generations of Cocke family members would be very pleased.

Similarly, the set of measured plans commissioned from Atlanta architect Thornton Marye for the Peachtree Garden Club's 1933 *Garden History of Georgia, 1733–1933* has proved to be of inestimable value to landscape historians—not just within the state, but in the region and beyond. Marye's drawing of the formal garden in the forecourt of a ruined nineteenth-century rural villa in northern Georgia was used as the authority for the recent rehabilitation of the massively overgrown boxwood frame of what is now, as it had been in the nineteenth century, a mixed parterre of flowers, trees, and shrubs typical of that period in the South. Because the Georgia survey also included a large section devoted to "modern" gardens—most of them distinguished estate gardens in the Beaux-Arts styles fashionable in the 1920s and 1930s—excellent documentation of this period survives, even though many of the landscapes documented in the book have been greatly changed, and others no longer exist.

If all history is, as we have come to understand, inevitably a form of mythmaking, it is fair to say that the men—the experts to whom the women of the garden clubs have always turned for the standards and design decisions that would inform their landscape preservation projects—deserve most of the praise or blame for the preservation philosophy that determined what was done, undone, or redone on the ground. The women sought and found other avenues of expression, action, and satisfaction in the same work. Their journeys of mutual exploration aimed at recovering and perpetuating regional traditions of family and place proved to be, for many, just the beginning of still more adventurous journeys of self-discovery and of service.

NOTES

1. Mrs. Mary Jones to Charles C. Jones Jr., 22 March 1858, in *The Children of Pride: A True Story of Georgia and the Civil War,* ed. Robert Manson Myers (New York: Popular Library, 1972), vol. 1, 400.

2. Charles B. Hosmer Jr. *Presence of the Past: A History of the Preservation Movement in the United States before Williamsburg* (New York: Putnam, 1965), 44.

3. Karen J. Blair, *The Clubwoman as Feminist: True Womanhood Redefined, 1868–1914* (New York: Holmes & Meier, 1980), 7.

4. William J. Murtagh, *Keeping Time: The History and Theory of Preservation in America* (New York: Sterling, 1993), 29.

5. Hosmer, *Presence of the Past,* 53.

6. Blair, *Clubwoman as Feminist,* 2–3.

7. Murtagh, *Keeping Time,* 30.

8. Blair, *Clubwoman as Feminist,* 2–5.

9. Ibid.

10. Carolyn Merchant, "Women of the Progressive Conservation Movement: 1900–1916," *Environmental Review* 8, no. 1 (1984): 57.

11. Alice G. B. Lockwood, ed. and comp., *Gardens of Colony and State: Gardens and Gardeners of the American Colonies and of the Republic before 1840,* 2 vols. (New York: Charles Scribner's Sons for the Garden Club of America, 1931, 1934).

12. See, for example, William R. Taylor, *Cavalier and Yankee: The Old South and the American National Character* (New York: George Braziller, 1961).

13. See Anne Firor Scott, *The Southern Lady: From Pedestal to Politics, 1830–1930* (Chicago: University of Chicago Press, 1970).

14. Diane Harris, "Cultivating Power: The Language of Feminism in Women's Garden Literature, 1870–1920," *Landscape Journal* 13 (Fall 1994): 113–23.

15. Marion Talbot, *The Education of Women* (Chicago, 1911), quoted in Sheila M. Rothman, *Woman's Proper Place: A History of Changing Ideals and Practices, 1870 to the Present* (New York: Basic Books, 1978), 69–70.

16. Medora Field Perkinson, *White Columns in Georgia* (New York: Bonanza Books, 1952), 278.

17. Hubert B. Owens, *Personal History of Landscape Architecture in the Last Sixty Years, 1922–82,* ed. Gail Karwoski (Athens: University of Georgia Press, 1983), 40.

18. Ibid., 47.

19. Richard Creek, *Gardens and Landscapes of Virginia,* text by Rudy J. Favretti (Little Compton, RI: Fort Church Publishers for the Garden Club of Virginia, 1993), 11.

20. Susanne Williams Massey and Frances Archer Christian, *Homes and Gardens in Old Virginia* (Richmond, VA: Garrett & Massie, 1931).

21. Edith Dabney Tunis Sale, ed., *Historic Gardens of Virginia* (Richmond, VA: James River Garden Club, 1923), viii.

22. *Landscape Architecture* 14 (January 1924): 148–49.

23. Harold R. Shurtleff, quoted in Hosmer, "The Colonial Revival in the Public Eye," *Presence of the Past,* 58.

24. Davyd Foard Hood, "To Gather Up the Fragments That Remain: Southern Garden Clubs and the Publication of Southern Garden History, 1923–1939," in *The Influence of Women on the Southern Landscape: Proceedings of the Tenth Conference on Restoring Southern Gardens and Landscapes* (Winston-Salem, NC: Old Salem, 1995): 174.

25. Fannie G. Campbell, in Sale, *Historic Gardens of Virginia,* 102.

26. Quoted in Rev. Douglas Seidel, "Progress Report on the Bell Garden and Documentation of an Ancient Musk Rose," *Magnolia* 14 (Winter/Spring 1999): 8.

27. Peggy Cornett, telephone interview by author, July 1, 1999.

"If Washington Were Here Himself, He Would Be on My Side"

Charles Sprague Sargent and the Preservation of the Mount Vernon Landscape

PHYLLIS ANDERSEN

"Resolved: That Mr. Sargent be authorized to direct the pruning, thinning and planting of trees so that, as far as possible, Mount Vernon may be restored to the condition in which George Washington planned and kept it. But that no well-shaped beautiful tree or flowering shrub shall be destroyed, except where they are interfering with other growth, which it is more important to retain."[1] In 1901 Charles Sprague Sargent (1841–1927), then director of the Arnold Arboretum, was asked by the regent of the Mount Vernon Ladies' Association, Justine Van Rensselaer Townsend, to give expert advice on the trees of Mount Vernon, the home of George Washington. Sargent made a site visit, asked for relevant historical documentation (in this case a copy of the list of plants Washington ordered from John Bartram in 1792), and requested complete control of the plantings of the estate. Mrs. Townsend demurred. Sargent's peremptory manner, his evident dismay at the condition of the trees, and his bold recommendations for removals and replacements intimidated the association. In broadening the scope of the association's initial request, then narrowly defined as aiding in the care of a few of Washington's trees, Sargent had clearly threatened their mission. "There was no allusion to the work of beautifying or adornment of any kind," wrote Mrs. Townsend of her request to Sargent, "for our love of Mount Vernon and its precious trees forbade us to think of any change in

Charles Sprague Sargent, director of the Arnold Arboretum, ca. 1904. Photograph by J. Horace McFarland. (Courtesy of the Archives of the Arnold Arboretum. Copyrighted by the President and Fellows of Harvard College)

the well known grounds of Washington's home." Sargent declined the position. He must have a "free hand," or he would take no part in the work.

The Mount Vernon Ladies' Association and Professor Sargent reconnected ten years later thanks to a new, more flexible regent, Harriet Clayton Comegys (1843–1927), and a softening of Sargent's view. Sargent's participation in the historic preservation efforts at Mount Vernon, which began in 1911 and continued until his death in 1927, has been virtually unrecognized, both in accounts of his career and in histories of Mount Vernon. Preserved in the archives of the association is the extensive correspondence between Sargent, Harriet Comegys, and Harrison Howell Dodge (1852–

1937), the superintendent of Mount Vernon from 1885 until his death in 1937; these documents make it clear that Sargent's work was broad in scope and went well beyond arboricultural recommendations.

The letters, notes, memos, and internal reports trace a struggle to overcome conflicts and develop a process to preserve a site of national significance, a struggle remarkably similar to the one the historic preservation community is undergoing today as it seeks to develop consensus on guidelines

Harriet Clayton Comegys, fourth regent of the Mount Vernon Ladies' Association from 1909 to 1927. (Courtesy of the Archives of the Mount Vernon Ladies' Association)

for preserving historic landscapes. Defining historical accuracy, balancing the protection of original features against the accommodation of the public, deciding how to replace plants of historic value—all these difficult questions surfaced during Sargent's work at Mount Vernon. While not easily resolved (compromise did not come easily to Sargent), the issues were clearly defined by Sargent's straightforward proposals for action. The personal tone of the letters in the Mount Vernon archives reveals the personalities of the participants. Sargent, writing from the Arnold Arboretum in Boston or from Holm Lea, his estate in Brookline, Massachusetts, was the irascible consultant, impatient with the pace of the process and the ineptitude of the Mount Vernon workforce. Harriet Comegys was patient and thorough, an excellent negotiator in spite of suffering all manner of ailments during her tenure as regent. And finally there was the sycophantic Superintendent, Dodge, whose need to please the ladies sometimes got in the way of his work on Sargent's projects.

The Mount Vernon Ladies' Association of the Union was formed in 1853 to preserve and restore the Virginia home of the nation's first president. The association is regarded by many as the first historic preservation organization in the country, and the story of its founding has been well documented in both the association's own versions and in less hagiographic renderings by others. The significance of the association's work is also discussed by Catherine Howett in another essay in this volume. Although historians of the preservation movement in the United States define the Mount Vernon Ladies' Association as the prototype of the house museum steward devoted to artifact recovery, the association should also be honored for its commitment, unusual for the time, to treat the buildings and the landscape of Mount Vernon as a single unit; the regents placed equal value on buildings, furniture, garden plans, and agricultural activities.

Like most historic preservation groups, the association was formed around the idea of rescue: the sagging roofs, the lawn waist-high with weeds, the neglected gardens. As if to reassure the association members of the validity of their acquisition, the early histories of the association's ownership of Mount Vernon are filled with the names of the dignitaries that visited: presidents and kings, minor European royalty, religious leaders, heads of exotic

Harrison Howell Dodge, superintendent of Mount Vernon from 1885 to 1937. (Courtesy of the Archives of the Mount Vernon Ladies' Association)

nations. To Sargent's consternation, each was encouraged to plant a tree. "If Washington had lived all this time he would use the ax, but the ladies believe in having two bad trees instead of one good one, and they have permitted a job lot of kings and princes to stick in blood-leaved Japanese maples and purple beech wherever they wanted to . . . the place needs a comprehensive landscape plan and the ax," Wilhelm Miller from the editorial department of *Country Life in America* wrote to Sargent.[2] By 1911 the association had outgrown the high emotion of its "save-and-rescue" stage and realized that further work would require careful thought and professional expertise. At this point, the group had not refined its mission beyond striving not to lose anything in hand.

Charles Sprague Sargent became the first director of the Arnold Arboretum of Harvard University in 1872 and held that position until his death fifty-five years later. His "austere purpose," to use his daughter's phrase, was to develop a collection of all the woody plants, both indigenous and exotic, that could be raised in the open air in Jamaica Plain, Massachusetts. The plant collection, begun in the 1870s, was initially gathered from North America and Europe. By the end of the nineteenth century, Sargent's collection policy had expanded to include the entire North Temperate Zone, with emphasis on China and Japan. The metamorphosis of this small scientific station into one of the world's leading study centers for woody plants was due to the expansiveness of Sargent's vision and the single-mindedness with which he pursued it.

Sargent's publications alone would have secured him a significant place in American landscape history. His fourteen-volume *Silva of North America,* published between 1891 and 1902, raised the study of American species to a new level of scholarship. The second edition of his *Manual of the Trees of North America,* published in 1922, was called "an old friend regenerated" and the "only complete guide to our native trees" by Stephen Hamblin, the plant specialist at Harvard's Graduate School of Design in a review in *Landscape Architecture Magazine.*[3] Sargent was also a leader in the effort to establish an American forestry policy. His *Catalog of the Forest Trees of North America* for the tenth census in 1884 and the plan he submitted to the New York State legislature for preserving the Adirondack forest placed him in the ranks of the nation's leading conservationists along with John Muir, George Engelmann, and Gifford Pinchot. His association with Frederick Law Olmsted Sr. resulted in a major contribution to the design of both the Arnold Arboretum and Boston's Emerald Necklace park system, of which the arboretum is a part.

In short, by 1911, when the Mount Vernon Ladies' Association of the Union sought advice from him for the second time, Sargent's own reputation, as well as that of the Arnold Arboretum as an institution of international standing, had been secured. His decision to work with the association was therefore based on patriotism and a deep sense of responsibility to a historic site rather than a desire to enhance his own prestige. In a letter to Harriet Comegys, he wrote, "You speak about compensation, a retainer, etc. Please dismiss any such subject from your mind. I consider it a great privilege and honor to be allowed to do anything in my power to restore the grounds of Mount Vernon to the condition in which they were when Washington was alive."[4]

Like most groups seeking help with historic preservation, the association first defined its needs in the narrowest sense: the trees, many planted by George Washington himself, needed professional care. Typical of Sargent, he redefined his role and, from the beginning, offered advice on the broader requirements for preservation: inventories of both plants and structures, restoration of specific features, vegetation management, and historical research to inform decision making.

The bowling green is Mount Vernon's central and strongest landscape feature. To quote garden historian Mac Griswold, "it is the armature of the entire design."[5] The inclusion of a bowling green in the design of Mount Vernon is attributed to Washington's reading of the British garden writers Philip Miller and Batty Langley. Washington owned a 1728 edition of Langley's *New Principles of Gardening,* a guide to the design of landscape features that describes the benefits and detailed design of a bowling green. Washington laid out a sweeping lawn edged by serpentine walkways lined with shade trees: Ohio buckeye, white ash, southern magnolia, mulberry, poplar. The trees both frame the view of the mansion and provide important shade for the walkways. He planted a wide range of species at close intervals, often in groves, with thick underplanting of shrubs. Sargent was sympathetic to this dense planting method, but it did force the association into some difficult decisions by the beginning of the twentieth century, when many of the trees planted by Washington had reached senescence, requiring extraordinary measures to sustain their lives. Moreover, trees planted by subsequent owners threatened the health of the original plantings, and volunteer trees had to be identified and removed. All of the now-predictable emotional reverberations attached to tree removal surfaced during Sargent's work with the association.

Sargent began to visit Mount Vernon at least twice a year, in the fall and in the early spring, and a routine soon evolved. Sargent would meet Miss Comegys at Mount Vernon, then she, Sargent, and Dodge would walk the grounds and discuss work to be done. Sargent would return to Boston and prepare work orders for the season ahead. In the early years he made detailed recommendations for saving, where possible, the remaining trees planted by Washington and for removing those that were beyond saving and were beginning to damage other historic plantings. Sargent also used his contacts from the Arnold Arboretum to order a substantial number of plants, primarily for mass plantings: native dogwoods *(Cornus florida),* yellowwoods *(Cladrastis kentukea),* and fringe trees *(Chionanthus virginicus)* were planted to enhance the woodland and park areas. He prepared both short- and long-term budget proposals, ordered bulbs from Holland and roses from England, and even sent plants to Mount Vernon from his own garden, Holm Lea. In all things, he offered advice, pithy and to the point. When Dodge turned to the U.S. Department of Agriculture for advice about the boxwoods at Mount Vernon, Sargent commented, "I have little confidence in the experts at the Dept. of Agriculture, it is always a good plan to leave well enough alone, especially in the case of old plants and old people."[6]

View of Mount Vernon, undated, probably the 1930s. (Courtesy of the Archives of the Mount Vernon Ladies' Association)

Sargent was primarily concerned with the woody plants of Mount Vernon and had little interest in the many separate gardens with herbaceous plants. He allowed himself to be drawn into garden projects only with great reluctance. In 1914 he prepared a list of "garden flowers" that would be suitable for planting at Mount Vernon, as this information was not available from Washington's diaries. Sargent's advice on the suitability of species was based on his knowledge of plant introductions, enhanced by the extensive library he was creating for the Arnold Arboretum. His recommendations added another level of expertise to the revitalization of the many separate garden areas of Mount Vernon that had been planted rather haphazardly with "old-time" flowers. Washington's taste for conservatory plants touched a particular chord with the Mount Vernon Ladies' Association. They diverted Sargent's attention from the grounds to long and difficult searches for exotic plants to fill the greenhouses and conservatory. Great pressure was put on him to locate orange and lemon trees as well as oleander, camellias, agaves, and pomegranates. Eventually Sargent refused further detective work, complaining that his pursuit of conservatory plants detracted from his real goal of saving the specimen trees and woodlands, the features at the heart of Washington's vision for the property.

The Mount Vernon Ladies' Association did not yet understand the dangers of appropriation; that is, in embracing the stewardship of the Mount Vernon landscape, they came to feel it was their personal garden to add to, embellish, "improve." This misplaced sense of proprietorship is not unusual: indeed, the tendency to "appropriate" historic landscapes is a frequent source of conflict between preservation professionals and committed amateurs. The members of the association were influenced by their own personal garden making in a period when horticultural display, enabled by the rich array of imported plants available in the nursery trade, was highly valued. Sargent pleaded, "You certainly would not hang a modern chromo on the walls of Washington's room because some important person gave it to you, and there doesn't seem to be much difference between a chromo on the walls and a purple modern tree in the garden. . . . No one more than I do want to preserve the grounds as Washington left them."[7] The association found it hard to separate their own motivations from that of Washington. Initially, Sargent, with a certain amount of politeness and reserve, tried to make the asso-

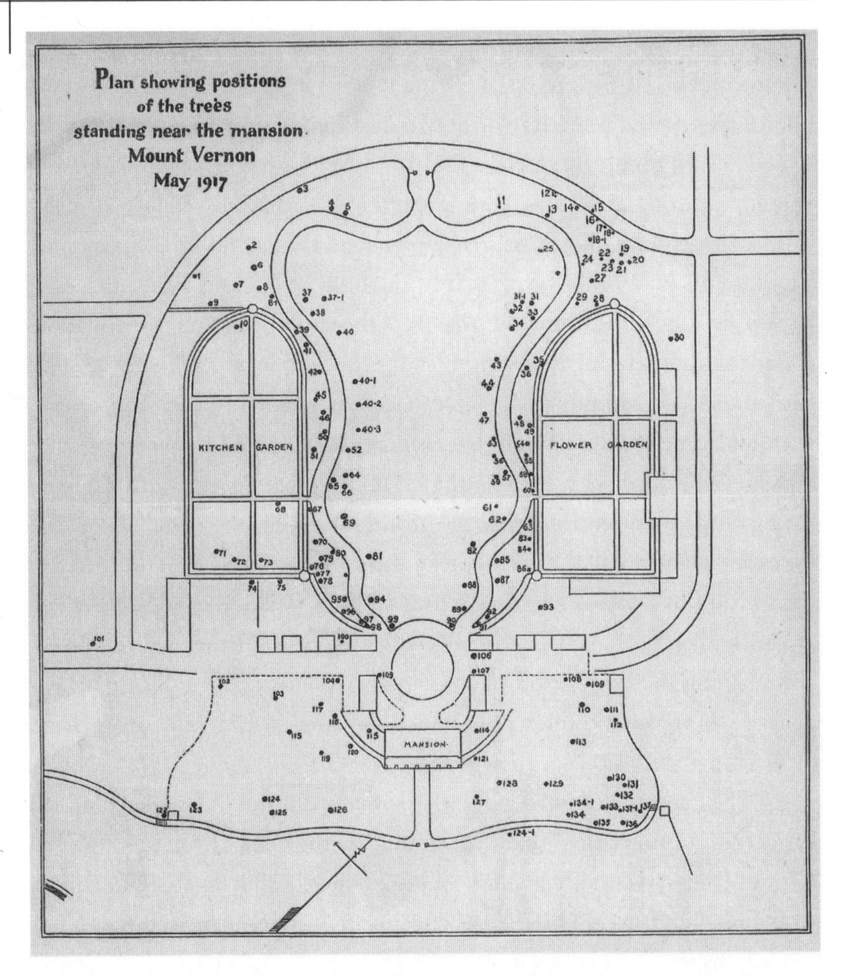

Plan showing positions of the trees standing near the Mount Vernon mansion from The Trees at Mount Vernon: Report of Charles Sprague Sargent to the Council of the Mount Vernon Ladies' Association of the Union, *May 1917. (Courtesy of the Arnold Arboretum Library)*

ciation understand the inappropriateness of some of their embellishments. In 1915 he reacted to the proposal for adding a new cutting garden some distance from the house by writing, "All these detached spots of cultivation more or less remote from the center increase work and are apt to be overlooked and neglected." Later, somewhat less patiently, he characterized as an eyesore the "new" greenhouse that had replaced the original one destroyed in a fire, and suggested that using it to grow flowers for sale to the public was somewhat lacking in dignity.

The demand from the public for continual floriferousness, appropriate or not, is a dilemma at many historic sites, and Mount Vernon was no exception. Roses were a continuing subject of debate throughout the sixteen years of correspondence; association members and others put pressure on Harrison Dodge and his garden staff to plant them. Sargent warned that few roses were available during Washington's lifetime, and those that were did not bloom more than once a season. He recommended the York and Lancaster roses and warned against 'Harrison's Yellow,' which was not available during Washington's time. In 1917 Sargent wrote that he had just discovered a rose brought to this country from England by Abigail Adams still growing in the garden of the Adams House in Quincy, Massachusetts. He noted that he would have a few plants propagated from that shrub for Mount Vernon since its age would have made it appropriate for Washington's garden.

Sargent had a special interest in restoring the Old Tomb area, using as his guide the writings of Washington and visitors to the property during his time. At Harriet Comegys's suggestion, he located a copy of Nathaniel Parker Willis's 1840 book, *American Scenery,* and he used the drawings by W. H. Bartlett of the tomb area to identify the trees existing at that time. Sargent pointed out the unsuitability of the existing sundial and the post and chains in front of the mansion, and he helped locate replacements appropriate to Washington's period. But most of all Sargent was concerned that the association's embellishments to both grounds and buildings would unnecessarily exacerbate the problem of long-term maintenance. "The thing to do is to reduce the cost of maintenance by permanent improvement," he wrote to Mrs. John Carter Brown in 1916.[8] To that end he recommended that little-used roads be removed, and he discouraged unnecessary paths and the proliferation of small outbuildings, each with a limited special use.

It is ironic that Sargent, the botanist-arborist-dendrologist whose far-ranging fieldwork made him famous as an international leader in forest policy and the preservation of scenery, should also have been the strict disciplinarian who demanded that the work of the association be based on historical

Postcard view of the tomb of Washington at Mount Vernon, undated, probably 1930s. (Courtesy of the Arnold Arboretum Library)

scholarship. He argued that "we should have at our command if possible every bit of information obtainable, that could in any way be of use in this important work of today, as well as for the Association's benefit in the future."[9] At his urging, the Boston Athenaeum prepared a bibliography of books and articles relating to George Washington and Mount Vernon based on their own catalog of Washington literature and the holdings of several other libraries, including those of Harvard University, the American Antiquarian Society, and the Library of Congress. The bibliography took the form of five thousand handwritten cards housed in a special wooden case that is now in the Mount Vernon archives, although like many bibliographic endeavors, its usefulness quickly diminished because it was not continually updated.

Elswyth Thane in her 1967 book, *Mount Vernon: The Legacy,* states that it was partly Sargent's use of Washington's diaries (the association had obtained typewritten copies of those in the Library of Congress) that motivated the Mount Vernon Ladies' Association to sponsor the diaries' first publication in 1925, edited by historian John C. Fitzpatrick. Sargent's correspondence with the association confirms his enormous interest in the diaries; he continually mined them for bits of information about both the plantings of Mount Vernon and its architectural features. He corresponded with Max Farrand, the Yale historian and husband of Sargent's former pupil, landscape gardener Beatrix Farrand, about the availability of Washington's writings. He prodded the association to acquire more original documents pertaining to Mount Vernon and, through his own acquaintance with antiquarian book dealers, acquired several documents himself that he later donated to the association. His interest in the historical documentation of Mount Vernon resulted in a short article for the journal *Rhodora* on celebrated botanist André Michaux's 1786 visit to Mount Vernon, which Washington had documented in his diaries.[10]

When plants become, to use art historian George Kubler's term, "prime objects" (as opposed to reproductions, replicas, or copies), they take on complex meaning well beyond their value as living plant material. The reincarnation of trees that were "witnesses to history" as souvenirs or talismans has become a familiar form of preservation. Seeds of historic trees are distributed to far-flung locations; dead trees reappear as commemorative bookends, paperweights, and sculptures.[11] Although this gives some in the preservation field a sense of unease, it cannot be disputed that the tree as icon engages the public attention, which can then be redirected to the larger issues of preservation. Although Sargent struggled to maintain a dignified context for his work, he did not dismiss the value of this appeal to public sentiment. "But no trees planted by man have the human interest of the Mount Vernon trees," he once said.[12]

A case in point is the so-called Washington Elm, which stood on the Cambridge (Massachusetts) Common for centuries and was so named because, as the story goes, George Washington took command of the Continental Army under the tree on July 3, 1775. The tree even bore a plaque to this effect. In October 1923 the Washington Elm fell, perhaps toppled accidentally by a worker trying to remove a dead branch. Given no reason to question the tree's historical association, Sargent secured a cross-section of the trunk and sent it to a plant anatomist at Harvard's Bussey Institution, who confirmed its age. After complicated negotiations between Sargent and the city of Cambridge, the cross-section was sent to Mount Vernon for display in the kitchen fireplace, a location the Cambridge city fathers thought inappropriate.

Postcard view of the Mount Vernon kitchen fireplace, early twentieth century. (Courtesy of the Arnold Arboretum Library)

Either unknown to Sargent, or perhaps dismissed by him, was detailed research compiled by Samuel Batchelder of Cambridge, published in the *Cambridge Tribune* in 1923. Batchelder very convincingly debunked the Washington association, stating that if Washington stood under the tree he did so to get out of the rain. Nevertheless, the cross-section of the tree remained at Mount Vernon for many years and was reproduced with an almost religious aura in brochures and postcards for the general public.[13]

A less questionable project was Sargent's effort to restore to Mount

Vernon the famous sago palm (*Cycas revoluta*) that Washington acquired from Pratt's nursery in Philadelphia. Washington grew the palm for many years in a small conservatory. A document in the archives of the Mount Vernon Ladies' Association states that it was sold after the death in 1802 of his widow, Martha, to a Mr. Peter De Windt of Fishkill-on-Hudson, New York, where it flourished for many years. In 1841 the palm was acquired by Henry Winthrop Sargent, a cousin of Charles Sargent, for the large conservatory on his Fishkill estate, Wodenethe, which passed in 1882 to his son Winthrop Sargent. At the request of Charles Sargent, who located the long-lost plant, Winthrop Sargent's widow donated it to Mount Vernon. The tree was installed at the Palm House at Mount Vernon but was quickly found to have outgrown the space during its time away. The roof was raised more than once, but after thriving for several years the tree began to fail. Numerous remedies and therapies were tried, but the plant died in 1934, mercifully after Sargent's death, since he had invested considerable time in prolonging its life. In 1941 a cutting from a still-thriving tree at Tudor Place in Washington, D.C., also acquired from Pratt's Garden at the same time as Washington's, was given to Mount Vernon, where it continues to grow today.

By 1922, Sargent, then eighty-one, was dismayed that work on the grounds of Mount Vernon had not progressed more quickly, and complained that decision making was needlessly slow. In November 1922 he wrote to Harriet Comegys, "It is a great regret that having devoted ten or twelve years of my best thoughts and attention to Mount Vernon I have been unable to secure the confidence of the Council to the extent of letting me carry out my planting plans. Tree removals are needed. I wish the Council had more imagination and more power to look into the future. The thing which I feel sure about in this matter is that if Washington were here himself he would be on my side."[14]

Sargent made his last visit to Mount Vernon in 1923. In June 1924 a major storm at Mount Vernon seriously damaged a tulip tree *(Liriodendron tulipifera)*, a sugar maple *(Acer saccharum)*, and Ohio buckeye *(Aesculus glabra)*, all planted by Washington. Sargent gave Dodge stern advice to use only the best arborist available to repair the damage. He wrote to Harriet Comegys that he might have growing in the Arnold Arboretum nursery some small cuttings from a Mount Vernon buckeye and that he would send one of them if it matched the one lost. By that time, however, Sargent's health was frail. Although he still went to his office at the Arboretum everyday, as the year progressed he admitted that he could not make the trip to assess the storm damage. Instead he sent the Arnold Arboretum's young superintendent of grounds, Christian Van der Voet, a horticulturist from Holland who had trained at Kew. Van der Voet made several trips to Mount Vernon in Sargent's stead.

Sargent remained involved through correspondence with the work at Mount Vernon until his death in March 1927. Harriet Comegys died a few months later. Thus ended a friendship based on mutual respect and commitment to the preservation of the Mount Vernon landscape. The only publication of Sargent's sixteen-year relationship with Mount Vernon was his inventory and condition assessment of the trees of the bowling green and around the mansion. *The Trees at Mount Vernon* was first published in 1917 as part of the *Annual Report of the Mount Vernon Ladies' Association.* It was updated and reprinted in 1926 as a separate document and was offered for sale at the property for many years. The report includes an introduction, a description and condition assessment of each tree, a scaled plan with all the trees located and numbered, and appendixes that include a list of the trees planted by Washington that had since disappeared.

Several of Washington's original trees remain at Mount Vernon—a great white ash, a tulip poplar—nurtured by Sargent and subsequent generations of consultants and gardeners. Washington's original trees are surrounded by many replacement plants and by the lush ornamental gardens, a significant concern of the present generation of curators and sponsors. But the survival of original trees reflects Sargent's admonition that "no care should be spared to preserve them, and as they pass away they should be replaced with trees of the same kinds, that Mount Vernon may be kept for all time as near as possible in the same condition in which Washington left it."[15]

Sargent's contribution to the landscape of Mount Vernon may not be highly visible in historic preservation literature; however, his rigorous approach to research and scholarship, his insistence on authenticity in both plant placement and replacement, his admonition to treat the site with a consistent sensibility—all set the stage for the work of landscape architect

Morley Jeffers Williams. Williams's work at Mount Vernon, beginning in 1931 just after Sargent's death, is described in an essay by Thomas Beaman later in this volume. Sargent's prolonged attempt to convince the association to separate nostalgia from meaningful renderings of historic ideas set the course for a new approach to preserving Washington's landscape. Never characterized as a sentimental man, Sargent was clearly moved by his participation in the preservation of Mount Vernon; its iconic status as a national landscape and the palpable presence of Washington in the original trees of the bowling green moved Sargent to attempt to transform the rather ragged site he first saw in 1911 into a more mature rendering of Washington's original vision.

NOTES

Some of the information contained in this essay was published in a different form in an article by the author, "Charles Sprague Sargent and the Preservation of the Landscape of Mount Vernon, or 'If Washington Were Here Himself, He Would Be on My Side,'" in *Arnoldia* 59, no. 1 (1999).

1. The Mount Vernon Ladies' Association of the Union, "Minutes of the Council," May 1901, in the Archives of the Mount Vernon Ladies' Association of the Union, Mount Vernon, Virginia.
2. Wilhelm Miller (editorial department, *Country Life in America*) to Charles Sprague Sargent, May 28, 1912, in the Archives of the Mount Vernon Ladies' Association.
3. Stephen Hamblin, review of *Manual of the Trees of North America,* by Charles Sprague Sargent, *Landscape Architecture* 12 (July 1922): 298–99.
4. Sargent to Harriet Clayton Comegys, October 2, 1914, in the Archives of the Mount Vernon Ladies' Association.
5. Mac Griswold, lecture at the Concord Museum, Concord, Massachusetts, May 13, 1999.
6. Sargent to Mrs. John Carter Brown, vice-regent from Rhode Island, December 28, 1911, in the Archives of the Mount Vernon Ladies' Association, Mount Vernon, Virginia.
7. Sargent to Brown, June 5, 1912, in the Archives of the Mount Vernon Ladies' Association.
8. Sargent to Brown, April 28, 1916, in the Archives of the Mount Vernon Ladies' Association.
9. Mount Vernon Ladies Association, "Minutes of the Council," May 1915, in the Archives of the Mount Vernon Ladies' Association.

10. "Washington and Michaux," *Rhodora: Journal of the New England Botanical Club* 17 (March 1915): 49–50.

11. For a discussion of trees and other Mount Vernon artifacts converted into souvenirs, see Karal Ann Marling, *George Washington Slept Here: Colonial Revivals and American Culture, 1876–1986* (Cambridge: Harvard University Press, 1988).

12. Charles Sprague Sargent, *The Trees at Mount Vernon,* rev. ed. (Mount Vernon, VA: Mount Vernon Ladies' Association, 1926). Originally published in Mount Vernon Ladies' Association, *Annual Report* (Mount Vernon, VA, 1917; rev. ed., 1926).

13. For a discussion of Batchelder and the myth of the Washington Elm, see Sheila Connor, *New England Natives* (Cambridge: Harvard University Press, 1994), 111.

14. Sargent to Comegys, November 22, 1922, in the Archives of the Mount Vernon Ladies' Association.

15. Mount Vernon Ladies' Association, *Annual Report* (Mount Vernon, VA, 1917), 46.

Morley Jeffers Williams

A Pioneer of Landscape Archaeology

THOMAS E. BEAMAN JR.

When historical archaeology was only a fledgling field, landscape architect Morley Jeffers Williams recognized the contribution the practice could bring to the study and restoration of historic landscapes. Once described as "a substantial, quick-speaking man with a brown moustache and a generally brown tweed appearance," Williams used archaeological evidence combined with documentary sources as methodological tools to research the historic landscapes of Stratford Hall and Mount Vernon in Virginia, in the 1930s, and Tryon Palace in New Bern, North Carolina, in the 1950s.[1] The results of these excavations yielded information that was used to interpret and guide the restoration of buildings, gardens, and landscape features at these historic sites.

Compiling a portrait of Williams's career is a difficult task for two reasons. First, as Williams's personal papers have to date not been located, sources that offer glimpses into his professional career are scarce. Therefore, as with an archaeological investigation, little pieces of evidence from meeting minutes, correspondence, and newspaper articles were used to piece together this portrait. The second difficulty is attempting to separate fact from fiction and hearsay. As Marc Antony observed in Shakespeare's *Julius Caesar,* "The evil that men do lives after them; the good is oft interred with their bones." During his career, several of Williams's professional decisions brought him into dispute with various individuals, notably Fiske Kimball, the restoration architect of Stratford Hall, and the J. A. Kellenberger family, members of the Tryon Palace Commission who were responsible for funding much of the restoration of Tryon Palace. These disputes and speculations are briefly reported in an attempt to present as impartial a recounting of Williams's professional work as possible.

Morley Williams's background in both civil engineering and landscape architecture undoubtedly contributed to his successful use of archaeology as a research tool.[2] This essay examines three specific cases of how Williams's archaeological research was used in the restoration of historic landscapes. The first case focuses on Stratford Hall, where excavations uncovered the design of the East Garden and period development to the west of the mansion. A second study discusses how the archaeology Williams conducted at Mount Vernon was used to document the evolution of the historic landscape. The third study details contributions the archaeological research made to the restoration of Tryon Palace. Williams's goals and discoveries at each of these sites are considered as well as the excavation techniques he employed.

STRATFORD HALL

It is not known when Morley Jeffers Williams first developed a research interest in historic gardens and landscapes in the southern United States. During summers and other academic breaks from 1931 until 1936, Williams, then an assistant professor in Harvard's Graduate School of Design (GSD), and a number of graduate students were actively involved in both documentary and archaeological field research on this topic. After many conversations with Williams, Bremer W. Pond, chair of Harvard's Department of Landscape Architecture, wrote, "I felt at the time that [Williams] was particularly well fitted for this phase of research, not so much from his previous historical work or knowledge, but on account of his power of concentration and his ability to get down to the actual facts of a case, searching out all possible records and authorities."[3]

In March 1931, Williams received a grant from the Clark Fund for Research in Landscape Design at Harvard to investigate "American Landscape

Design as Exemplified by the Plantation Estates of Maryland and Virginia, 1750 to 1860." In May, he traveled throughout Virginia and Maryland making topographic surveys of historic plantations, which included Gunston Hall, the home of George Mason, and Woodlawn, George Washington's gift to his granddaughter Eleanor Custis. That summer, Williams was also asked to prepare drawings of Mount Vernon to be used in an exhibition to celebrate the bicentennial of George Washington's birth. Williams and two assistants began a systematic survey of Mount Vernon in July, and over the winter he prepared drawings. His 1931 survey of Mount Vernon is very important for another reason, for many archaeologists believe that this was the first time Williams used archaeology as a source to identify hidden elements of historic landscapes.[4]

Based on his initial surveys in the summer of 1931, the Garden Club of Virginia asked Williams to complete the research on the landscape of Stratford Hall begun by Arthur Shurcliff in 1930. The club agreed to fund the investigation by paying for hired labor and for the time of Charles Coatsworth Pinkney, a graduate student in the GSD who served as Williams's field assistant and conducted the archaeological excavations at Stratford Hall in the summer of 1932. Williams contributed his time gratis to the project, though he later acknowledged that it was a second grant from the Clark Fund that allowed him to do so.[5]

Whereas Arthur Shurcliff initially investigated the similarities and differences between the brick, mortar, and types of bonding used in various walls and pavements at Stratford Hall, Williams focused his early research of the site solely on the physical features of the east garden and landscape. In June and July 1932, Pinkney supervised the archaeological excavation "with occasional assistance and suggestions" by Williams, while local unskilled African American laborers constituted the crew of excavators. Williams, like Shurcliff and many other early archaeologists who worked on historic sites, favored narrow trenches excavated to subsoil as his primary exploratory research method. It is likely Williams learned this technique from Shurcliff, his mentor at Harvard who used the same methodology in the initial work at Stratford Hall. Narrow trenches allowed archaeologists to locate physical features of the cultural landscape efficiently over large areas by not having to move great amounts of earth.[6]

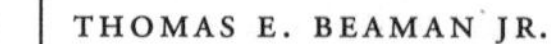

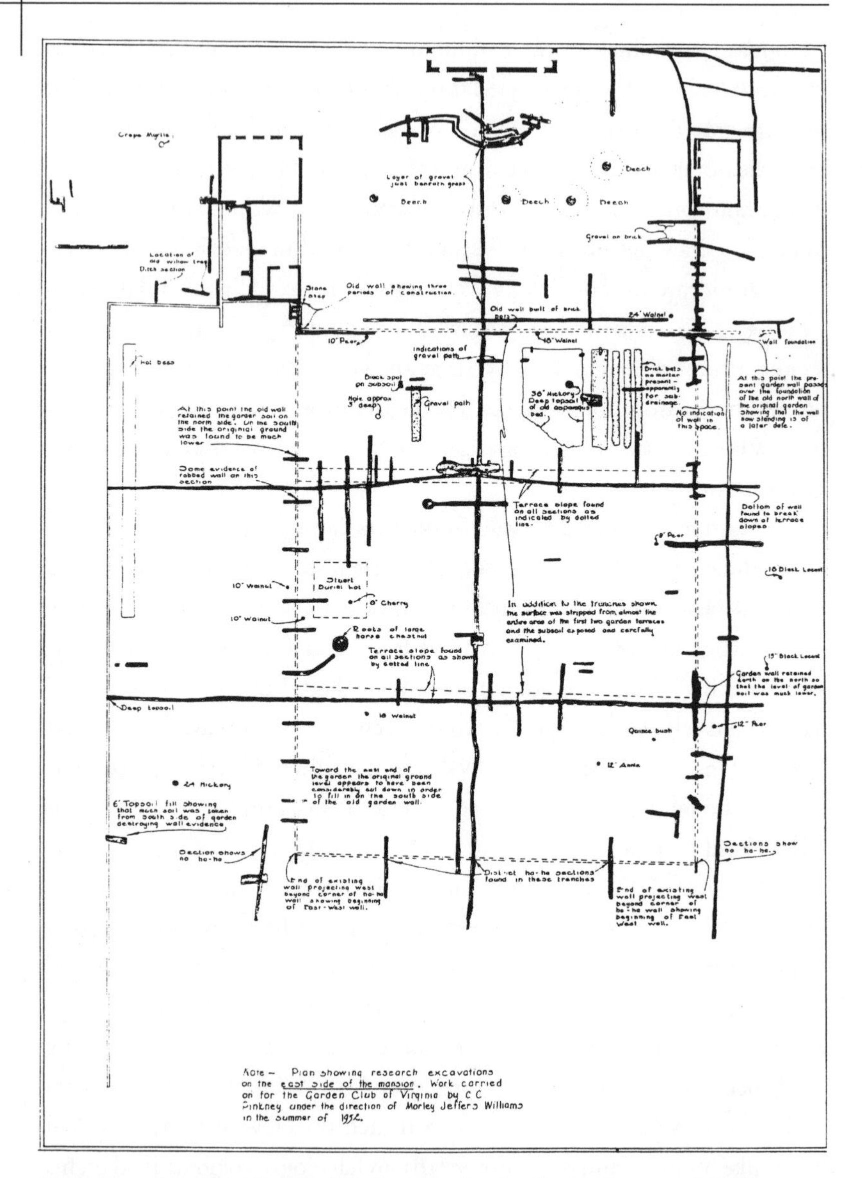

Excavation plan of the Stratford Hall east garden by Charles Coatsworth Pinkney under the direction of Morley Jeffers Williams, 1932. (Courtesy of the Jessie Ball duPont Memorial Library, Robert E. Lee Memorial Association, Inc., Stratford Hall Plantation)

Williams's first goal was to determine if the east garden was terraced. Through a single east-west trench dug the length of the garden, he identified two terrace slopes, which were then confirmed through the use of north-south cross trenches. He also discovered the ruins of the northern and southern garden walls in trenches as well as the remains of a ha-ha wall and ditch to the east of the garden. Evidence of two side paths within the garden was found, but no evidence of a central path. Areas of brickbats with no evidence of mortar were also discovered, which Williams interpreted as being part of a drainage system for the garden. Additionally, he noted that small white stones had formerly covered the area between the main house and the garden. He also explored the areas to the north and south of the garden and the area between the ha-ha wall and the Lee family burial vault but found nothing of note.[7]

Pinkney made additional archaeological discoveries outside the east garden that summer. He found that the south lawn had no slope and was at its original level. In the center of this area, he located a small brick foundation, which Williams interpreted as the setting for a sundial pedestal. A buried wall on the southern end of the lawn was confirmed as a ha-ha wall. Pinkney also found evidence of gravel drives both to the south of this ha-ha wall and to the north of the main house.[8]

By combining Shurcliff's previous investigations, Pinkney's excavations, and documentary research, Williams identified the layout, walls, and terracing of the east garden, as well as the original approach to the mansion and the view from the mansion to the Potomac River. Based on these findings, the Garden Club of Virginia asked Williams to design the plans for the restoration of the east garden. Both the club and the Robert E. Lee Memorial Foundation accepted these plans. Their only change to the design was the removal of the garden houses, as Fiske Kimball, Stratford Hall's director of restoration, considered them not to be authentic to the period. As a result, Williams and Kimball disagreed over who was responsible for the restoration of the garden walls. Was it the responsibility of Kimball, whose contract with the Robert E. Lee Memorial Foundation stated that he was in charge of the restoration of the main house and other structures, or the obligation of Williams, whose agreement with the Garden Club of Virginia placed him in charge of the entire garden restoration? The Robert E.

Lee Memorial Foundation and the Garden Club of Virginia interpreted the garden walls and proposed garden houses as structural, which made it Kimball's final decision. The dispute was settled quickly, and the garden houses were removed from the plans. Williams apparently bore no ill will toward any party involved with the decision. Based on both the archaeological evidence and documentary research, Williams's overall designs for the Stratford Hall landscape were implemented almost immediately. Williams spent the summer of 1933 supervising the reconstruction of the east garden. The north and south vistas from the main house were also restored based on Williams's designs at this time.[9]

In addition to his work at Stratford Hall in 1932, a second Clark grant allowed Williams to continue his surveys of plantations in Virginia and Maryland, including Monticello. Williams was encouraged by Kimball's previous studies there, and his initial goal was to survey the property to locate and record evidence of the inclined roads or "roundabouts" that Jefferson designed for Monticello. During this survey, he was able to locate the walks and several planting beds on the west lawn. It is not known if Williams conducted or oversaw any archaeology at Monticello, although it is likely that he may have. He noted that there was no gravel found under the sod for the walks, which sounds very similar to the excavations at Stratford Hall that same summer.[10]

Pinkney conducted additional archaeological excavations at Stratford Hall from August to October 1934, primarily to measure the extent of development to the west of the main house. He unearthed parts of the foundations of the former stable and springhouse, as well as an entrance road and brick pavers at the west entrance of the main house. Kimball used these discoveries in designing the restored stable, springhouse, and west entrance. Pinkney also located several areas of fired earth and brick wasters—interpreted as brick kilns—and an abandoned nineteenth-century icehouse, which likely dated to Mrs. Elizabeth McCarty Storke's ownership of Stratford Hall from 1826 to 1879. These excavations in the late summer and fall of 1934 were the last conducted under Williams's supervision at Stratford Hall, although in 1938 he did make several additional recommendations for the restoration of the grounds based on the archaeological investigations and other plantation layouts.[11]

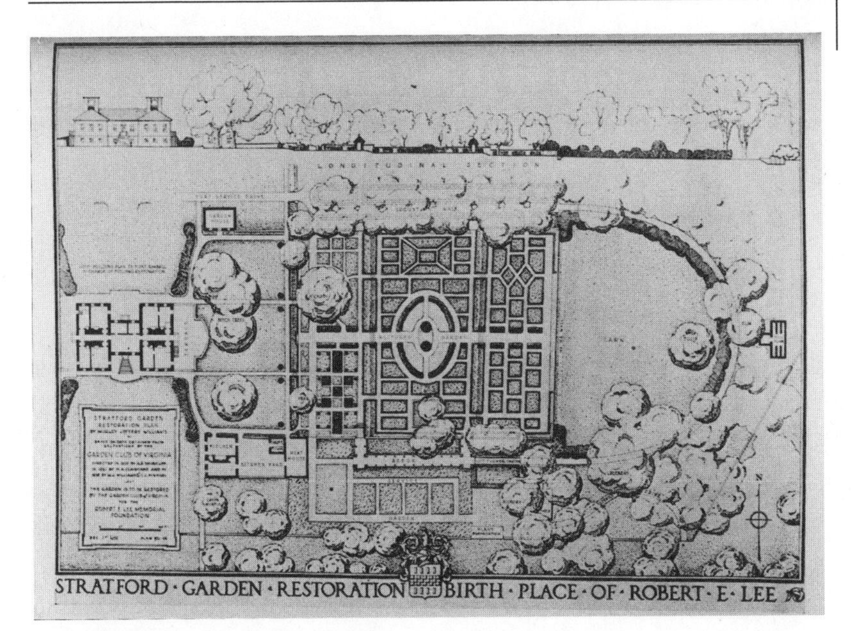

Restoration plan of the Stratford Hall east garden by Morley Jeffers Williams. (Courtesy of the Jessie Ball duPont Memorial Library, Robert E. Lee Memorial Association, Inc., Stratford Hall Plantation)

Pinkney's weekly written progress reports reveal several interesting observations about the field techniques used in the 1934 excavation. First, as with Shurcliff's earlier excavation, the primary field methodology was trenching. Second, Pinkney noted that Williams recommended taking "records by level" in each section of the trench, indicating an awareness of the importance of stratigraphy in archaeological research. He mentioned few artifacts beyond brick and mortar in the reports yet was certainly aware of them. He dated the icehouse to the Storke period by a large gray jar fragment with a blue pattern similar to those found in the main house at the time of the restoration.[12]

However, it is doubtful that many artifacts were collected or saved, as these excavations were intended to identify landscape patterns and architectural details for restoration purposes. This is a decided contrast to modern archaeological practices, where all artifacts recovered in an excavation (regardless of its purpose) are kept as both diagnostic markers and for use in further social and cultural studies. Recent excavations conducted at Stratford Hall by archaeologists from Mary Washington College in Fredericksburg, Virginia, confirm that several of Williams's and Pinkney's backfilled trenches, relocated near the main house and in the west garden area, regularly contained artifacts in the backfilled soil.[13]

MOUNT VERNON

Morley Williams's archaeological work at Mount Vernon differed from his excavations at Stratford Hall, where Fiske Kimball directed the restoration and Arthur Shurcliff initiated the excavations two years before Williams arrived. At Mount Vernon, Williams was the first to conduct archaeological excavations at the site and was in charge of the restoration. His primary goal was to determine the ages of buildings and landscape features in order to understand the evolution of this historic landscape. Though he wrote no reports for his archaeological research at Mount Vernon, Williams's excavations are well documented in meeting minutes and in extensive notes and drawings on file at this historic site. Even with new theoretical perspectives and additional evidence from recent excavations, findings from these early archaeological studies continue to play a vital role in modern interpretations of the Mount Vernon landscape.[14]

Williams conducted his introductory survey of the Mount Vernon landscape in 1931, supported by the Clark Fund grant he had received to study the organization of southern plantations. He drew two conclusions from this survey. First, Williams proposed that Washington's Mount Vernon was consciously designed to resemble the shape of a shield, outlined by the walls of the deer park, the two east ha-ha walls, the south wall of the vegetable garden and the north side of the flower garden, and by the curving west ends of these gardens. Second, Williams was able to identify three distinct phases in the development of the plantation: the period prior to George Washington's acquiring the estate (ca. 1735–54); the period of Washington's marriage (ca. 1758–75); and the period following the marriage (ca. 1775–99), "when expanding social obligations called for greater space and elaboration."[15] This second conclusion guided Williams's later archaeological exploration of Mount Vernon—the dating of past landscape elements to developmental phases or time periods in the evolution of the landscape.[16]

Williams was able to delineate these three phases in the development of Mount Vernon not only from the excellent documentary records available but also from the archaeological discovery of four foundations of early dependency buildings: a kitchen, washhouse, dairy, and storehouse. These foundations, two of stone and two of brick, were located on the west side of the main house, stretching out diagonally from the northwest and southwest corners and connecting to the house by low walls. These buildings apparently dated to the period in which Washington's father, Augustine, or his half brother, Lawrence, owned the property (ca. 1735–39 and ca. 1740–52, respectively). Extant sources indicate this was the first time Williams used archaeological evidence in formulating ideas on the development of historic landscapes. He also spent part of the summer of 1934 further exploring these four foundations.[17]

During the summer of 1935, Williams focused on the archaeological investigation and restoration of the kitchen garden at Mount Vernon. Unfortunately, no evidence of the original planting beds and paths was identified during the excavation. The design Williams chose for the restoration was based on Washington's account books and period garden books.[18] That same summer Williams was also involved in historical research of the White House grounds as background information for a report by the Olmsted Brothers firm for a possible redesign of the landscape, a project discussed at length by Cynthia Zaitzevsky elsewhere in this volume. This research led Williams to disagree with the placement of the Jefferson Memorial south of the Washington Monument on the White House axis. Williams wrote, "If the ideas of Washington and [Pierre Charles] L'Enfant are sacred, the view south of the White House should be kept open. The river view exists and cannot be ignored." To preserve L'Enfant's symmetrical plan of the Mall and the river view, Williams believed that a more logical place for the Jefferson Memorial was across the Potomac River and to the west of the river view.[19]

In the winter of 1935–36, Williams was asked to join the staff at Mount Vernon as the director of research and restoration. He taught courses at the

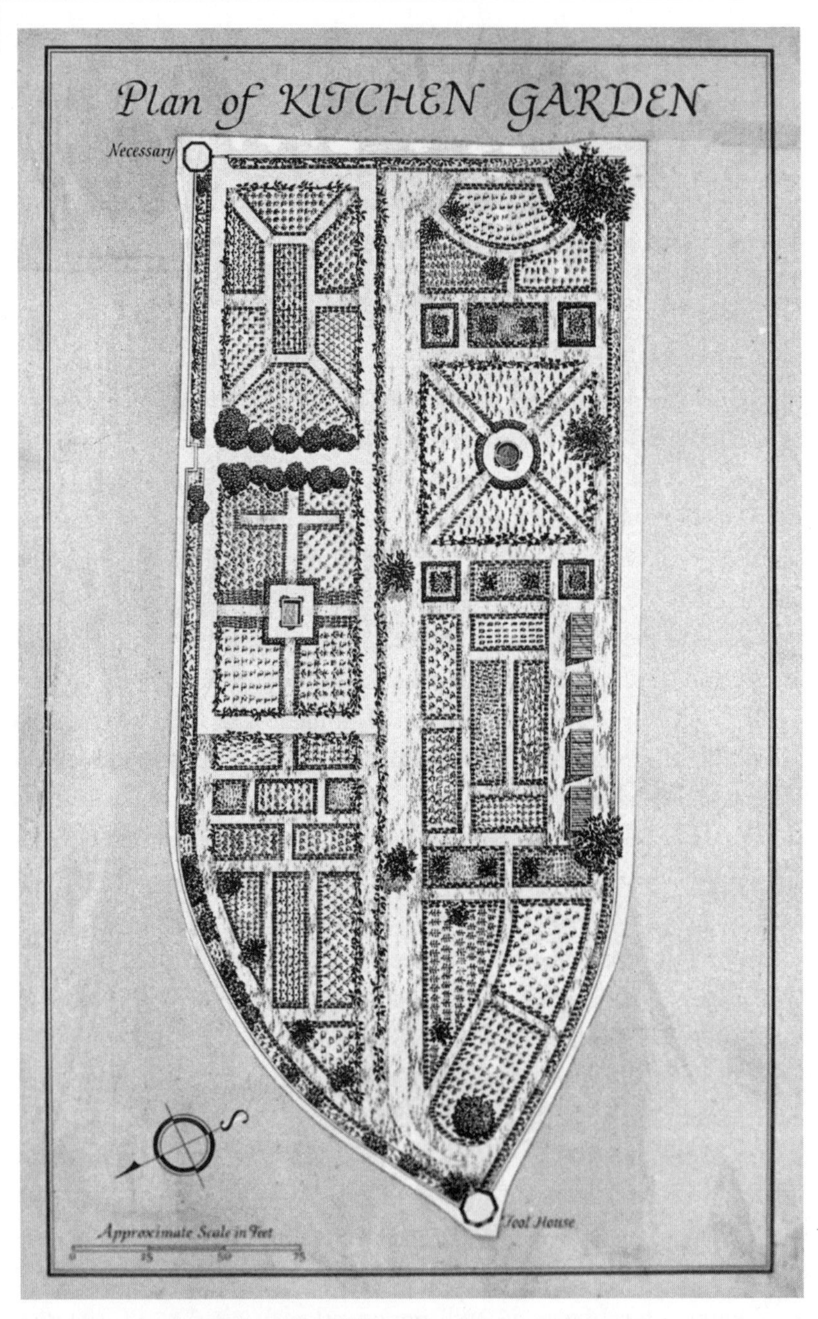

Restoration plan by Morley Jeffers Williams for the Mount Vernon kitchen garden, 1935. (Courtesy of the Mount Vernon Ladies' Association)

Harvard GSD during the spring semester of 1936 and then resigned to begin his directorship. Over the next three years, Williams oversaw the continued investigation of archaeological features and documentary research necessary to begin the restoration of Mount Vernon to the era depicted in Samuel Vaughan's 1787 drawing of the property, the period chosen for the restoration. He focused his research on identifying the periods to which the buildings and landscape features at Mount Vernon dated, an integral part of interpreting any historic landscape.[20]

In 1987, Dennis J. Pogue, currently serving as director of restoration at Mount Vernon, prepared a summary overview of Williams's investigations as part of a background study of previous archaeology on the property. Pogue classified Williams's research into three separate categories. First, Williams tested the bowling green and upper and lower gardens to identify past garden and landscape designs. Second, he led restoration-related excavations in the stable yard, the icehouse on the east lawn, and the north and south ha-ha walls. Finally, Williams investigated the archaeology of a greenhouse, a blacksmith shop, the dung repository, a carpenter shop, and a nineteenth-century icehouse in the stable yard. This research confirmed the existence of buildings and landscape designs shown on the 1787 Vaughan plan of Mount Vernon.[21]

Based on Williams's archaeological findings, he replaced the posts that delineate the grass circle on the west front of the mansion, but little else was restored during his brief tenure as director. The one exception to this minimal intervention is the reconstruction of the kitchen garden, which was not based on archaeological evidence but relied instead on account book entries and period garden books. Although Williams probably expected his studies to be utilized in the future as additional elements of buildings and landscape features were restored, he apparently was more concerned with understanding the evolution of Mount Vernon's historic landscape than the immediate restoration.[22]

Williams's field drawings and notes of the excavation at Mount Vernon provide insight into his archaeological methodology. Not surprisingly, his techniques were very similar to those that he and Pinkney used at Stratford Hall, where trenching was the primary investigative tool. Archaeologists have excavated a number of these trenches more recently, such as in the

1993 excavation of the dung repository. Williams's profile drawings of trench walls reflect his awareness of stratigraphy, and in some cases, he made an attempt to date various strata with changes in the Mount Vernon landscape. Williams designed his excavations to date and gather restoration information on the buildings and landscape features and used artifacts simply as a guide to dating strata. He kept only a few exemplary pieces, such as a brass "Custis raven" that was part of an animal bridle found during the testing of the blacksmith shop. Like his archaeological trenches at Stratford Hall, Williams's exploratory trenches at Mount Vernon contained artifacts redeposited from his earlier excavations.[23]

In 1939, Williams left Mount Vernon after Charles Cecil Wall succeeded Col. Harrison Dodge as its director. Rumors persist at Mount Vernon even today that Williams had aspirations to the position, even to the extent of designing the director's house in 1935. The fact that Williams dated (and eventually married) Nathalia Uhlman, a graduate student assisting in the restoration research, reputedly cost him the directorship. However, to date no tangible evidence has been located to support these anecdotal accounts of Williams's departure from Mount Vernon.

TRYON PALACE

Morley Williams spent 1940 and 1941 conducting independent research on eighteenth-century manuscripts and newspapers in the Library of Congress and elsewhere. During this period, he and Nathalia became the parents of two children, Richard MacKinsey and Brooke Curtis. Nathalia had trained as an architect at the Massachusetts Institute of Technology and the Fontainebleau School of Architecture in France. From 1941 until 1947, the Williamses operated a private practice in Bluemont, Virginia. In September 1947, Morley Williams joined the faculty of the North Carolina State College (now University) School of Design in Raleigh as a professor of landscape architecture. The next year he succeeded E. G. Thurlow as head of the Landscape Architecture Department.[24] Yet in early 1952, at the age of sixty-five, Williams again left academia for another restoration project, that of Tryon Palace, the opulent pre-Revolutionary, Palladian-villa style home of loyalist governors William Tryon and Josiah Martin in New Bern, North Carolina.

Williams faced a greater challenge in the restoration of Tryon Palace than in his previous excavations at Mount Vernon and Stratford Hall. The former colonial royal governors' residence and landscape was to be restored by the Boston architectural firm of Perry, Shaw, and Hepburn, Kehoe and Dean, which oversaw much of the restoration work of Colonial Williamsburg. Based on Williams's former expertise in interpretation and restoration of historic sites, he was hired in 1952 by William Perry as his local representative both to direct the physical research and to oversee day-to-day operations. The problems inherent in restoring the site were multiple. After the palace burned in 1798, the property was subdivided into lots and sold. From the early nineteenth century until the early 1950s, numerous houses and outbuildings occupied these lots, all of which would have to be relocated or torn down as part of the restoration. Two streets had long been extended over the former palace property, one of which, George Street, went directly through the former location of the main building. Only the brick shell of the palace's west wing, which served as the stable in the eighteenth century, remained. Archaeological research would be needed not only to confirm the details of British architect John Hawks's 1767 structural plans but also to provide architectural details of the interior and the landscape for restoration purposes.

Christopher Crittenden, director of the North Carolina Department of Archives and History Section, and George Ross, director of the North Carolina Department of Conservation and Development, recommended Morley Williams to William Perry as a logical candidate to conduct the initial physical research for the Tryon Palace project. Though it is not clear how Crittenden and Ross knew Williams, all were active members in the North Carolina Society for the Preservation of Antiquities, an organization that strongly supported the palace restoration. Perry expressed his enthusiasm for the recommendation to the Kellenbergers, noting that Williams's "experience at Mount Vernon, Stratford, and elsewhere seems to qualify him admirably for this important preliminary work."[25]

Williams supervised the archaeological investigations of Tryon Palace and its grounds in 1952–54 and again in 1958–59 as other cultural features were discovered during the development of the landscape. Unlike his previous work at Stratford Hall and Mount Vernon, Williams collected a large quantity of artifacts during his excavations at the palace. He failed to process and catalog the artifacts, however, and his inability to complete the promised excavation reports resulted in the end of his association with the palace restoration in 1962. Although he completed one photographic album with captions on the restoration of the east wing, containing little information on the excavation of that structure, he prepared no technical summaries or public report on the excavations. Unfortunately, to date, no written reports or records of the artifact analyses from Williams's work at the palace have been located. Stories continue to circulate that Williams's last act before he died was to have all his personal paperwork destroyed, including his completed reports on the palace project, though this is unlikely. Based on records that do exist for the archaeological investigation, it is more likely that Williams, at the age of seventy-five when he left the palace project in early 1962, never completed these reports.

However, numerous photographs on file at Tryon Palace Historic Sites and Gardens in New Bern effectively document the excavation and site restoration, and basic descriptions of many structural remains can be compiled from the daily work reports (which served as field notes), correspondence, and meeting minutes. In addition, there are two extant drawings of the main building and east wing foundation. The main building of the palace was located under the surface of George Street, but only the east and west foundation walls, part of a stairway partition, and portions of original interior basement walls remained. Both the southeastern and southwestern basement rooms had dirt floors. Structural remnants of the east wing foundation, which served as the palace's kitchen, were also found and excavated. The original west wing, which was the stable for the palace, was an extant structure at the time of the restoration and did not require extensive archaeological investigation. Additional elements of the original palace landscape were also discovered, including footings of the original colonnades and palisado walls (probably iron fences), storm drains, a well near the east wing, three privies, and a surface of the original entrance drive. No evidence was found of the outbuildings added by Governor Josiah Martin in 1771 and 1772. Williams also discovered evidence of a nineteenth-century cistern and

Excavations at Tryon Palace prior to the reconstruction of the main building, c. 1953. A pattern of systematic trenching used to uncover structural features is visible in the background. In the foreground can be seen the east foundation wall of the main building. (Courtesy of the North Carolina Office of Archives and History, Raleigh, North Carolina)

a foundation constructed of ballast stone believed to date to the settlement of New Bern in the early eighteenth century.[26]

Williams's archaeological research confirmed details of Hawks's plans as accurate, and the restoration proceeded. William Perry's preservation philosophy guided the restoration of Tryon Palace: "The nature of the 'Restoration' requires that all sound portions of original walls be preserved. Exposed surfaces are visible after construction is completed. This has been the essence of the work at Williamsburg."[27] The west wing of Tryon Palace was repaired and restored to its original function as a stable. The east and west foundation walls were the only structural remains of the original main building considered durable enough to use in the reconstructed main building. The east wall was leveled at the sixteenth brick course. Similarly, the west wall was leveled at the eighteenth brick course. These walls were then repointed and damp-proofed. Additional courses of brick were later added to protect the original foundation walls before reconstruction began. These two original foundation walls are still visible inside the reconstructed main building. The remaining architectural features were deemed too weak to be used and were removed. No original brick features were used in the reconstruction of the east wing. The other period architectural features discovered through archaeological research, the colonnades and palisado walls, privy foundations, and Hawks's drainage system, were repaired and restored. A pigeon house was built without archaeological evidence.[28]

As plans for restoration developed, disputes arose as to how the work should proceed and were manifested in two competing restoration philosophies of the era: should the restoration reflect the extant archaeological evidence, or should it proceed based on what some believed Governor Tryon would have *wanted* it to be? Architect William Perry favored the latter approach. Historian William S. Tarlton researched Perry's plans and discovered that they originally lacked the two pentagonal privy buildings. Moreover, they showed a different arrangement of how the palisado joined the sentry houses. The plans also illustrate a different configuration of stone steps for the north entrance of the main building than the archaeological evidence reveals. Perry planned a cement floor for the southeastern and southwestern basement rooms, which originally were dirt. Of the pieces of marble recovered during the excavation, the percentages and types did not correspond to Perry's plans for the marble floor of the main foyer. Shards of the original window glass were greener and more irregular than the window glass planned for use in the reconstruction. Recovered fragments of the original plaster revealed only plain struck molding, while the architectural plans allowed for the use of floral motifs, foliated patterns, egg and dart ornamentation, dentils, triglyphs, medallions, rosettes, and other elaborate geometric designs in plaster.[29]

Crittenden disagreed with this restoration philosophy. He believed that restoration should be carried out to resemble the original buildings as closely as possible. Tryon Palace commission member and highway chair

A. H. Graham stated that Perry should be allowed to go as far with the restoration "as his architectural conscience will permit him to go."[30] Williams defended Perry in a letter to the editor of the *Raleigh News and Observer*. While stating that the available physical evidence is being followed "meticulously by the architect whenever it applies," he noted that the "restoration problem, in the fields where evidence is wanting, is not a simple matter of asking for more money to create more beauty. It is rather the problem of drawing the line at some point between the austere and the lavish."[31]

This and other statements made by Williams in his letter give a clear indication of his preservation philosophy. Williams believed in the integration of the physical evidence recovered through archaeological investigation, as evidenced in his previous restoration plans at Stratford Hall and Mount Vernon. The problem occurred where physical evidence was lacking. At Tryon Palace, the problem centered primarily on the interior decor, which was destroyed in the 1798 fire. Citing physical evidence in the form of recovered glass and ceramic tableware fragments, Williams pointed out the "sensitive regard to [following the] metropolitan fashion" of the original Palace residents.[32] This regard for contemporary high socioeconomic style, combined with evidence noted in similar British residences of the period, led Williams to support Perry's vision of the restored Palace as more elaborate than exact.

The executive committee of the Tryon Palace Commission, meeting in February 1955, unanimously approved a revised set of plans for a less ornate structure. It is not certain to what extent the committee considered Tarlton's analysis of Perry's plans. When the artifacts from the palace excavation have been completely analyzed, a similar study of interior decorations based on archaeological evidence is merited. What can be stated with certainty is that in planning the restoration, the committee carefully considered the archaeological data of interior furnishings as well as structural remains.[33]

Williams's excavation methodology at Tryon Palace both resembles and departs from his previous archaeological investigations at Stratford Hall and Mount Vernon. Williams again used diagonal trenching to locate structural remains and to search for landscape features, though the nature of the restoration project eventually prompted total excavation of the main building and east wing. The crew that Williams hired to help with the physical research and excavation was composed primarily of eight to twelve African American males from the New Bern area. Williams trained these men in excavation techniques, though archaeology was only a small part of their jobs. Their other duties were to clear debris from the site, cut grass, unload lumber, assist carpenters and masons, and haul dirt and brickbats off-site.

To determine the nature of artifacts in planning the interior decoration, all the excavated soil was sifted through fine-mesh screens. It appears that the screening was thorough, as recent investigations reveal that Williams's trenches contained no artifacts. Restoration specialists also sought artifacts to place in a museum room planned for the basement of the reconstructed main building. Unfortunately, the 191 boxes of artifacts that date both to the palace and post-palace period have virtually no contextual information other than simple labels reading "East Wing" or "Palace." Perry noted that Williams established a grid system across the entire palace property, and that certain interesting artifacts were plotted in situ, though at this time no documentary or photographic evidence provides a clue to the grid system or how Williams may have plotted artifacts within that grid. Archaeologists hope that some form of a "Rosetta Stone" will be discovered to decipher Williams's grid and link the surviving artifacts to a proper archaeological context.[34]

There are minor references made to stratigraphy in the palace daily reports. Repeated references in Williams's notes from Stratford Hall, Mount Vernon, and Tryon Palace certainly indicate his awareness of stratigraphy. However, the daily reports do not indicate or suggest that Williams practiced the technique of stratigraphic investigation or considered each stratum and its artifacts independently during excavation and analysis. The poor contextual information of the recovered artifacts may support this notion. These factors and his work at the other sites indicate it is likely that Williams was more concerned with the larger restoration questions and issues of these projects.

Morley Williams was also responsible for researching and designing gardens for Tryon Palace. A formal parterre garden, a small, private parterre garden intended solely for the enjoyment of the palace occupants, a kitchen herb garden, and a vegetable garden were built as part of the restoration. Archaeologists have found no evidence of garden walkways, beds, or walls in any of the documentation related to the excavation of the palace grounds. Claude Joseph Sauthier's 1769 maps of New Bern showed formal parterre gardens to the north of the palace, and a later drawing by traveler Francisco de Miranda illustrated formal gardens to the south of the palace. The restored gardens do not fit either the location or parterre arrangements shown in these figures. With no archaeological evidence on which to base his plans, Williams tried to balance the idea of an accurate restoration with the desire to create an aesthetically pleasing garden for the modern visitor. The results are gardens that Williams designed solely after English plans of picturesque, naturalistic landscapes of the 1760–70 period.[35]

By 1962, Morley Williams's association with Tryon Palace had dissolved. The conclusion of this association is often misunderstood. Though very satisfied with his archaeological investigations and the design and development of the site landscape, the Kellenbergers and the Tryon Palace Commission had become increasingly frustrated with Williams for not completing the processing of the recovered artifacts or reports on the excavation and restoration, all of which he had promised to do. Beginning in 1957, May Gordon Kellenberger began reminding Williams to write a report on his research on the palace. However, at this time Williams was busy supervising the construction of the landscape. Hiring several individuals to work with Williams in the processing of the artifacts produced few results. Following the completion of the Tryon Palace landscape, Williams had become involved in other projects, including returning to Harvard to lecture. In 1961, an increasingly frustrated Mrs. Kellenberger wrote, "Now, five years have passed since construction was finished, Mr. Williams is endeavoring to put together data which should have become the property of the state long ago."[36] The Kellenbergers even wrote William Perry of the architectural firm, asking him to withhold any final payments with Williams until a number of issues were settled.[37] Finally, in December 1961, Williams returned all the artifacts to Tryon Palace, noting, "It is a great relief to be free of the responsibility for the safety of this truly valuable collection."[38]

THE PAST AND PRESENT OF LANDSCAPE ARCHAEOLOGY

Morley Jeffers Williams's archaeological investigations of the landscapes of Stratford Hall, Mount Vernon, and Tryon Palace serve as excellent examples of early historical archaeology in the United States. The first archaeological explorations occurred on notable historic sites and were primarily used to substantiate and supplement facts found in written records. Such explorations were often led by historians or landscape architects, and the data collected in these investigations were primarily used to restore and interpret these sites for the public. The use of archaeological techniques in architectural and landscape studies represented cutting-edge research technology for Williams and many of his contemporaries, such as James Knight, Arthur Shurcliff, John Cotter, and J. C. Harrington.

Though the efforts and accomplishments of these early pioneers were not forgotten, the archaeological study of historic landscapes largely reemerged in the late 1970s and 1980s, the result of a deepening interest in historic preservation and as a natural outgrowth of many modern concerns, such as the interaction between humans and the natural environment. In the 1980s, William M. Kelso's archaeologically based interpretations of the landscapes at Carter's Grove, Kingsmill, and Monticello served as seminal works to a new generation of archaeologists, demonstrating the potential that archaeology had in the study of landscapes. While Williams and his contemporaries favored selective trenching to cover large areas, Kelso's studies demonstrated to archaeologists that the most effective technique to detect subtle features of historic landscapes is to excavate large areas at one time. Larger areas may provide a more complete picture than smaller investigations. Individual walls may be seen to form complete structures, and walkways may be noted through larger defined areas, such as garden beds. From a cultural resource management perspective, where time and budget are of greater concern, the practice of exploring larger areas allows an archaeological site to be more thoroughly explored, defined, and recorded than selective trenching would reveal.[39]

The term "landscape archaeology" has predominantly been used to represent the archaeological study of anything beyond the doors of a historic residence. From this broad definition, three topical areas of study have emerged. First and foremost is the study of gardens, which traditionally have been the most common landscape feature to be archaeologically investigated. While most garden archaeology is undertaken to provide documentation for future restoration, several studies have attempted to move beyond restoration to consider aspects of ideology and gender within garden design. A second topic of landscape archaeology is the study of buildings and cultural features (such as a ha-ha wall or fence) within rural or urban landscapes. This has mainly concentrated on formally designed estates but is rapidly expanding to include vernacular landscapes as well. While this type of landscape archaeology often has been conducted for restoration purposes and to understand the evolution of the landscape, occasionally it has revealed the cultural forces and ideologies behind the changes. The third and least common, though no less fruitful, topical area of landscape archaeology is the study of settlement patterns, the location of residences and industries on a larger scale. The majority of such settlement pattern studies are either regionally based, such as an area of a state, or geographically based, such as a river basin.

Even today, the vast majority of published case studies in landscape archaeology have focused on the grounds of historic houses, museums, or private property. The excavations in these case studies usually have been restoration oriented and funded through preservation organizations, universities, museums, or private donations. They have involved many different methodological techniques, including trenching, area excavation, mechanical stripping of areas, and remote sensing; on a larger scale, aerial photographs and satellite imagery (GIS) are used, as well as analytical techniques such as seed, pollen, and phytolith analyses. Much of the methodology these studies advocate remains untried in the realm of federally mandated compliance archaeology, which comprises the vast majority of the current archaeological research in the United States. There are several reasons why contract companies infrequently conduct landscape studies: time and funds are usually limited; few sites are deemed significant enough for mitigation; and often only a small portion of a larger site is mitigated. In addition, many landscape architects are unaware of the potential contributions archaeology has to offer landscape studies. There are certainly exceptions, but unfortunately these often remain hidden from the larger communities of archaeologists and landscape architects in isolated compliance reports and never see broader publication.[40]

Numerous articles in modern academic journals and other publications attest to the continuing interest and the broadening focus of landscape archaeology. In addition to the continued search for structures and landscape features, modern archaeologists emphasize the importance of stratigraphy and the analysis of recovered artifacts to unlock social and cultural information about the former occupants of a site. With the development of new paradigms, there is also a greater interest in the diverse aspects of landscapes, such as the roles of ideology and gender in the design and care of historic gardens. Modern archaeologists may take advantage of many technological advances in the study of landscapes. Remote-sensing devices, such as ground-penetrating radar and proton magnetometers, and soil resistivity tests can be used to identify buried components of landscapes without the time and expense of archaeological excavation. Paleoethnobotany, which includes seed, pollen, and phytolith analyses, has made it possible to identify the family, genus, and species of many varieties of historic plants and trees for more accurate botanical restoration.

However, the objective of landscape archaeology—to understand cultural impressions made on the natural landscape—remains essentially unchanged since Morley Jeffers Williams began his work in the 1930s. Even with advanced methods and new theoretical perspectives, it is ironic that with the great interest in historic preservation, archaeology—by its nature an inherently destructive process—remains one of the best tools available to investigate and understand the cultural development of historic landscapes.

NOTES

The author wishes to express his gratitude to the following people, who discussed, shared, and confirmed information about Morley Williams: William L. Beiswanger, Virginia Burgess, Robert P. Burns, Susan Cahill, Dottie Haynes, Judy Hynsen, Dean Knight, Perry Mathewes, Dennis Pogue, Laura Lee Sampson, Peter Sandbeck, Douglas Sanford, Minerva Smith, Brian A. Sullivan, and Esther White. He also thanks Charles A. Birnbaum, Mary V. Hughes, Linda F. Carnes-McNaughton, Charles R.

Ewen, John J. Mintz, Pam Robbins, and Patricia Samford for their comments on earlier drafts of this study.

An account of Williams's work at Tryon Palace was previously published in an article by the author entitled "Fables of the Reconstruction: Morley Jeffers Williams and the Excavation of Tryon Palace, 1952–1962," in *North Carolina Archaeology* 49 (2000): 1–22.

1. *Boston Evening Transcript,* May 2, 1934. In 1717, acting governor of Virginia Charles Lee purchased the land for Stratford Hall Plantation, the boyhood home of Robert E. Lee from 1807 to 1811. The estate of Mount Vernon, granted to George Washington's great-grandfather John Washington in 1674, was the first president's home from ca. 1754 until his death in 1799. Tryon Palace, built by English architect John Hawks in 1767–70, was the home of royal governor William Tryon until 1771; Josiah Martin, the second royal governor to reside at the palace, left in 1775 at the beginning of the American Revolution.

2. A biographical sketch of Williams that further details his early life and career training can be found in Thomas E. Beaman Jr., "Morley Jeffers Williams," in *Pioneers of American Landscape Design,* ed. Charles A. Birnbaum and Robin Karson (New York: McGraw Hill, 2000), 455–57.

3. Bremer W. Pond to Mrs. Fairfax Harrison, June 19, 1933, Archives of the Robert E. Lee Memorial Association, Jessie Ball duPont Memorial Library, Stratford Hall Plantation, Stratford, Virginia.

4. Morley Jeffers Williams, "The Evolution of the Design of Mount Vernon," *Landscape Architecture* 22 (April 1932): 165–77; North Carolina State College News Bureau, information form, 1948, Biographical file, North Carolina State University Archives, Raleigh.

5. Morley Jeffers Williams to Mrs. E. R. Newell, May 28, 1935, and Williams, "Stratford Excavations, Summer 1932" (copy), both in Archives of the Robert E. Lee Memorial Association; Morley Jeffers Williams, "The Restoration of Stratford: Three Drawings," *Landscape Architecture* 23 (April 1933): 175–77.

6. Arthur A. Shurcliff, "Report on Investigations and Observations Made in Regard to Brickwork and Mortar at Stratford Hall, Prepared for the Stratford Garden Committee, Garden Club of Virginia" (copy), and Morley Jeffers Williams, "Stratford Excavations, Summer 1932," both in Archives of the Robert E. Lee Memorial Association.

7. Williams, "Stratford Excavations, Summer 1932," 1–3. As defined by architectural historian Carl R. Lounsbury, a *ha-ha* is a cultural barrier designed to keep livestock or wild animals in a pasture or wilderness away from a plantation's "pleasure grounds." Ha-has are constructed to make the plantation appear to be an extension of the "pleasure grounds," so that there is no visual interruption of the landscape. At Stratford Hall, the ha-ha was a sunken fence style, where a short fence was placed in the bottom of a ditch, but the top of the fence did not extend above the ground level. Carl R. Lounsbury, *An Illustrated Glossary of Early Southern Architecture and Landscape* (New York: Oxford University Press, 1994), 172.

8. Williams, "Stratford Excavations, Summer 1932," 3.

9. Williams, "The Restoration of Stratford"; Dorothy Hunt Williams, *Historic Virginia Gardens: Preservations by the Garden Club of Virginia* (Charlottesville: University Press of Virginia, 1975), 20; Morley Jeffers Williams to Fiske Kimball, October 24, 1932, and Fiske Kimball to Morley Jeffers Williams, October 26, 1932, both in Archives of the Robert E. Lee Memorial Association; Ethel Armes, *Stratford Hall: The Great House of the Lees* (Richmond, VA: Garrett & Massie, 1936), 506–11.

10. Morley Jeffers Williams, "The Gardens at Monticello," *Landscape Architecture* 24 (January 1934): 65–72.

11. Charles Coatsworth Pinkney to Morley Jeffers Williams, "Weekly Reports of Excavation Progress, 1934," and Williams, "Comments to Accompany the Preliminary Study for the Stratford Grounds Restoration," 1938, both in Archives of the Robert E. Lee Memorial Association.

12. Pinkney to Williams, "Weekly Reports of Excavation Progress, 1934"; Pinkney to Williams, "Weekly Report," August 4, 1934; Pinkney to Williams, "Weekly Report," September 1, 1934; all in Archives of the Robert E. Lee Memorial Association.

13. Douglas W. Sanford to author, April 12, 1999, author's collection. For a more comprehensive review of the history of archaeological investigations at Stratford Hall, see Douglas W. Sanford, "Landscape, Change, and Community at Stratford Hall Plantation: An Archaeological and Cultural Perspective," *Quarterly Bulletin of the Archaeological Society of Virginia* 54 (March 1999): 2–19.

14. Dennis J. Pogue, "Archaeology at George Washington's Mount Vernon: 1931–1987," file report no. 1, 1988, 3–6, Archaeology Department, Mount Vernon Ladies' Association, Mount Vernon, Virginia; Dennis J. Pogue, "Mount Vernon, Transformation of an Eighteenth-Century Plantation System," in *Historical Archaeology of the Chesapeake,* ed. Paul A. Shackel and Barbara J. Little (Washington, DC: Smithsonian Institution Press, 1994), 101–14.

15. Williams, "Evolution of the Design of Mount Vernon," 170.

16. Williams, "Evolution of the Design of Mount Vernon," 172–74; Morley Jeffers Williams, "Washington's Changes at Mount Vernon Plantation," *Landscape Architecture* 28 (January 1938): 62–73.

17. Pogue, "Archaeology at George Washington's Mount Vernon," 3–6.

18. Williams, "Washington's Changes at Mount Vernon," 72.

19. Morley Jeffers Williams, "A Site for a Memorial," *Magazine of Art* 31 (May 1938): 268–70.

20. Williams, "Washington's Changes at Mount Vernon," 62–73. A virtually complete change of the landscape, gardens, and outbuildings and an enlargement of the main residence of Mount Vernon were documented by visitor Samuel Vaughan in 1787. George Washington himself attested to the accuracy of Vaughan's drawing, and its accuracy has been repeatedly confirmed through archaeological investigations at the estate. Pogue, "Archaeology at George Washington's Mount Vernon," 18.

21. Pogue, "Archaeology at George Washington's Mount Vernon," 3–6; Williams, "Washington's Changes at Mount Vernon," 66.

22. Mount Vernon Ladies' Association of the Union, "Minutes of the Council," *Annual Report, 1937* (Mount Vernon, VA, 1937), 42–43, copy in the Archives of the Mount Vernon Ladies' Association; Williams, "Washington's Changes at Mount Vernon," 72.

23. Dennis J. Pogue, "Archaeological Investigations at the Mount Vernon Dung Repository (44Fx762/15), An Interim Report," file report no. 5 (1994), 10–13; Mount Vernon Ladies' Association, "Minutes of the Council," *Annual Report, 1937*, 42.

24. Williams, information form and undated news clipping, *Raleigh News and Observer*, both in Biographical file, North Carolina State University Archives.

25. William Perry to Mr. and Mrs. J. A. Kellenberger, April 11, 1952, Kellenberger Papers, Tryon Palace Historic Sites and Gardens, New Bern, North Carolina, hereinafter cited as Kellenberger Papers.

26. Palace Daily Reports 55, 56, 62, 69, 86, 91, 98, 99, 103, 169, 176–79, 189, 238, 446, 735; Morley Jeffers Williams, "Palace Proper, Scale 1 in.=4 ft., December 19, 1953"; Williams, "Site Report of the East Wing of Tryon's Palace, New Bern, North Carolina" (1961); William Perry, "Progress Report, August 29, 1952"; William Perry, "Status of the Reconstruction of and Accounts for West Wing and East Wing as of November 30, 1953" (1954); William Perry to Mr. J. A. Kellenberger, July 12, 1956; all in Kellenberger Papers.

27. William Perry, "Progress Report, March 22, 1954," Kellenberger Papers.

28. William Perry, "Status of the Reconstruction of and Accounts for West Wing and East Wing as of November 30, 1953"; William Perry to Mr. J. A. Kellenberger, August 13, 1954; William Perry, "Documents and Specifications for Reconstruction and Restoration of Tryon Palace, New Bern, North Carolina," 1955, all in Kellenberger Papers. *Repointing* is a term that commonly refers to stabilizing and remortaring a brick wall for continued use or reuse.

29. William S. Tarlton, "Tryon Palace Plans and Specifications, Additional Statement (from the State Department of Archives and History), November 10, 1954," Kellenberger Papers.

30. Unsigned editorial, *Raleigh News and Observer,* July 6, 1954.

31. Morley Jeffers Williams, letter to the editor, *Raleigh News and Observer,* July 9, 1954. For a thorough discussion of this debate, see Blackwell P. Robinson, *Three Decades of Devotion: The Story of the Tryon Palace Commission and the Tryon Palace Restoration* (New Bern, NC: Tryon Palace Commission, 1978), 71–78.

32. Williams, letter to the editor, July 9, 1954.

33. Tryon Palace Commission, "Minutes of the Executive Committee of the Tryon Palace Commission, February 11, 1955," Kellenberger Papers.

34. William M. Kelso, Nicholas M. Lucketti, and Margaret C. Wood, "Preliminary Archaeological Investigations of the Eighteenth-Century Gardens at Tryon Palace, New Bern, North Carolina" (Williamsburg, VA: James River Institute for Archaeology, 1994), 9. Two trenches attributed to Williams's explorations were also uncovered on the north lawn during the 1999 Archaeology Field School conducted

by East Carolina University's Department of Anthropology. William Perry, "Progress Report, August 29, 1952"; Perry, "Progress Report, September 24, 1952"; Palace Daily Report no. 43, August 19, 1952, all in Kellenberger Papers.

35. Williams discussed this period of design for the palace gardens at the dedication of the Maude Moore Latham Garden on April 8, 1961. Robinson, *Three Decades of Devotion,* 158.

36. Mrs. J. A. Kellenberger to Dr. Christopher Crittenden, October 27, 1961, Kellenberger Papers.

37. J. A. Kellenberger to William Perry, May 15, 1961, Kellenberger Papers.

38. Morley Jeffers Williams to Mrs. J. A. Kellenberger, January 2, 1962, Kellenberger Papers.

39. William M. Kelso, "Landscape Archaeology: A Key to Virginia's Cultivated Past," in *British and American Gardens in the Eighteenth Century,* ed. Robert P. Maccubbin and Peter Martin (Williamsburg, VA: Colonial Williamsburg Foundation, 1984), 159–69; William M. Kelso, *Kingsmill Plantations, 1619–1800, Archaeology of Country Life in Colonial Virginia* (Orlando, FL: Academic Press, 1984); William M. Kelso and Rachel Most, eds., *Earth Patterns: Essays in Landscape Archaeology* (Charlottesville: University Press of Virginia, 1990).

40. Anne Yentsch and Judson M. Kratzer, "Techniques Used by Historical Archaeologists to Study American Landscapes and Gardens," *Journal of Garden History* 17 (January/March 1997): 47–53.

"The Fading Landscape"

Arthur A. Shurcliff's Evolving Perceptions of Landscape Preservation

ELIZABETH HOPE CUSHING

Scholars examining historic preservation issues in the twentieth century are frequently confronted with the shifting sense of "history," the different theories and strategies that evolve in light of new evidence and new attitudes, as well as the slight alterations in perspective, the minute amendments we make, in the face of these fluctuations. Those who speculate upon decisions made by and about early preservationists and conservationists would do well to reflect upon the axiom that viewpoints toward the past are subject to a continuous flow of reassessment and change.

Certainly one of the most important icons of early twentieth-century preservation history was John D. Rockefeller Jr.'s transformation of the small, rural town of Williamsburg, Virginia, from its pre-Depression quietude into the utterly altered, bustling corporate entity of the Colonial Williamsburg Foundation. The team Rockefeller's agents gathered for the task consisted predominantly of northern architects and historians (residents called it the "second Yankee invasion"), among them the Boston landscape architect Arthur A. Shurcliff (1879–1957). He came to the project at the suggestion of the architects in charge of the restoration, Perry, Shaw, and Hepburn, also from Boston. Already a seasoned practitioner in all aspects of landscape practice, at fifty-eight years of age Shurcliff had spent years developing exquisite sensibilities to the natural and man-made worlds he inhabited and helped to shape.

Arthur A. Shurcliff in 1905, at the age of thirty-six. (Courtesy of a private collection)

He was born Arthur Asahel Shurtleff (the name change occurred in 1930, in order, he said, to conform to the ancient spelling of the family name) into a loving and nurturing family consisting of his parents, Sarah Ann and Asahel Milton Shurtleff, and four siblings. The Shurtleff home in Boston was filled with music, art, and literature; the five children were encouraged to engage in a cultivated life that included a profound respect for history, both familial and national, and for handcraft. Asahel Shurtleff taught all his children woodworking in his shop on the fourth floor of their Beacon Hill home. Many aspects of handcraft, in particular woodworking, remained serious avocations for Shurcliff throughout his life. After his marriage in 1905, he and his wife, Margaret Homer Nichols Shurcliff, also a woodworker, built a small summer house in Ipswich, Massachusetts, which they proceeded to expand over the years, carving all the interior decoration and crafting most of the furniture themselves.

Two major influences in Shurcliff's cultural life pervaded his body of writings on preservation and restoration through the years: the Arts and Crafts movement, which hit Boston full force with the 1897 exhibition at Copley Hall, and the Colonial Revival wave that washed over the city at the time of the Philadelphia Centennial Exhibition in 1876 and held sway for decades afterward. The Arts and Crafts movement began in England as a reaction to what were perceived as the dehumanizing and degrading aspects of industrialization. Championed by internationally known worthies such as art critic and writer John Ruskin and the most notable practitioner of handcrafted decorative arts, William Morris, the movement spread rapidly around the world. Cantabrigian Charles Eliot Norton, Harvard University's first professor of fine arts and a personal friend to Ruskin, was instrumental in bringing the aesthetic principles to Boston, serving as founding president of the Society of Arts and Crafts, Boston, which was inaugurated the same year the exhibition was held.[1] This reverence for old-fashioned methods of production and pre-industrial life patterns was quickly adopted around the United States, and the effects of its principles and products reverberated through the years to come.

The Colonial Revival aesthetic, also a retrogressive movement, concentrated on preserving, restoring, and revering bygone times, places, and objects. In a different manner it, too, was a reaction to industrialization: horror at the explosion of urban spaces, the influx of a massive immigrant labor force (the first disruption of the perceived order since the initial settlement of white Europeans had displaced the native population), and a distinct sense that this rapid transformation was quickly destroying all evidence of the homogeneous, historical, and understandable fabric of predominantly small-town American life.

For many in New England the two movements ran parallel, eventually becoming entwined as the years went by. The antique and the historical went hand in hand with reverence for handcrafted objects and simplified, rural life. Certainly these trends were reinforced for Arthur Shurcliff by his family's interests.

Above all other influences, however, his life was steeped in a deeply resonating love and understanding of the natural world. During his formative years, the Shurtleffs instilled in him an abiding affection for rural scenery, touring about the countryside surrounding Boston during all seasons of the year and removing the family to various nearby country retreats in summer, including Shurcliff's personal favorite, the Riddell farm at Waverly (now Belmont), Massachusetts.

This pastoral refuge was home to the Waverly Oaks, aboriginal trees growing on an ancient glacial drumlin made famous first in the verses of Boston poet James Russell Lowell. Later the area was the subject of Boston landscape architect Charles Eliot's second preservation project: the establishment of the Boston Metropolitan Park Commission, a follow-up to the Trustees of Public Reservations (currently known as the Trustees of Reservations), the 1891 association that Eliot scholar Keith N. Morgan states served as the "model for subsequent conservation and historic preservation and organizations here and abroad."[2] At Waverly, Shurcliff later wrote: "Tree and flower names were taught us by our father and mother, from whom we learned to regard with awe the enormous trunks and spreading branches of the Waverly Oaks, the twilight croaking and trills of Beaver Brook frogs, sunset color, the spell of landscapes to the sight and to the ear, the sound of rain, leaves, thunder, bells, and the waterfall. . . . We were taken on many long walks over nearby hills and sometimes to distant ponds."[3] These oaks remained so significant to Shurcliff that he made at least annual visits there, including proposing to his future wife in the lower branches of one of them.

The youthful enthusiast spent every moment he could walking and bicycling in the countryside around Boston, thoroughly familiarizing himself with the natural world and with small-town New England life. It is not surprising that both Emerson and Thoreau were his idols from an early age or that he turned to their works throughout his life, eventually writing books of his own meditations.

Shurcliff's forays into the country were frequently made alone, but he also went with his father or with friends. Every autumn the Shurtleff family made a pilgrimage to the mountains of New Hampshire, where Shurcliff hiked and camped throughout his life. He frequently canoed and kayaked on the Charles River in vessels he designed himself, camping as he went along. Everywhere he went he carried a sketchbook and paints, recording his observations and the multitude of matters that caught his interest, another habit he retained well into old age.

The autumn of 1889 found Shurcliff matriculating at the Massachusetts Institute of Technology (MIT), intending to pursue a five-year course in mechanical engineering, for the bright and ingenious young man was foreordained to join his father in the family business of inventing and manufacturing fine surgical instruments. It did not take him long, however, to realize that his interests lay in another direction. With the dispassionate hindsight of fifty years, he wrote in his autobiographical sketches: "Because of the wide public interest in the landscaping of the Chicago World Fair . . . my thoughts turned to Landscape Architecture. Yet there was a stronger reason for this turn, being my interest in country scenery, landscape sketching and painting, natural history, touring-a-wheel [bicycling], camping, mountain climbing, and in the journals of Thoreau,—these influences led me away from mechanics toward scenery, toward planning and construction for the scenes of daily life."[4] One must turn to his journals for a sense of the quiet desperation he felt as he wrestled with the issue throughout his training at MIT. In the spring of his final year, 1894, anguish erupts from the generally stoical twenty-four-year-old as he writes in his journal following a trip to the textile mills at Lawrence, Massachusetts, with his class: "Heavens! Am I a mechanical engineer? Am I to do such awful work? How about the trees? How about the sky? I have forgotten them all."[5]

Instead he decided to consult with eminent Brookline, Massachusetts, landscape architect Frederick Law Olmsted Sr. It was at the Olmsted firm that he encountered Charles Eliot, who helped him cobble together a two-year program at Harvard College, because no formal school of landscape study existed at the time. Eliot, the bright star of the office, took Shurcliff under his wing, informally supervising his work at Harvard. When the young man graduated with a second B.S. in 1896, he immediately apprenticed himself to his mentor and worked with him during the short space of time before Eliot's tragic, premature death of meningitis the following year.

Shurcliff was devastated but continued at the firm for seven more years, gaining a thorough grounding in all phases of landscape practice before setting up his own office in 1904. The effects of Eliot's early training stayed with Shurcliff for the rest of his life, and he always contended that the Olmsted brothers, John Charles and Frederick Law Olmsted Jr., versed him generously and well. In 1899 Shurcliff aided Frederick Law Olmsted Jr. in establishing the nation's first four-year program in landscape architecture at Harvard, where he taught until the demands of his own practice forced him to resign reluctantly in 1906. Those sources of preparation, combined with his in-depth engineering training, made him an extremely knowledgeable practitioner when he finally set out on his own.

Once Shurcliff was established in his practice, his interests in the natural and antique worlds, always present, appear to have taken a deeper course. It is significant that Charles Eliot published a series of articles in 1889 for the influential periodical *Garden and Forest* entitled "Six Old American Country-Seats," in which he endeavored to record significant older American country places. It is likely that Shurcliff read and was inspired by Eliot's articles, as he was so often influenced by Eliot's thoughtful approach to landscape issues.

In 1897 he made one of the many excursions he took with his friend Robert Bellows, bicycling from Massachusetts through Rhode Island to Connecticut, sketching and photographing old places. According to Shurcliff's journal, they stopped "at many a graveyard to make rubbings and to question old men with canes about the times and men gone by."[6] By 1898 he and certain friends were making it a practice to tour old towns around the Boston area, including an excursion in the spring that he described as "fleeing the city and seeking fields dotted with blossoming apple trees and farming villages of quaint houses."[7] That summer and the previous one, Shurcliff had requested that his father photograph old houses and farms during their annual sojourns in New Hampshire and Nantucket.

That year he also extended his explorations to include American gardens. During an expedition to Concord, Massachusetts (a frequently visited mecca, as it was the home of his two transcendental heroes), Shurcliff made pencil sketches of gardens he considered to be genuine eighteenth-century designs, creating lists of what he understood to be the "old-fashioned" plants he found therein.

That August found Bellows and Shurcliff on the road again as they took their bicycles by train to Newburyport, an early seaport along the

Asahel Milton Shurtleff's 1898 photograph of the Jethro Coffin House on Nantucket Island. (Courtesy of a private collection)

northern coast of Massachusetts. After thriving in the nineteenth century, the town fell into economic decline, a fact that had the effect of preserving it to a remarkable degree. The subtitle of Shurcliff's ubiquitous, pocket-sized journal reveals his predominant interest: "The Log of 5 Days in Newburyport" was, he wrote, "dedicated to an old box hedge."[8]

As well as enjoying the natural beauty of the countryside and the nearby ocean, the two young men made gravestone rubbings and scouted out the old houses in the area, Newburyport being a rich source of architecture. For Shurcliff there was a particular interest in the old gardens he found. "Wednesday morning," he writes, "saw me in the old-fashioned gardens of the heart of the town. These old places although now gone to decay are filled with a kind of golden glory which is lacking in the new gardens. The old lattice trellises and ruined box hedges and even the weedgrown paths seem to have the glamor [sic] of the olden days that are only to be lived over again in books or in these old gardens themselves." Not only is Shurcliff expressing his certainty that these are authentic gardens from the past, but he goes on to imbue them with a special aura found only there: "I confess that I feel the presence of the old worthies more in the garden than in the houses. The flowers planted by my old bonneted dame and her rough-cheeked gardener are still blooming and the weeds are guilty with fear that the fingers long since fallen to dust will root them from among the roses."[9]

The Newburyport log contains plans, a list of plants he was informed were "old-fashioned," and photographs of old gardens, chief among them what he calls the Brockway garden, later to appear in Alice G. B. Lockwood's 1934 *Gardens of Colony and State* as the Osgood-Brockway garden. Lockwood acknowledges her dependence upon Shurcliff's earlier research, including reproducing a list of plants he found growing there. Her source may have been his original "Log," or perhaps his first lengthy published piece, "Some Old New England Flower Gardens," written for the December 1899 issue of *New England Magazine,* where he quotes extensively from his journal. In that article he declares that the east garden of the house is in what he calls "a remarkable state of preservation." With an observation that directly links him to Arts and Crafts garden design, Shurcliff writes of the space: "It is surrounded by a high close fence heavily clothed in vines, and no one could imagine from without that such a garden existed; it is as much removed from the street and its traffic as a room in the house itself . . . there is evidence that the garden is regarded by the household as part of their daily life, and there is no suggestion that it is a place for display or that it is a fanciful ornament." Interweaving this concept with what he perceives the colonial garden to be, he concludes that the Brockway garden "may fairly be called a type of the old-fashioned garden: the long narrow plan, the central walk, the terraces, the presence of flowering trees in the flower borders, the arbor, and the seclusion high border screens are to be found in nearly every example."[10] The accompanying garden plans are framed with Arts and Crafts style borders. What becomes clear in this article is the unselfconscious co-mingling of Arts and Crafts and Colonial Revival concepts, a

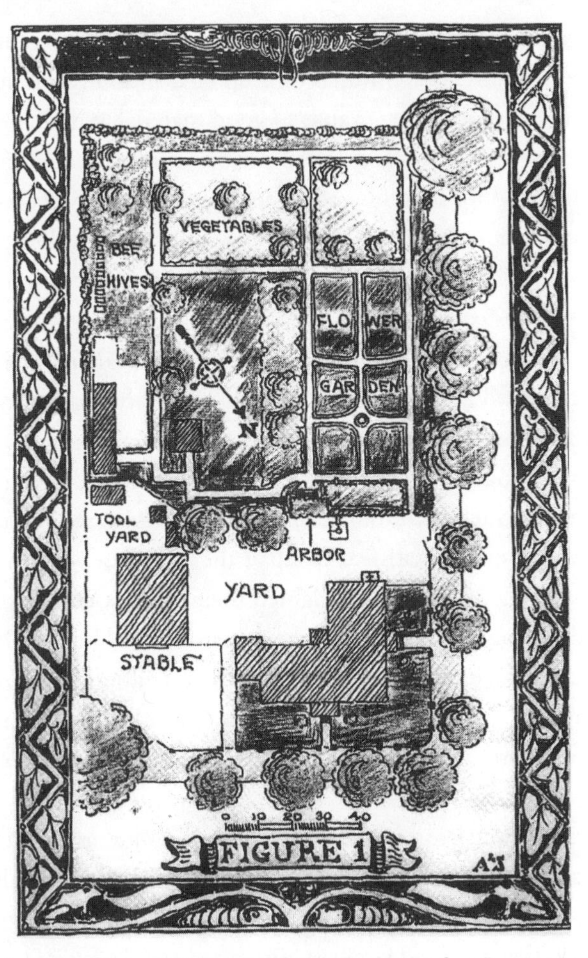

An illustration from "Some Old New England Flower Gardens," written in 1899 for New England Magazine. *Border design shows Shurcliff's affinity for the Arts and Crafts movement.*

modus operandi he continued to employ both in his writing and in his design work. Arts and Crafts and Colonial Revival ideals interwove in Shurcliff's mind, creating the basis for the personal beliefs and professional preservation principles he espoused.

It is interesting that Shurcliff chose for his first major publication an article that reflects his longtime interest in the historical past, signaling the emergence of his own theses about "old-fashioned" gardens within that context. Clearly he believed that towns such as Newburyport, which remained in many ways unchanged from their eighteenth- and nineteenth-century appearance, were often repositories of unspoiled antiquity. He states at the beginning of his article that "thanks to good material and good workmanship," many houses from the colonial period have survived intact, and he remarks on the continuing interest in the American past reflected in their current preservation. In prose replete with Colonial Revival reverberations he adds:

> That we have cared to find out what manner of men went before us and that we have come to like them better than we have liked any other men is proved by the interest which we are taking in every description of colonial record and the care with which such records are being preserved and reproduced. We are not satisfied to repair the old houses and mend their quaint furniture and brighten their candlesticks; we are building houses so much like them that a critical housewife of the time of King George would find them faultless. . . . Every record and tradition is precious, and we eagerly make them a part of life today.[11]

Shurcliff is quick to admit that the colonial garden, as the most ephemeral of relics, has for the most part "slipped away with the loving hands that once cared for it." He believes that not all have disappeared, however, for strong, stable New England family tradition preserved a few of them despite the loss of the fortunes that had originally created them. "The very reserve and quietness of these families," he opines, "are proof that ancestral traditions are strong within them." Making clear his reverence for those very traditions he continues: "But perhaps the greatest proof that the old appealed to them more than the new is found in the fact that they cared for their old gardens. Time could not tarnish their flowers, and there was no reminder in them of the dilapidation that threatened the ancestral house-hold. Larkspur and Canterbury Bells were the same, rich or poor. When poverty pressed hard, the flower garden was the last thing to give evidence of it, and the utilitarian uses to which the ground could be put were allowed to encroach last of all upon its precincts." Shurcliff acknowledges that searching in the 1890s reveals mostly traces of these gardens. "Many of them," he writes, "are overgrown with grass, and the outlines of the old walks are only to be discovered by tufts of box edging here and there." He goes on to state unequivocally, however, that "many of them are well preserved, and these constitute a real resource to the household. They are cared for like precious things."[12]

This is crucial to understanding Shurcliff's life-long conception of colonial American gardens and the context for his later historic preservation work. He believed that it was still possible to find the outlines, or sometimes even more complete examples, of actual eighteenth-century gardens, and he considered that the plans he reproduced for *New England Magazine* were genuine examples. "It has been my good fortune," he states firmly, "to discover several flower gardens of this kind in northeastern Massachusetts." As a last argument he concludes by stating, "The designs have doubtless undergone changes since those days, but the fact that the flowers have not suffered by the intrusion of modern varieties, and that the cast-iron fountain and urn are not to be found in them, are some evidence that except for the devastation of time they remain substantially unmodified in design."[13]

Also in 1898 Shurcliff was finally able to afford the first of many study trips to Europe. Charles Eliot had counseled him to travel abroad as soon as possible in order to familiarize himself with planning, landscapes, parks, and ancient places, particularly in England, and the Olmsteds were also eager for him to experience English and European parks and landscapes. Shurcliff began the process by bicycling in France and England, absorbing the atmosphere and retracing some of Eliot's steps. This and subsequent trips to England were to have a profound effect upon the historic preservation theory he propounded for the rest of his life.

In a July 1902 *House and Garden* article entitled "Two Nantucket Gardens," Shurcliff addresses the issue of colonial authenticity and continuity once again. Despite the vicissitudes of time, he is certain that the few old gardens left on the island are authentic, in particular what he refers to as the King and Sanford gardens. In his article Shurcliff demonstrates the decided quirkiness of Colonial Revival logic. "Sad to say," he writes, "they were built at a comparatively recent period, the early part of the century being the date ascribed to them." Undeterred by that news he goes on to report that "fortunately there is evidence to support the tradition that they were copied from much older gardens in their prime." Unfortunately for modern scholarship, he does not elaborate upon what that evidence might be. He does go on to detail what he considers to be the "important features of the designs," including formality, seclusion, and what he calls the dependence placed upon box hedges to mark off "the main outline of the garden's pattern and to give character to designs which without hedges would have rather suffered than have been improved by the presence of flowers in the ill-defined panels between the paths. Indeed the only considerable architectural effect in the gardens results from the use of this box plant in ribbons, strings and knobs."[14] Shurcliff held the conviction that boxwood served as a ubiquitous colonial hedge and decorative device consistently throughout his preservation practice.

Again in "Two Nantucket Gardens," he weaves in Arts and Crafts concepts, emphasizing the garden as an extension of the indoors, providing outdoor rooms for living:

> Their designers seem to have realized the value of a direct relation between the garden and the house, and the effectiveness of a formal design in the garden itself. . . . The garden is treated as a modified extension of the house-plan in which clipped box edging, clearly defined walks, symmetrically placed arbors and vine-clad fences repeated the structure and ornaments of the indoor dwelling. Distracting views of adjoining houses and traffic were screened from sight by high boundary fences, walls, and plantations which extended the privacy of the house into the garden.[15]

After a tour of England in 1902, Shurcliff, who had become a member of the Society of Arts and Crafts, Boston, the year before, published in 1903 an article in Gustave Stickley's newly formed magazine, *The Craftsman,* in which he describes another aspect of his concept of the colonial ideal, dear to his heart all his life: the early farmstead. He photographed and drew plans for farms around Rowsley in Derbyshire, including that of Mrs. Anne Hibbs. Praising what he called the "organic fitness" of living on the land,

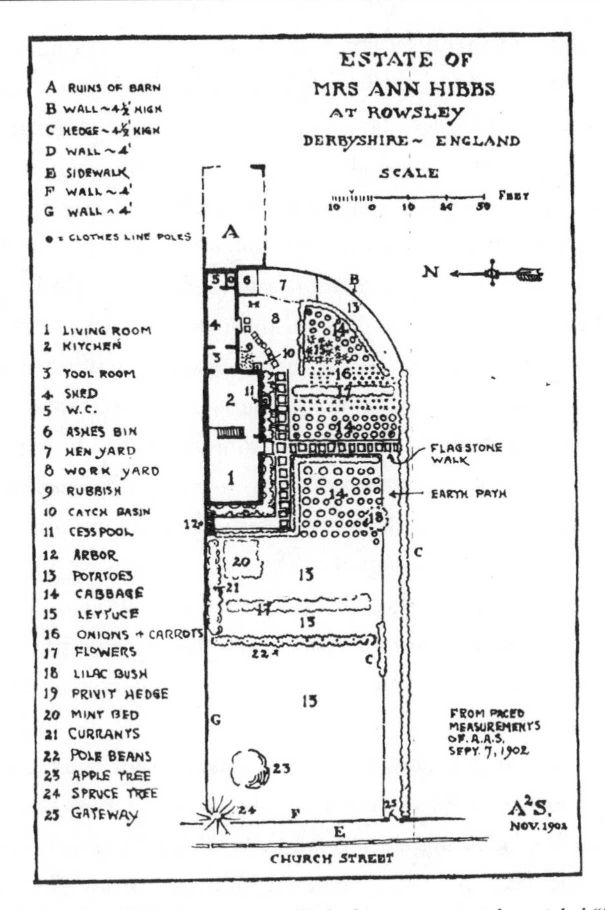

The plan of Mrs. Ann Hibbs's property published in a 1903 article entitled "The Grounds of an English Villager's Cottage," written for The Craftsman.

remote from modern life, expressing thoughtful contemplation of the price paid for civilization and modernization, and perfectly reflecting his own ambivalence, he writes: "To an American who believes that success and advancement depend upon a lively trade intercourse between two communities, and who has lived under conditions which approximate such a state, the appearance of many of the Old-World towns which have not suffered oppression Embraced degradation and the characteristics of their inhabitants are a revelation." For Shurcliff the revelation is not confined to landscape or architecture but embodies all aspects of rural life, including its inhabitants. The visiting American, he writes "sees fields, houses, furniture, clothes, faces and manners which are so beautiful and captivating as to make him feel a new regard for the human family. He may not, on the whole, retract his belief in the desirability of machine manufactures, and trade, but he will be led inevitably to reconstruct his notions of what ultimate ends his own efforts and his times should try to achieve."[16]

Nor does Arts and Crafts "fitness" encompass all that is on Shurcliff's mind in this essay. Essential to comprehending his future landscape preservation practice is knowing he believed throughout his life that to examine these isolated, rural, turn-of-the-century English hamlets was to see American villages of the eighteenth century: "The country about Rowsley remains in many ways unchanged in appearance from its aspects a hundred or more years ago, and its inhabitants are perhaps as much concerned to-day with the ancient occupations of the farmer, stock-raiser, joiner, smith and millwright as they were in the period of the early Georges."[17] Shurcliff made frequent trips to England during his years with the Williamsburg project, photographing all manner of things including fences, gates, stiles, walls, and outbuildings. Reports were prepared after each trip, complete with detailed information and photographic records.

Shurcliff's keen interest in, and appreciation for, farmscapes clearly persisted; in 1915 he writes of another Rowsley farm, J. G. Burnett's Wye Farm, in an article for *Landscape Architecture* entitled "An English Farm Group." He begins the piece in a telling manner: "Tourists visiting the countryside of England are generally too intent upon a round of 'seats' and 'places' to spare time to visit crofts and farms of yeomen. To those who enjoy landscapes and simple architecture, however, the unfading memory of England is of farms and cottages. Views of splendid mansions, polite forecourts, and magnificent gardens deliberately seen, fade away, but merest glimpses of whitewashed houses, quaint dooryards, orchards, fields, and meadows, remain fixed in the memory."[18] He praises what he calls the hollow-square formation of farm buildings, extolling both the quadrangle and the U-shaped configurations for utility, beauty, and harmony with its surroundings.

By 1917 that interest in old-country farmscapes has leapt the Atlantic with Shurcliff's article entitled "A New Hampshire Farm Group of 1805," written again for *Landscape Architecture.* Here he opens by lamenting the decline of the New England farm, correctly postulating that the westward migration and the lure of the city had depleted the ranks of potential farmers. Using the Willis K. Daniels farm in Plainfield, New Hampshire, a longtime favorite of his, he celebrates the ancient farms that are left, stating that "Their planning is still the best planning." According to Shurcliff, the old farmers "were, if anything more keenly concerned with their environment than we are, and consequently, it is natural for us to look up to them as masters in their art."[19] He loved the outbuildings as well as the layout of this farm, and over the years he wrote letters to Blanche Daniels requesting detailed descriptions of the buildings and their uses, along with other minutia such as the types of "skeps," eighteenth- and nineteenth-century bee shelters made from twisted and woven straw, that her father and grandfather had used in the bee house.

Sensitive, attuned, and nature loving, Shurcliff articulated longstanding affection and concern for the American farmscape. As a child and young

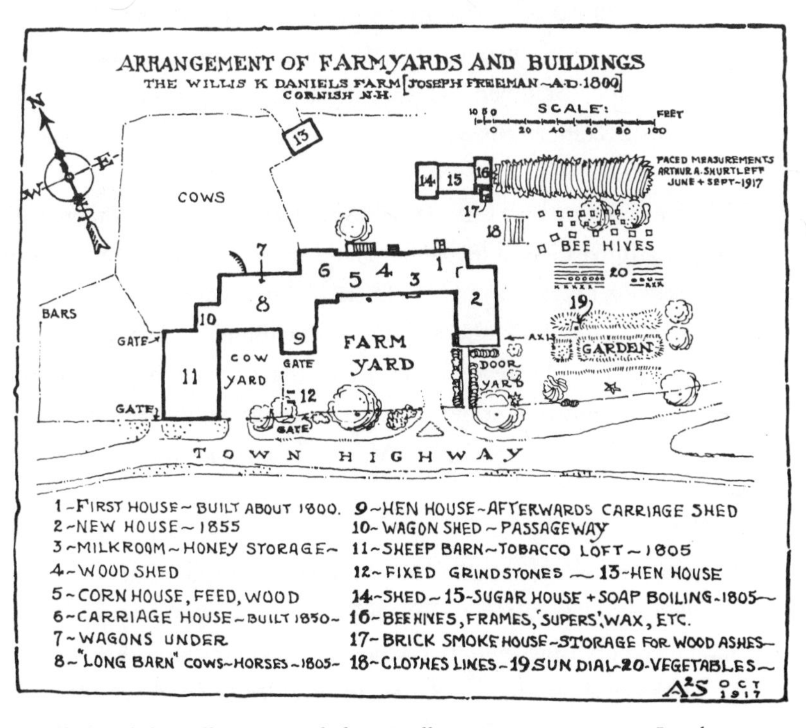

Shurcliff used the Willis K. Daniels farm to illustrate a point in a 1917 Landscape Architecture *article, "A New Hampshire Farm Group."*

adult, he had explored and even venerated the easily accessible countryside surrounding Boston. There survives from around 1905 an unpublished draft entitled "A Fading Landscape," which is worth quoting at length. The passing of the traditional agricultural community was at the forefront of many people's concern, but Shurcliff is remarkable in his farmscape preservation proposal. In the manuscript he declares:

> There is now fading away upon the borders of our New England cities a type of landscape which has not been recorded in our parks and reservations. Woods and fields upon hill and in valley, brooks, ponds and seashore have been set apart forever for public enjoyment but in their transfer from private into public control they have lost a quality upon which they once depended for a large part of their charm. While real perpetuation has been denied this landscape in the field, a partial but lasting record has been accorded it in the pictures, songs and stories which it has inspired. This fading landscape is the farming landscape which had its beginning at the heads of our ancestors in colonial times.

Shurcliff goes on to say how fortunate those alive in 1905 are that there still exist many charming and viable "old farm landscapes" that continue to "bear an organic relation to the ground. . . . There are hundreds of farms in which the old spirit that once built and maintained the thousands that have gone to the wall is still alive. There are corner stones that have not been removed. There we may not only feel the old ancestral pulse but we may enjoy through it a rarely beautiful landscape." Then Shurcliff continues with the following suggestion:

> There are museums in which old weather vanes and purgers, candlesticks and psalters are saved against time for ages that have given up using them but which live to think about them and to write about them. Among our great land of parks could we not spare one as a kind of eddy or brick cement in our own lives in which we could save one of these old farms. I believe

> the antiquarian interest in such a park would fall far short of its landscape interest. The principles of landscape architecture in such a park would be understood by all of us. We should discover that such a park was mother to all the parks.[20]

Sixteen years later, in 1921, writing in his Harvard Twenty-fifth Reunion Class Report, Shurcliff takes a moment to reflect on the passing of open space in the Boston area and the consequences of development upon civilization:

> In our freshman days of 1892 the open country lay near the College. . . . Hundreds of acres of farmland and woods in North Cambridge, Waverly, and East Watertown could be reached in a half-hour's walking. . . . The occupation of a large part of this open ground near the College has taken place since 1896 by the construction of streets, single-family dwellings, apartment houses, dormitories, halls, museums, the Stadium, locker buildings, boathouses, a great power station . . .
>
> These changes near the College are characteristic of similar changes which have taken place over the entire district about Boston, between the second and fourth or fifth mile circles.

Shurcliff, who in his writings was generally given to optimism or silence concerning any misgivings he might have, concludes: "To what extent the encrustation of the earth with structures, above and below the ground, can proceed without detriment to the spirit and vigor of men is likely to become known in this vicinity within a hundred years if the present rate of growth continues."[21]

The year 1930 brought a tercentenary celebration to Boston that included a memorial volume entitled *Fifty Years of Boston.* Shurcliff, now sixty years old and having lived through significant transitions from Boston as a quiet, urban backwater to the bustling modern metropolis it was becoming, was called upon to record his view of those alterations in a chapter entitled "Everyday Life in Boston: Its Changing Aspects." In it he writes:

> Before 1900 much open country surrounded Boston within fifteen miles. Every traveler who journeyed from town to town passed through long reaches of landscape in which pastures, cultivated fields, woodlands, extensive salt marshes, fresh water swamps and rocky hills were common sights. Cambridge was separated from Boston, from Brookline, from Belmont and from Somerville by such free spaces, including much tidewater. The individuality of the built-up section of every city and town was accented by the undeveloped lands which surrounded it and which lent local suburban color and interest to each urban center. . . . To the upcoming generations of Bostonians this ancient loveliness of the individual villages, towns and cities will be a picture which can only be imagined, for no drawings or photographs show it. Maps of those days will eke out the fancy and will give a hint of the good fortune of the men of 1900, who did not need to make long journeys to find "natural" beauty.

Having assured the reader that in noting the various changes, "we do not condemn; we merely note," Shurcliff also declares that "In 1930 most of the nearby cities and towns, owing to the upbuilding of their surrounding free spaces, have lost the individuality and (to our eyes) the beauty which they possessed a third of a century ago." And yet, with typical optimism, his message is not altogether doleful. Writing of the efforts to preserve open space and safeguard the older fabric of the city, Shurcliff concludes: "It should be recorded of Boston in 1930 that her citizens of today have been among the first in America to awaken to an appreciation of the handiwork of the early men of this country and to take part in that most modern of all planning movements which attempts to save the ancient work from destruction and to preserve it to enrich our own times. The day is fast approaching when a city cannot call itself modern if it lacks evidence of this practical appreciation and understanding of its own origins."[22]

By 1936 Shurcliff was not above appealing to the material side of human nature in a small article entitled "A Word to Tradesmen and Real Estate Men of Country Towns," in which he encourages local storekeepers to trade on the current tourism vogue for quaint old country towns. "Little by little" he writes, "some of the more enterprising towns are learning that it pays to give up strident, raucous displays of brilliant colors and bizarre architecture and are remodeling their stores and signs wholesale to recall 'old times.' . . . The atmosphere of early history and the quiet life of early times makes an appeal which brings visitors from every state. In other words, this atmosphere is a dollars and cents asset. It must be conserved now, if it is not to be lost forever."[23]

As the development of Shurcliff's philosophy is traced through the years, it becomes clear that the physical environment he was so influential in creating at Colonial Williamsburg was strongly informed by his early experiences of rural and small-town life and by the ruminations about landscape, nature, and early American culture that consistently thread through his writings and his practice. He was a man steeped in the cultural heritage of his times, who translated that legacy continuously in the rapidly changing era in which he lived. His principles of landscape preservation perfectly reflect the basic values he adhered to and practiced all his life, opening an invaluable window upon how one of the most important early practitioners envisioned his mission and embodied it in his life and work.

NOTES

1. The socialist aspects of the Arts and Craft movement, deeply rooted in Morris's philosophy, did not take hold in America.

2. Keith N. Morgan, "Held in Trust: Charles Eliot's Vision for the New England Landscape" (Bethesda, MD: National Association for Olmsted Parks, 1991), 1.

3. Arthur A. Shurcliff, *Autobiography of Arthur A. Shurcliff* (Cambridge, MA: Sarah Shurcliff Ingelfinger, Hubbard Park, 1981), 5.

4. Ibid., 16.

5. Arthur A. Shurcliff (then Shurtleff), Journals, vol. 3, February 15, 1894, private collection, Cambridge, Massachusetts.

6. Arthur A. Shurcliff (then Shurtleff), "Log of Bicycle Tour through III States," July 1897, Houghton Library, Harvard University, Cambridge, Massachusetts.

7. Arthur A. Shurcliff (then Shurtleff), "Log V Days in Concord: Log of a 5 Days Stay in Concord Written at Odd Minutes on the Knee of Arthur A. Shurtleff, May 1898," May 22, 1898, MS Am 1424 (3), by permission of the Houghton Library, Harvard University.

8. Arthur A. Shurcliff (then Shurtleff), "Log of 5 Days in Newburyport, August 1898, Dedicated to an old box hedge," August 3, 1898, MS Am 1424 (2), by permission of the Houghton Library, Harvard University.

9. Ibid.

10. Arthur A. Shurcliff (then Shurtleff), "Some Old New England Flower Gardens," *New England Magazine,* December 1899, 434, 424–25.

11. Ibid., 422.

12. Ibid., 423.

13. Ibid., 423, 426.

14. Arthur A. Shurcliff (then Shurtleff), "Two Nantucket Gardens," *House and Garden,* July 1902, 314, 317–18.

15. Ibid., 313.

16. Arthur A. Shurcliff (then Shurtleff), "The Grounds of an English Villager's Cottage," *The Craftsman,* April 1903, 11.

17. Ibid., 12.

18. Arthur A. Shurcliff (then Shurtleff), "An English Farm Group," *Landscape Architecture,* April 1915, 120.

19. Arthur A. Shurcliff (then Shurtleff), "A New Hampshire Farm Group of 1805," *Landscape Architecture,* October 1917, 19, 20.

20. Arthur A. Shurcliff (then Shurtleff), "A Fading Landscape," private collection, Cambridge, Massachusetts, 1–3. Shurcliff notes on the manuscript that it was written "about 1905."

21. "Arthur Asahel Shurtleff," *Harvard College Class of 1896 Twenty-fifth Anniversary Report [Number VI]* (Cambridge: private printing, 1921): 524–25, by permission of the Harvard University Archives.

22. Arthur A. Shurcliff (then Shurtleff), "Everyday Life in Boston: Its Changing Aspects," *Fifty Years in Boston* (Boston: Boston Tercentenary Committee, 1930), 685–86, 701, 686, 706.

23. Arthur A. Shurcliff, "A Word to Tradesmen and Real Estate Men of Country Towns," *A Handbook on Conservation* (Concord, MA: Rumford Press, 1936), 15.

"Californio" Culture and Landscapes, 1894–1942

Entwining Myth and Romance with Preservation

DAVID C. STREATFIELD

The publication in 1894 of Helen Hunt Jackson's novel *Ramona* played a critical role in initiating a new and highly romanticized enthusiasm for the "Old California" of the "Californios," Spanish-speaking individuals born in California. Interest in this culture's past quickly attained mythic proportions. The myth assumed an unbroken Hispanic tradition of Spanish soldiers, benevolent Franciscan padres who ministered to and cared deeply for the native Indians, and a dignified manorial tradition of dons, living in unpretentious courtyard ranch houses with simple flower-filled gardens.[1] This mythic view of the Californio past was almost entirely *invention* rather than *discovery.* However, it was not a minor regional phenomenon but was part of a national anti-modernist movement, allied with the Arts and Crafts movement, that was concerned about the rise of industrialism, European immigration, and the growth of new urban settlements.[2]

The principal design manifestations of anti-modernism were architectural revivals: Colonial Revival in the eastern states, Spanish Colonial Revival in California, and the Santa Fe style in New Mexico. Each of these revivals used the past selectively, idealizing obvious and attractive physical design features at the expense of the less pleasant social contextual issues. However, the Spanish Colonial Revival went beyond these tendencies and was an invention, with its initial and subsequent borrowings from Baroque Mexico and Andalusian Spain, neither of which had been used as sources by the Californios themselves. The garden landscapes associated with these revivals cut across the specific revival styles and involved what May Brawley Hill has called, in a book by that title, "Grandmother's Gardens," old-fashioned flower gardens.[3]

By the beginning of the twentieth century, Californio culture was marginalized, and many of their structures and designed landscapes had been drastically changed, abandoned, or allowed to slide into a ruinous condition. However, like many myths, this one was partly based on a real past. This phenomenon has been examined by several scholars, but the degree to which preservation activities were embedded in the imagined world of "Old California" has not been seriously studied.[4]

This essay briefly discusses the creation of the myth and then focuses on the disparity between Californio culture, its mythic reinterpretation, the subsequent impact on designed landscapes, and how the myth became entwined with preservation and landscape conservation activities. This neglected history was initiated largely by amateurs who also wrote some of its earliest interpretive histories. Their passionate devotion and principled work raises critical questions about possible roles of the amateur in the current highly specialized world of preservation.

MYTHMAKING AND RESTORATION

Mrs. Helen Hunt Jackson devoted the last six years of her life to the plight of the California Mission Indians. In 1883, together with Abbot Kinney, she wrote a report for the Department of the Interior that focused on the Indians' land rights.[5] However, *Ramona,* which was published in the following year, vaulted the issue onto the national stage. This very readable and romantic work portrays the Indian heroine and hero as victims of white greed and cruelty. Ironically, the novel's broader impact was not to address the plight of the Indians but to construct a mythic past of California's mission period as a time of resplendent peace and contentment presided over by the mission padres and accompanied by an unbroken continuity of a simple, unostentatious, but graceful mode of manorial ranching life.

At the end of the nineteenth century the missions were crumbling

Rancho Camúlos, Piru. Photograph by Charles F. Saunders, appearing in Alice B. Lockwood, Gardens of Colony and State, *1934. (Courtesy of the Garden Club of America)*

ruins, and the ranch house thus became the principal material evidence of this glorious past. Jackson's description of the typical ranch house was based on her visits to Rancho Camúlos, near Piru, and Rancho Guájome, in San Diego County. She writes of "the representative house of the half barbaric, half elegant wholly generous and free-handed life . . . under the rule of the Spanish and Mexican viceroys." This tradition was centered on the U-shaped single-story ranch house with verandahs overlooking a simple formal garden with a central circular space defined by clipped Monterey cypress hedges around a fountain. The verandah walls were lined with large red water jars filled with "fine geraniums, carnations and yellow-flowered musk." Vines clambered up the verandah posts, "some growing in great bowls swung by cords from the roof of the verandah, or set on shelves against the walls." Beyond were extensive fruit orchards and vineyards. "Nothing was to be seen but verdure or bloom, or fruit." Jackson's romantic description of a house and garden created in 1856, after Californio control of California had passed to Americans, assumed that it represented an unbroken, continuous cultural and design tradition extending back to the Spanish period.[6]

Other writers commented on the similarity between the foundation of the United States and the beginning of the Spanish presence in California. Thus the Hispanic past could be appropriated as a model for regional design because its simple dignity was rooted in the local past. California's short history and the light presence of the Californios on the land also led to the invocation of other cultures and the selective mining of these design traditions to serve the national anti-modern search for a corrective order to the ugliness of industrializing America. California was seen as a physical place of great beauty with the promise of opportunities to forge a unique relationship between humanized place and the landscape. Charles Dudley Warner compared the California landscape to that of Italy. Charles and Henry Greene created some of the finest Arts and Crafts environments in the country, evoking Japanese architecture and gardens in their Pasadena houses. Berkeley poet Charles Augustus Keeler called for a fusion of the Orient and the Mediterranean traditions of Italy and Spain, while landscape designer Bruce Porter looked both to Spain and Italy for formal ordering principles.[7]

CALIFORNIO LANDSCAPES: RESTORATION AND MYTHIC REINTERPRETATION

The Spanish settlers who entered California in 1769 created a colonial landscape of civilian pueblos, with sites for houses, orchard and garden plots, presidial or military cities, and a chain of twenty-one missions controlled by the Franciscan order, which were conceptually transitional institutions. This settlement pattern, like all prior Hispanic colonies, used the Laws of the Indies to site the pueblos and presidios and the mission churches and their estates.[8] But collectively the Californio landscape constituted the crudest provincial outpost of the immense and far-flung Spanish empire. This fact was conspicuously ignored by Jackson and other writers at the end of the nineteenth century. The disparity between the real and imagined worlds of the Californios can be best understood by examining each landscape type separately and their subsequent treatment in the twentieth century.

THE MISSION

The mission was a large feudal institution intended to convert the native Indians to Christianity and raise them to the status of *gente de reson,* which unfortunately never happened. A typical mission comprised the church, padres' quarters, guards' rooms, and workshops planned around an enclosure. In addition, there was an Indian village, a walled garden, and orchards.[9] Harold Kirker has documented how the Franciscan padres emphasized the central role of a conservative religious orthodoxy by adhering to Spanish architectural traditions derived from Roman and Moorish colonists. However, the padres' knowledge of these conventions had been weakened by cen-

Map of California missions from Rexford Newcomb, The Old Mission Churches and Historic Houses of California: Their History, Architecture, Art and Lore, *1925.*

turies of modification and adjustment to regional circumstances elsewhere in the Spanish empire: "Spain's architecture reached California at least third hand."[10] In this respect, the Spanish colonization of California differed from the English colonies on the East Coast, where the settlers introduced intact building traditions.

Possessing a crude monumentality, the mission churches were the most impressive features of the Californio world, since they were the only structures built out of stone or kiln-burned brick. Their simple dignity was complemented by colonnaded walks linking the conventual buildings and the simple formal gardens.

The missions controlled immense surrounding tracts of land that became the industrial sector providing tallow, beef, wool, and horses for the pueblos and presidial towns. Legally this land belonged to the Indians, and colonists were only permitted to use it for a decade. At that time the land was to be handed over to the Indians. This ambitious and enlightened colonial program did not succeed, and the missions assumed full control of the ranches on behalf of the Indians, who provided free labor.

The missions were not popular with early Protestant visitors, who were deeply offended by Catholic practices and found nothing to admire except the great abundance of flowers and produce in the mission gardens.[11] Antipathies also existed within the Hispanic community. Spanish Californians resented the republican sentiments of the Mexican regime that supplanted the mission system's clerical feudalism in 1810. However, it was not until the Declaration of Secularization in 1833 that the immense mission ranch lands were transferred to private hands through grants of ranchos.

Unfavorable assessment of the Californios began to change in the 1860s when several writers started to reexamine Hispanic culture more favorably. Elizabeth Hughes criticized the crassness and vulgarity of contemporary industrial American society and suggested that the reforming intentions and industrial organization of the mission system could serve as a superior model for creating new communitarian ideals. Hubert Bancroft attempted a fairer assessment of the Hispanic past that acknowledged many of its weaknesses.[12]

By the early 1900s the missions were the most conspicuous remnants of the Californio world, although most of the structures were in advanced stages of dereliction, and their gardens had completely disappeared. Despite their pathetic condition, the simple, robust dignity of many churches was still impressive. The only church to survive intact, since the Franciscan fathers had never left, was the masonry church at Santa Barbara, situated high above the unimpressive little American town that had replaced the original presidio. Helen Hunt Jackson, who visited in 1882, expressed a widely shared sentiment in her admiration: "It is an inalienable benediction to the place. The longer one stops there the more he is aware of the influence on his soul, as well as of the importance in the landscape of the benign and stately edifice."[13]

PRESERVATION INITIATED

Charles Fletcher Lummis, a flamboyant easterner, attempted to correct Jackson's romanticized past in his role as editor of *Land of Sunshine,* renamed *Out West,* by shifting attention to the missions. While Lummis shamelessly promoted the Southland, as the region south of the Tehachapi Mountains has always been known, as a tourist mecca, his magazine was notable for his rigorous insistence on the use of original source materials.[14] Early issues of *Land of Sunshine* contained articles describing individual missions, which were followed by editorials that began to address the possibility of an organized attempt to safeguard them, not only for their intrinsic worth as valuable emblems of the past but as potential tourist attractions. Lummis's December 1894 editorial declared, "There is to be no accursed 'restoration'—*preservation* is the watchword. . . . A society will be incorporated," whose charge would be to raise permanent funding for the conservation of "the finest ruins in The United States."

In December 1895 the Landmarks Club was founded "to preserve from further decay and vandalism the old Missions of California: to assist in the restoration of such of the old Mission buildings as may be found adaptable for use in harmony with their original purposes; and to safeguard and conserve other historic monuments, relics and landmarks of the States."[15]

This voluntary organization had a large board of directors, including architects Sumner Hunt and Arthur B. Benton. By 1904 the club had tripled

Ruins of Mission San Juan Capistrano prior to stabilization, from Rexford Newcomb, The Old Mission Churches and Historic Houses of California: Their History, Architecture, Art and Lore, *1925.*

in size and included several socially prominent individuals including Caroline Severance of Los Angeles; George Marston of San Diego; Harrison Gray Otis, owner of the *Los Angeles Times;* and Mrs. Phoebe Apperson Hearst, whose family owned the *San Francisco Examiner.*[16] The organization's varied projects were financed by dues and contributions from these sympathetic individuals.

The Landmarks Club did not attempt to protect the entire chain of twenty-one missions but only the more derelict ones in the Southland, such as Missions San Diego, San Juan Capistrano, and San Fernando, and the Asistencia at Pala, all of which were in a semi-ruinous condition. The club leased each of these structures until 1912, when its preservation activities declined significantly.[17]

Arthur B. Benton and Sumner Hunt served as the club's architects, and Lummis was a consultant historian. Mission San Juan Capistrano was the first to receive attention. The chapel and kitchen building were reroofed with tiles, and breaches in the walls were repaired. Portions of the front corridor and some two hundred feet of the patio corridor and the adjoining colonnades and walls were stabilized with bolts. Some four hundred feet of the cloister garth colonnades were temporarily reroofed and waterproofed with gravel and asphalt until old tiles could be found. The great stone church's remaining pilasters were buttressed, and the roof of the adobe church was covered with tiles. By December 1896, this mission had been stabilized for a cost of $1,400.00, all of which had been raised through subscriptions and voluntary contributions.[18] However, it was not until the late 1920s that gardens were created by Father St. John O'Sullivan.

Conspicuously ignoring the much earlier work of the Mount Vernon Ladies' Association of the Union, the Landmarks Club took great pride in being the first organization in the country to undertake preservation without any public funding and noted that without its intervention the stabilized missions "would have been merely shapeless mounds of adobe mud." Proud presentations of this work also inspired women in Wisconsin and Texas to start landmark programs in their states.[19]

The most successful of all the Landmarks Club projects was the rehabilitation of the Asistencia at Pala, which combined sensitive architectural restoration with cultural reinvigoration. The little church was reroofed with the original tiles on new rafters of peeled pine from the upper sections of Mount Palomar. This outpost of Mission San Fernando had been created to serve an outlying group of Indians. In 1902 a group of Cupeño Indians moved here from their rancheria at Warner's Ranch together with Indians

Restored Asistencia, Pala, from Rexford Newcomb, The Old Mission Churches and Historic Houses of California: Their History, Architecture, Art and Lore, *1925.*

Garden at Mission San Juan Capistrano, 1923. Photograph by Charles F. Saunders, appearing in Alice B. Lockwood, Gardens of Colony and State, *1934. (Courtesy of the Garden Club of America)*

from San Felipe. In 1910 the Episcopal Church built a school for teaching lace making to Indian women. Thus Pala continued to serve an authentic Indian community allied to its Spanish-Mexican past.[20]

The early mission restorations are notable for the modest interventions into the structures, but little attention of any kind was paid to the treatment of the mission gardens. It was not until the 1920s that some of the gardens were restored. At this time, Father St. John O'Sullivan continued the restoration of Mission San Juan Capistrano, which culminated at the end of the decade in his design of new gardens.

In 1932 landscape architect Charles Gibbs Adams commented, "Knowing all we do of these things, I feel that the so-called 'restoration' we have made of some Mission gardens are nothing short of pitiful."[21] The first serious mission restoration occurred in 1935 when the ruins of Mission Purísima La Concepcíon, near Lompoc, were acquired by the state from Santa Barbara County as a park. The National Park Service undertook an extensive renovation of the buildings and site as a Civilian Conservation Corps (CCC) project with 170 boys. This mission site had been protected from demolition by the Union Oil Company early in the century, but the structures had deteriorated so much that the existing adobe walls were taken down, and new adobe brick walls were constructed around concealed concrete pillars. Primitive tools were used to reproduce the visible parts of the structures. The boys molded 110,000 adobe bricks and 32,000 roofing tiles, since it was assumed they had the same level of building expertise as the original Indian workmen.

The pear orchard was re-created using cuttings from the sole surviving tree in the original orchard. Grapevines from the original vineyard were transferred from a newer site. The principal mission garden was re-created around the original fountain using authentic plants such as hollyhocks, Castilian roses, and medicinal herbs. A nursery was established to replant the outer areas of the grounds with some 15,000 shrubs and trees. Lester Rowntree, the noted horticulturist, plant collector, and writer, commented very favorably on this, saying that "the array of native shrubs assembled there is unequaled by any commercial nursery."[22] Animals were later introduced in fenced paddocks around the buildings. Today the "re-created" dignity of the church, monastic buildings, simply planted garden, orchards, and grazing animals evokes the larger visual landscape of a feudal mission more powerfully than any other remaining mission in California.

Mission La Purísima Concepcíon, Lompoc. Photograph by author.

RANCHO

The rancho played an extremely limited role in Spanish California. The provision forbidding private ownership of ranches was eased in 1786, but only a very small number of land grants were issued. It was not until the Secularization Act of 1833 that the enormous mission-controlled lands were transferred into private ownership. Individuals, mostly retired soldiers of little social standing, and Yankee traders could petition the governor for a land grant. A conspicuous exception was the grant of Rancho San Julían in Santa Barbara County to Capítan José Antonio de la Guerra y Noriega, governor of the Santa Barbara Presidio and a member of an old and distinguished Spanish aristocratic family.[23] Thus, the true golden age of the Hispanic Californian ranch lasted from 1833 until the onset of a disastrous drought in 1862. It was a period of *dolce far niente,* or sweet idleness, when huge herds of cattle guarded by mounted vaqueros roamed over unfenced ranch lands, leaving the ranch owner little to do but bask in a form of Virgilian contemplation.

For Yankees this relaxed pastoralism was economically unsound. The Mexican dons valued the past rather than the present and had no interest in planning for the future. Indeed, the dons saw work as a prelude to pleasure, happily viewing their huge herds of cattle as the zenith of pastoralism, while Yankees saw the untilled landscape as a missed opportunity. As Leonard Pitt observed, this classic clash between conflicting cultural values had no clear basis for resolution.[24] By the end of the nineteenth century, all ranches combined crop cultivation with raising sheep and cattle.

By the 1860s very few Mexican families owned ranches, owing to legal ownership problems coupled with severe drought conditions. This wholesale transfer of ranch land from Californios to prosperous easterners resulted in significant changes to the existing ranch houses. In the Mexican period, a typical ranch house was invariably a small adobe structure, often without glazed windows, doors, or wooden floors, which served as a secondary structure providing temporary shelter for the owner's occasional visits. Most lacked any significant garden development, as Edwin Bryant noted in 1846: "It is a peculiarity of the Mexicans that they allow no shade or ornamental trees to grow near their houses." The restored Hugo Reid adobe house at Rancho Santa Anita, Arcadia, recaptures the modesty and crudity of such establishments. Very few possessed courtyards, and these were not pleasure gardens but work yards, the largest being the entry court at Rancho Los Cerritos, Long Beach, built by Don Juan Temple.[25]

The new American ranch houses were simple but dignified structures that synthesized the basic Mexican adobe house with the more elegant and comfortable wooden colonial house type with sash windows and wood floors, introduced to California at Monterey, former capital of Alta and Baja California, by Thomas Larkin. Don Juan Temple's house at Rancho Los Cerritos, Long Beach, is the most ambitious example of this synthesis in the Southland. Associated with this new house type, the courtyard pleasure garden enclosed by the wings of the ranch house is really an American invention in which American and Mexican gardening traditions were also conflated. The gardens at Rancho Camúlos, near Piru, and Rancho Guájome, near Vista, which inspired Jackson's description in *Ramona,* were not examples of a continuous Hispanic garden tradition. Instead they fused simple Mexican gardens with formal New England gardens and their old-fashioned flowers. The large walled garden at Rancho Los Cerritos recalled the formal gardens of Massachusetts that Temple had known as a boy. However, whereas the garden at Rancho Camúlos was a similar synthesis, it has a different cultural meaning since it represents acceptance of new Yankee standards by a Mexican family.[26] Several Mexican ranch house gardens were remodeled in the 1920s. The garden at Rancho Los Alamitos, Long Beach, is a classic example of what was thought to be a typical Spanish-Mexican garden. It was widely admired during this period. Its creator, Florence Green Bixby, gardened continuously here from 1909, when her husband inherited the ranch, into the mid-1930s. A series of simply detailed, flower-filled garden enclosures, created to overlook the pastures, were designed successively by Paul Howard, Florence Yoch, and the Olmsted brothers.[27]

The age of the house at Rancho Camúlos—its core being the oldest surviving adobe house in the Southland—led visitors in the 1920s and 1930s into believing that they were seeing garden spaces similar to those of "Old California." The "Old Garden," with its simply detailed raised circular tank similar to those in mission gardens, and the large paved patio beneath an

Fountain of the "Old Garden" at Rancho Los Alamitos, Long Beach. (Courtesy of Rancho Los Alamitos)

immense pepper tree believed to have been planted in the 1840s by Don Abel Stearns, the ranch's Mexican owner, recalled the simplicity of mission gardens. Furnished with Navajo rugs and wicker chairs, it provided a comfortable outdoor family living room and space for entertaining guests, although it was quite unlike the service yard that almost certainly existed here in the Mexican period.

Florence Green Bixby's simple gardens with their exuberant flower planting expressed her own modest personality, passionate love of plants, and straightforward, appropriate gardening techniques and were not part of a serious attempt to evoke Hispanic gardens. Only by realizing from hard experience that she was living in a land of little rain did her gardens recall the vanished Hispanic world. However, she used this insight to restrain ambitious and inappropriate design proposals by the Olmsted Brothers such as their proposed use of lawns in her rose garden and a broad Italian cypress–lined avenue marching across a pasture. For English garden writer Marion Cran, the gardens at Rancho Los Alamitos represented "Old California," a perception reinforced by landscape architect Charles Gibbs Adams's supervision of the gardens in what he called the "ancient manner." But although the gardens had nothing to do with the Californios, their "ancient manners" were continued in the modest and generous hospitality that Florence Bixby and her husband extended to their ranch hands and friends, a hospitality beautifully evoked by their eldest daughter, Katherine Bixby Hotchkiss, in her reminiscences, *Christmas at Rancho Los Alamitos.* Some of their annual parties were attended by three hundred people, a fact that led Florence Bixby's obituarist to describe their life as being lived on a "grand and patriarchal scale."[28]

Ralph Cornell's design for the garden space that remained at Rancho Los Cerritos was even further removed from the character of the original garden. Don Juan Temple's garden of the 1840s was the most elaborate ranch garden created in Mexican California. Llewellyn Bixby Jr., who purchased what remained of this ranching establishment in 1929, transformed the massive two-story ranch house into a comfortable modern house.[29] Cornell's garden design, reinforcing this straightforward ahistorical character, retained only the large trees, added flowering trees in the belief that color should not be limited to flowering annuals, and created a vine arbor. This simple design is almost identical to the gardens that he created for new houses elsewhere in the Southland.

The restoration of El Molino Viejo, San Marino, was much closer in spirit to real Californio Spanish and Mexican gardens. This simple building was designed by Father José María Zalividea and built in 1816 as one of two water mills for Mission San Gabriel.[30] After El Molino Viejo was used first as a house and then as a clubhouse lounge for the Huntington Hotel golf course, Archer Huntington gave it to Mrs. James Brehm, who was a younger sister of Florence Green Bixby and who hired contractor Frederick L. Ruppel to restore the structure for use as a house.

Ruppel had become interested in old building technologies while working at Mission San Juan Capistrano. He carefully probed the structure to determine how it had been altered by the successive owners but was unable to determine the original forms of all the details. In such instances he drew from his extensive knowledge of mission building techniques. The structure was protected with the purchase of additional land, and landscape architect Katherine Bashford was commissioned to provide an appropriate setting for the old building. Bashford's simple walled garden extended around two sides of the house, and its modest layout of rectangular plots filled with old-fashioned flowers and orchard trees recalls the simplicity of mission gardens.

More scholarly examination of ranch houses and later gardens also began in the 1920s. At the beginning of the twentieth century, several writers had written admiringly and romantically about the missions and surviving ranch houses. Of these writers, Charles Francis Saunders, who moved to California early in the twentieth century from Pennsylvania, became a serious student of gardens and native plants. Although lacking formal training in botany or horticulture, he devoted much of his time to writing about the state's native flora and cultural past. In the early 1920s, just prior to its sale to Mr. and Mrs. Rüpel in 1924, he visited Rancho Camúlos and interviewed Señora del Valle, the daughter-in-law of Jackson's model for Señora Moreno in *Ramona.* This thoughtful interview and his roughly drawn garden plan were the basis for his brief description in Alice Lockwood's *Gardens of Colony and State.*[31]

Rexford Newcomb, professor of architecture at the University of Illinois, began careful measurement of mission churches and houses in California and New Mexico in 1912. He measured the buildings, photographed and sketched them, and interviewed the fathers at Pala, San Juan Capistrano, and Santa Barbara. He also did archival research at the Archivo General de Indias in Seville. This scholarly work culminated in his book on this subject published in 1925, which established the first accurate record of these structures prior to the creation of the Historic American Buildings Survey (HABS) program in the following decade.[32]

Further insights into later nineteenth-century gardens were made by amateur writers with a keen appreciation of the value of the memoir as a form of history. The San Francisco Garden Club commissioned a number of short histories of gardens in the city and adjacent communities in the Bay Area from older members in the 1930s. While none of these meet current standards of scholarship, they are nevertheless important records of plants grown in gardens during the second half of the nineteenth century.[33] Landscape architect Charles Gibbs Adams, regarded as the foremost authority on gardens of the Spanish and Mexican eras in the Southland, wrote articles based on early sources such as diaries and other records of early travelers such as Captain George Vancouver and Captain J. F. G. de la Perouse: "Gardens of the Spanish Days of California" and "Spanish Influence in California." H. M. Butterfield of the Extension Service at the University of California, Berkeley, performed an invaluable service to later garden historians by assembling a large collection of nineteenth-century nursery catalogs, now housed in the Bancroft Library at the University of California, Berkeley. These catalogs served as the basis for a series of articles including "The Introduction of Eucalyptus into California" (1938), "History of Ornamental Horticulture in California" (1965), and "Estates in California" (1969).

PRESIDIAL TOWNS AND PUEBLOS

While the Laws of the Indies produced elegant cities in many South and Central American countries, Californio cities were notable for their crudeness and lack of elegance. This can be attributed to the fact that Alta California was mostly settled by Spaniards from rural Mexico rather than the Iberian Peninsula and to the widespread use of adobe blocks. An 1876 article in a Santa Barbara newspaper deplored the surviving ugly Hispanic houses since they were "built of the Ochre-colored adobe, thatched with reeds, windowless, doorless, smokey and half-eaten by the attacks of the winter rain."[34]

The earliest restoration of a house in a presidial town occurred in 1908 when architect Hazel Waterman was commissioned by the Spreckels Company, the sugar-refining company that also owned the Hotel Coronado, to restore the decayed Casa Estudillo in San Diego's Old Town. This large U-shaped house, which later acquired the title of "Ramona's Marriage Place" from Jackson's novel *Ramona,* was built in 1829 but had become a virtual ruin by the early twentieth century. The Spreckels Company hired a publicist to promote the myth that Ramona had been married in the house and ran tours to the house from the Hotel Coronado.[35]

Waterman's approach to restoration was enlightened and almost scholarly because she was determined to restore the house authentically. She obtained information on how old adobe structures had been built from old manuscripts, photographs, and interviews with elderly local residents, coupled with visits to sites such as Mission San Juan Capistrano and the Pio Pico adobe house near Whittier.[36]

From this detailed research, she concluded that only Mexican laborers should be employed to mold the adobe brick by hand. A native worker was found who was familiar with making bricks "in the old way," and he taught the other workers how to knead the adobe into moist bricks that were baked in the sun for a number of weeks. She also incorporated leftover materials from old buildings. Despite the fact that large brick tiles were not found on any of the floors, her interviews confirmed that they had been used. New tiles were fashioned for the floors and the roof using the old methods. She used "materials intended for wharf piles and telephone poles, provided by the Spreckels Company, cut to required dimensions, hand shaped and then aged by soaking in the mud flats of the bay" to replace the badly rotted roof beams.[37]

However, while the restoration of the building was conducted with remarkable sensitivity, the garden was treated in a most cavalier fashion, its planting resembling a lush, late-Victorian garden. Waterman either did not recognize or consciously ignored the fact that the courtyards of Californio houses were workplaces. However, even if Waterman had attempted to apply the same scholarly standards to this space, it is doubtful that this would have been accepted by the Spreckels Company, whose interest in the restoration was to create an attractive destination for the Hotel Coronado's guests. At all the surviving Californio houses more of the physical fabric remained, and virtually none of the original planting survived. Early visitors' accounts provided only scanty accounts of garden arrangements at any of the Spanish or Mexican houses. Even Rexford Newcomb commented favorably on the garden in his otherwise admirable book, *Old Mission Churches and Historic Houses of California.*

The Panama-California Exposition held in San Diego in 1915 endorsed the widespread adoption of the Spanish Colonial Revival style as the dominant design mode throughout the Southland in the prosperous 1920s. Initially Bertram Goodhue adopted the flamboyant churrigueresque style for its ability to confer dignity to public spaces; however, he quickly moved away from this and adopted a simpler and increasingly more abstract mode that was remarkably close to Irving Gill's austere designs.[38]

In Santa Barbara, designers looked to the Andalusia region of Spain for inspiration. This was the most extreme form taken by the Californio myth, since it did not remotely resemble anything that the Californios had created. However, it was appropriate that it was employed more vigorously in Santa Barbara, since this community retained more of its Hispanic heritage than any of the other Spanish pueblos and presidial towns. In the Mexican period, the Franciscan fathers there did not leave, unlike most of the other missions, and the population of the region contained a larger proportion of Hispanic citizens. After California became American, a typical gridiron plan was laid out with street names commemorating the three cultures that lived there: the Chumash Indians, the Spanish, and early Americans. The surviving Hispanic buildings were not popular, however, and outwardly the small city was thoroughly American in appearance, with all new buildings being built in currently fashionable styles. Helen Hunt Jackson found the town to be "undistinguished . . . like any other of a dozen New England towns . . . stodgy . . . correct, . . . and uninteresting."[39]

The surviving crude adobe houses were not admired until 1896, when the *Daily Press* expressed the hope that more discretion would be exercised in destroying them, "for these old landmarks lend to the city a picturesqueness and a local color regarded with interest by travelers and tourists." In 1909 the Civic League advocated the preservation of the large de La Guerra mansion, which novelist Gertrude Atherton admired enormously, "What a house! There is nothing like it in this country."[40]

The creation of the Santa Barbara Community Arts Association in the 1920s translated the city's imagined elegant Spanish past into a false Andalusian imagery that incorporated some remnants of the real past. This association was founded by Irene and Bernhard Hoffmann, who persuaded other prominent social figures to support the organization's new artistic vision for the city. In 1922, with the assistance of Dr. Henry Pritchett, a former president of MIT and the president of the Carnegie Foundation, the Plans and Planting Committee, one of four subcommittees of the association, obtained a grant of $25,000 a year for ten years for civic improvements. This committee skillfully guided physical planning and design in the city center during the 1920s, advocating the creation of a City Planning Commission and an Architectural Review Board responsible for design controls. They sponsored one of the best small homes programs in the nation and organized tours of estates in Montecito.[41] The careful preservation of this urban vision was achieved by the continued scrutiny of proposed developments by the Plans and Planting Committee under the leadership of Pearl Chase, Bernhard Hoffmann's chief assistant, until her retirement in the 1980s, a remarkable example of enlightened civic activism.

The association's most famous accomplishment, conceived by Bernhard Hoffman and designed by James Osborn Craig, was the El Paseo shopping center and the adjoining public square with the new City Hall. This complex of shops and artists' studios, incorporating Casa de La Guerra and the two Gaspar Orena adobe houses, represents the zenith of the Jacksonian mythology. The large, U-shaped Casa de La Guerra, which had been occupied by the family since it was built, was clapboarded in the late nineteenth century and was completely remodeled into a stuccoed Spanish hacienda with a simple raised garden occupying the original entry courtyard. Until 1943 one wing of the building was occupied by Miss Delfina de La Guerra, who continued to dispense traditional Hispanic hospitality, while antique shops occupied the remaining wings. Approached by the new Street of Spain, the courts and garden at the rear of the mansion were transformed into a public plaza that served as the focal space for artist studios, restaurants, and antique shops. This complex of buildings and public spaces was, in fact, one of the most distinguished national examples of urban design in the 1920s, ironically built upon a completely false idea of the original Hispanic character.[42]

The other two adobe houses were restored and became antique and furniture shops, with simple tiled patios designed by landscape architect Lockwood de Forest Jr., who also designed another small garden for the restored adobe house that served as Bernhard Hoffmann's downtown office. With its small lawn and clustered Italian cypress trees, it emphasized the inherently romantic approach adopted by most garden designers. De Forest also designed the patio at the Museum of Natural History around three

City Hall, Santa Barbara. Photograph by author.

existing oak trees in a highly evocative manner to sustain Floyd Brewster's attempted re-creation of a Spanish hacienda.[43]

In the following decade, the proposed plan of landscape architect Emerson Knight for the central part of the presidial town of Monterey, the former capital of Alta and Baja California, united issues of landscape interpretation and historic preservation. The principal thrust of his report was his advocacy of leaving untouched the great crescent-shaped waterfront: "Nature here, pleads to be left undisturbed so that its beauty may at least approach the feeling of pristine grandeur. In sheer glory of scale, it seems to excel all other crescent beaches in California." Knight insisted that parked cars, concessions, intensive recreational facilities, and a sea wall should not be permitted. Instead he proposed a broad promenade along the curving seafront, connecting with a walk through the town that would enable visitors to see the finest surviving historic structures. "Accordingly the beach promenade might serve as a prelude to the historic journey, or may become particularly effective at the close of a review of old historic houses, as a mirror for reflection, enhancing and even intensifying the memory of so rich an experience." Monterey had an exceptionally large number of structures of considerable architectural and historical significance dating from the

Mexican and early American periods, including Colton Hall, the Royal Presidio Chapel, the Custom House, Casa Amesti, which was beautifully restored for her own use by prominent interior decorator Frances Elkins, and the Larkin House.[44]

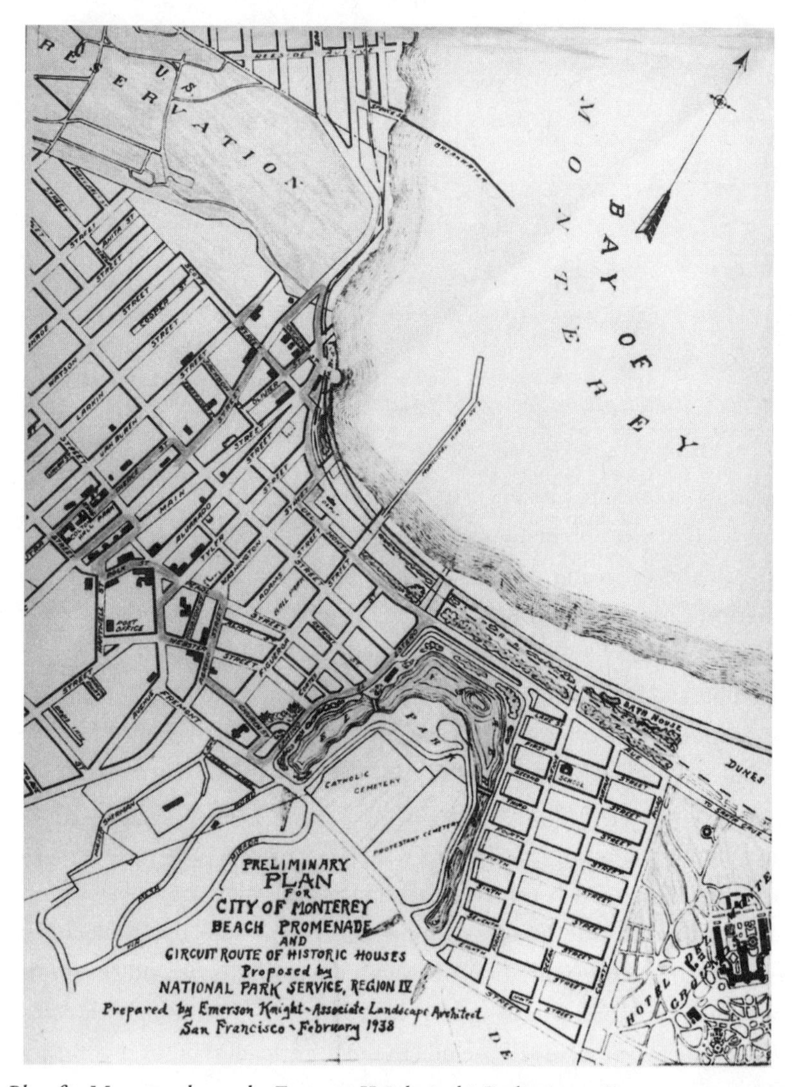

Plan for Monterey drawn by Emerson Knight in his Preliminary Report concerning the Master Plan for Historic Monterey, *1938. (Courtesy of the Emerson Knight Collection [1954–1], Environmental Design Archives, University of California, Berkeley)*

CALIFORNIA NATURAL LANDSCAPES

The Californios made few changes to the natural landscape other than using edible plants. Concern over the disappearance of native plants, unlike the protection of Hispanic structures, attracted little attention. The sublime mountain landscapes of the California Sierras had been universally extolled since the 1870s, but appreciation of natural landscapes closer to cities was largely limited to expeditions to view blooming wildflower meadows. Charles Lummis was a pioneer in anticipating the fragility of these plant communities. His own garden at El Alisal, his three-acre estate in Highland Park, was a remarkable essay in plant conservation as well as being an early attempt to revive Hispanic architecture. The house was built partly out of boulders hauled by Indian workers from the local creek and positioned around an existing sycamore tree, and the simple courtyard almost evoked a genuine Spanish workplace. However, Abigail Van Slyck has pointed out that despite Lummis's intentions, this was a nineteenth-century house in its spatial arrangement. He also retained the grove of thirty sycamores from which the house took its name and the wildflower meadow, which occupied the bulk of the garden space. Lummis delighted in its jumble of colors and the myriad number of wildflowers. However, this garden model was not popular, and the large number of bungalow gardens created in the first decades of the twentieth century by designers such as E. O. Murmann used a broad panoply of styles.[45]

Englishman Theodore Payne led the most focused attempt to conserve native plants, which he first encountered as gardener to Madame Mojeska on her estate in Santiago Canyon, Orange County, and which he then tried to cultivate in gardens. After opening a nursery in Los Angeles, Payne realized the full magnitude of the effects of the rapidly urbanizing Californio landscape. He recalled "when the State was almost covered with wild flowers. Wherever you looked or stepped there were acres of purple owl's clover, yellow tidy tips, golden poppies. But often returning later to a favorite haunt, I would find that many of them had disappeared completely."[46]

Payne advocated passionately for a widespread use of native plants for the rest of his life, cultivating and selling them in his nursery, using them in his designs for private and public gardens, lecturing and writing about them in horticultural journals. In 1915 he designed a five-acre demonstration garden in Exposition Park, Los Angeles, that contained a reproduction of a natural landscape with groves of sycamores, oaks, redwoods, and pines, together with native shrubs, perennials, bulbs, and annuals. He also created gardens on several estates in Montecito and Santa Barbara between 1910 and 1930 using only native plants. The most extensive example was at Mrs. Lora Knight's estate, Cima del Mundo, in east Montecito. Theodore Payne clothed the sensuously undulating topography of this 140-acre estate with extensive plantings of wildflowers, and the stream banks were planted with native trees and shrubs. However, his native gardens on other estates were never part of the principal garden space and vied for visitors' attention with simulated Italianate parterres, Spanish patios, and rose gardens.[47]

The creation of the Blaksley Botanic Garden in Santa Barbara considerably advanced public exposure to and scientific study of native plants. The idea of an experimental garden of native California plants was first promoted by ecologist Dr. Frederick Clements. But it was a passionate lecture on California wildflowers, delivered to the Montecito Garden Club by Theodore Payne, coupled with projected plans for a housing development in upper Mission Canyon, that led to the creation of the garden. It was the first public garden in California dedicated to the display of and research on native plants. The fifteen-acre site in Mission Canyon was highly suitable since it contained a variety of topographic settings with different microclimates and soils, a dramatic view of La Cumbre Peak, and the most substantial remains of the mission aqueduct and the dam constructed in 1807.[48]

The Blaksley Botanic Garden's first director, Dr. Elmer J. Bissell, laid out a series of displays of native plants adapted to their physical settings, ranging from arid, sunny ecosystems for cacti and succulents to the damp coolness of redwood forests. These early design developments were accomplished with great sensitivity, the winding paths, natural planting, and carefully placed rocks evoking an atmosphere of undisturbed tranquility.

The garden was expanded considerably in the 1930s as a result of a substantial gift by Mrs. Robert Woods Bliss. This necessitated an overall master plan that was developed between 1937 and 1942 by landscape architect Lockwood de Forest Jr. and landscape gardener Beatrix Farrand. De Forest battled with Farrand over the appropriateness of introducing formal elements, such as the axial courtyard around which the garden's office buildings and library were grouped, and a long, straight flight of steps leading down into the garden from the parking lot and aligned on the founder's rock. The principal feature of the plan, which was largely executed by Farrand, was a large wildflower meadow that opened up to a broad view of La Cumbre Peak. Farrand also recommended that the archaeologist at Mission Purisima advise on the repair of the mission dam in order to assure an appropriate level of craftsmanship.[49]

This garden had a considerable impact on visitors, who could see and appreciate native plants growing in settings similar to their native habitat. The displays were intended to assist homeowners in broadening their plant palettes. This research function inspired Mrs. Susannah Bixby Bryant to found Rancho Santa Ana Botanic Garden, a similar institution dedicated to the study of native plants and their adaptability for planting in gardens and public spaces, on her ranch in the Santa Ana River Canyon. Theodore Payne selected the spectacular site, and the Olmsted Brothers did the detailed site planning. To provide greater public accessibility the plants were moved to a new site in Claremont in 1952, where the garden became closely associated with Claremont College. Frederick Law Olmsted Jr. deplored this move, but Philp Munz, the garden's director, insisted that the original site was not a good one for a native plant garden.

The greatest care for the preservation and maintenance of a natural landscape occurred at Point Lobos (Punta de los Lobos Marinos, or Point of the Sea Wolves), one of the most beautiful and scientifically important sites on the California coast. It was widely believed that Robert Louis Stevenson had based Spyglass Hill in *Treasure Island* on this rugged promontory projecting out into the ocean after visiting it in 1879. The site is of considerable ecological importance, since it has several colonies of sea mammals, is the natural habitat of the brown pelican, and is the southern limit of the Monterey cypress. E. P. Meinecke, a plant pathologist, believed that the grove of Point Lobos cypresses was the only wild grove left and recommended limiting the number of visitors. Frederick Law Olmsted Jr., who was working on the California State Park plan, proposed giving it special treatment as a "museum piece" to prevent damaging trampling by the public. This concept was later endorsed by Dr. John C. Merriam, president of both the Carnegie Institution and the Save-the-Redwoods League, who argued that state protection similar to that of a museum would remove the site from political pressures. The Olmsted firm continued to play a significant role in the protection of Point Lobos by providing site planning and analytical surveys that were advanced for their time. Olmsted questioned creating a nursery on the site and recommended, instead, collecting cones from the Point Lobos cypresses for seed propagation to be carried out at "a reliable and well-established nursery."[50]

Olmsted shared the concerns of the consulting scientists about proceeding with caution until more ecological information could be obtained. In 1934 he outlined an approach of continuous and systematic note taking of the salient landscape features, detracting factors, observation positions, and temporary variable climatic factors. He proposed that his assistant George Vaughan prepare a careful record after two to three months of continuous observation, which could serve as a basis for "yard by yard mapping" by scientists.[51] In January 1935, a program was drawn up for preparing a base map, photographic map, oblique aerial photographs, detailed record maps at a scale of forty feet to the inch, and an "Inventory of Esthetic and Inspirational Value." The scientists were anxious for Olmsted to define the visual and sublime properties of Point Lobos. Olmsted discriminated between sensual and intellectual landscape impressions by suggesting that sensual impressions were entirely visual in nature, while intellectual impressions were concerned with meaning.[52]

Olmsted was assisted by George Vaughan, a young Harvard graduate, who lived at Point Lobos for seventeen months. Vaughan developed a detailed understanding of the site by recording its visual character under widely varying climatic conditions, especially the dense fogs that enveloped the site in the summer, and knowledge of its disturbed nature caused by a history of fire, cattle grazing, and trampling by visitors and workers.[53] He also searched for photographic records to supplement his visual analysis.

By closely observing the development of cypress seedlings, Vaughan began to question Frederick Clements's theories about succession on the site. Olmsted encouraged Vaughan to study the presence on the site of types of *Baccharis pilularis*, an aggressive member of the chaparral plant community. A recently published scientific paper suggested that it would be appropriate to limit the spread of the *Baccharis pilularis* by encouraging a less aggressive member of this genus.[54]

CONCLUSION

The appearance of the myth of the Californios was inevitable. The discovery of California at the end of the nineteenth century as a place of unparalleled opportunities demanded a usable set of ordering principles to guide new developments. The widely shared anti-modernist sensibility ensured an attempt to appropriate a local past. The real landscapes of the Californios had little to offer the search for new ordering principles. Thus, the myth that appeared served this purpose by misinterpreting the surviving material evidence. The adoption of Andalusian imagery in the 1920s was the final culmination of romantic distancing from the less pleasant truths of the past. This cultural distancing also affected Californio descendants. Leonard Pitt has pointed out how descendants of Spanish Californians have been unwilling to admit that their ancestors were of mestizo descent, or that their ancestors' land grants were of Mexican, not Spanish, origin.[55]

The distance between the reality and myth of Californio culture confirms that myths are usually grounded in some historic truth, but the capacity for inventing a past appears to spread across many cultures. The rediscovery of the Golden Age that occurred in Italy in the Renaissance was as much *invention* as a true *recovery*. This almost certainly means that the use of history has often been a process not so much of actually recovering the past as seeking an alternative direction with which to improve the present. Actual or perceived failure has no place in such an enterprise, which partly explains the reluctance of both Californios and Americans to explore the repressive or other unsuccessful aspects of the Californio past. This selective pursuit of an idealized past venerates only those achievements that have obvious dignity or elegance, such as the mission church or the ranch house, without wishing to inquire too deeply about their social circumstances or origins.

What is remarkable, however, about the Californio mythic development is the incorporation of preservation activities. Preservation practices inevitably evolve over time, but the early practices presented in the treatment of Californio missions are remarkable for the modesty of the interventions undertaken. In part this reflected the amount of available funding, but it may also reflect a hitherto unrecognized romanticism on the part of the restorers intuitively drawn to partially decayed structures.

Related to this modest treatment of structures is the apparent lack of interest in the appropriate treatment of designed gardens. In marked contradistinction were the pioneering conservation attempts of Theodore Payne, Lockwood de Forest Jr., and Lester Rowntree. Their work is notable for their testing of the adaptability of native plants to gardens in ways that anticipated and complemented the work of scientific institutions such as the Santa Barbara Botanic Garden and the Rancho Santa Ana Botanic Garden.

In these ways the California experience of addressing the conservation of the material aspects of a prior cultural tradition differs significantly from the work discussed by other authors in this volume. There was no site in California comparable in age, historical significance, or physical condition to any of the New England colonial gardens or Mount Vernon. Indeed, part of the cultural meaning of the myth is a suppressed desire to find comparable significance in the ruined world of the Californios. California's mission churches attained national significance because they were constructed at the time of the country's founding.

Equally remarkable is the prominent role of amateurs in early California preservation activities. To some extent this reflects the very small number of professionally trained landscape architects practicing in California in the first three decades of the twentieth century. Charles Fletcher Lummis, Bernhard Hoffmann, Pearl Chase, Charles Saunders, and some early landscape designers, such as de Forest and Knight, had either no or very little formal professional training. Much of the early writing about the world of the Californios and the subsequent American period was done by amateurs gathering materials in the form of personal recollections that might have otherwise disappeared. Their contributions should not be ignored or ridiculed because they do not rise to modern standards of scholarly excellence. Their vision and their persistent commitment to the necessity of preserving and recording the past were exemplary and are similar to the dedicated work of southern women discussed by Catherine Howett elsewhere in this collection.

This raises important questions about the future of the amateur in preservation, an arena that has become highly professionalized. Are there roles that amateurs can still play in writing about the past? Certainly the nonspecialist will always play a critical role in publicly supporting the work of professionals. But the amateurs who have written for decades in journals such as *Garden History* suggest that the amateur may still contribute to the writing of the past, by recognizing the importance of past place-making activities through interviews and gathering materials that might otherwise be lost.

The appearance of the myth of the Californios and its subsequent development in the first four decades of the twentieth century are an important part of California history, revealing changing attitudes toward the past and the treatment of its material remnants. An instructive comparison can be made between the careful restoration and interpretation of Florence Green Bixby's gardens at Rancho Los Alamitos and the proposed restoration of a similar romantic garden at nearby Rancho Los Cerritos to the earliest period of its history. At the former garden, the layered nature of its history is valued in a way that acknowledges the value of Bixby's very romantic view of the past. By contrast, the proposed restoration at Rancho Los Cerritos will completely eliminate a similar garden as having no cultural value. Both houses and gardens epitomize the evolution of the romantic Californio myth into the 1920s, yet these opposing contemporary reactions to valuing and interpreting this recent past confirm the tensions and ambiguities that still exist in preservation efforts today.

NOTES

1. Helen Hunt Jackson, *Ramona* (Boston: Roberts Brothers, 1884). One of the best discussions of the Californios is in Leonard Pitt, *The Decline of the Californios: A Social History of the Spanish-Speaking Californians, 1846–1890* (Berkeley and Los Angeles: University of California Press, 1966). The mythmaking aspects of Hispanic California are discussed in Kevin Starr, *Americans and the California Dream, 1850–1915* (New York: Oxford University Press, 1973).

2. T. J. Jackson Lears, *No Place of Grace: Antimodernism and the Transformation of American Culture, 1889–1920* (New York: Pantheon Books, 1981).

3. For English Colonial Revival on the East Coast, see Karal Ann Marling, *George Washington Slept Here* (Cambridge: Harvard University Press, 1988); for the Spanish Colonial Revival in California, see David Gebhard, "The Spanish Colonial Revival in Southern California (1895–1930)," *Journal of Architectural Historians* 26, no. 2: 289–305; for the Santa Fe Style, see Chris Wilson, *The Myth of Santa Fe: Creation of a Modern Regional Tradition* (Albuquerque: University of New Mexico Press, 1997); Abigail A. Van Slyck, "Mañana, Mañana, Racial Stereotypes and the Anglo Rediscovery of the Southwest's Vernacular Architecture, 1890–1920," in *Gender, Class, and Shelter: Perspectives in Vernacular Architecture V,* ed. Elizabeth Cromley Collins and Carter L. Hudgins (Knoxville: University of Tennessee Press, 1995), 95–108; and May Brawley Hill, *Grandmother's Garden: The Old-Fashioned American Garden, 1865–1915* (New York: Abrams, 1995).

4. Starr, *California Dream;* Gebhard, "Spanish Colonial Revival"; Harold Kirker, *California's Architectural Frontier: Style and Tradition in the Nineteenth Century* (1960; reprint, Salt Lake City: Peregrine Smith Books, 1986); Harold Kirker, *Old Forms for a New Land: California Architecture in Perspective* (Niwot, CO: Roberts Rinehart, 1991).

5. Abbot Kinney and H. H. Jackson, "Report on the Condition and Needs of the Mission Indians" (Washington, DC: U.S. Office of Indian Affairs, 1884).

6. Jackson, *Ramona,* 6.

7. Charles Dudley Warner, *Our Italy* (New York: Harper Brothers, 1893); Randell L. Makinson, *Greene and Greene* (Salt Lake City: Peregrine Smith, 1977); Charles Keeler, *The Simple Home* (1904; reprint, Santa Barbara: Peregrine Smith, 1978), 11–16; Bruce Porter, introduction to *Stately Homes of California,* by Porter Garnett (Boston: Little, Brown, 1915), ix–xv.

8. For the Laws of the Indies, see Dora P. Crouch, Daniel J. Garr, and Axel I. Mundigo, *Spanish City Planning in North America* (Cambridge, MA: MIT Press, 1982).

9. Kurt Baer, *Architecture of the California Missions* (Berkeley and Los Angeles: University of California Press, 1958), 40–42.

10. Kirker, *Old Forms,* 9.

11. Sir George Simpson, *Narrative of a Journey round the World during the Years 1841 and 1842,* 2 vols. (London: H. Colburn, 1847), 1:408.

12. Elizabeth Hughes, *The California of the Padres; or, Footprints of Ancient Communism* (San Francisco: I. N. Choynski, 1875); Hubert Bancroft, *California Pastoral, 1769–1848* (San Francisco: History Company, 1888).

13. Helen Hunt Jackson, *Glimpses of California and the Missions* (Boston: Little, Brown, 1903), 100.

14. For Lummis's numerous activities, see Edwin R. Bingham, *Charles F. Lummis: Editor of the Southwest* (San Marino, CA: Huntington Library, 1955); Marco

Newmark, "Charles Fletcher Lummis," *Historical Society of Southern California Quarterly* 32 (March 1, 1950): 52; Van Slyck, "Racial Stereotypes," 98–100.

15. Quoted in Bingham, *Charles F. Lummis,* 104.

16. "Landmarks Club," *Land of Sunshine* 6 (December 1896): 25–26.

17. "The Landmarks Club," *Out West* 18, no. 1 (January 1903): 88–89.

18. Karen J. Weitze, "Arthur B. Benton," in *Toward a Simpler Way of Life: The Arts and Crafts Architects of California,* ed. Robert Winter (Berkeley and Los Angeles: University of California Press, 1997), 192; Arthur Burnett Benton, "The Work of the Landmarks Club of Southern California," *Journal of the American Institute of Architects* 2, no. 10 (October 1914): 469–81.

19. Charles F. Lummis, "Saving Our Great Monuments," *Out West* 24, no. 3 (March 1906): 245; *Out West* 22, no. 1 (July 1905); and "The Landmarks Club," *Out West* 18, no. 2 (February 1903): 216.

20. "The Landmarks Club," *Out West* 18, no. 5 (May 1903): 624; Turbese Lummis Fiske and Keith Lummis, *Charles F. Lummis: The Man and His West* (Norman: University of Oklahoma Press, 1975): 90–91.

21. Charles Gibbs Adams, "Gardens of the Spanish Days of California," *Annual Publications, Historical Society of Southern California* 15 (1932): 347–55.

22. Lester Rowntree, *Flowering Shrubs of California* (Stanford: Stanford University Press; London: Humphrey Milford, Oxford University Press, 1939): vii.

23. A. Dibblee Poett, *Rancho San Julían: The Story of a California Ranch and Its People* (Santa Barbara: Fithian Press, Santa Barbara Historical Society, 1991), 8–38.

24. Pitt, *Decline of Californios,* 10–19.

25. Pitt, *Decline of Californios,* 83–103 (northern ranches), 104–19 (southern ranches); quote is taken from Edwin Bryant, *What I Saw in California, Being the Journal of a Tour in the Years 1846, 1847* (New York: D. Appleton; Philadelphia: George S. Appleton, 1849), 385; William Montgomery, "Studies in Southern California Landscape History Applied to the Development of Rancho Los Cerritos" (unpublished Master of Landscape Architecture thesis, California State Polytechnic University, Pomona, 1976).

26. Charles F. Saunders, "California," in Alice G. B. Lockwood, ed. and comp. *Gardens of Colony and State: Gardens and Gardeners of the American Colonies and of the Republic before 1840* (New York: Charles Scribner's Sons for the Garden Club of America, 1931, 1934), 2:391–402; Kirker, *California's Architectural Frontier,* 16.

27. David C. Streatfield, *California Gardens: Creating a New Eden* (New York: Abbeville Press, 1994), 161–68.

28. Marion Cran, *Gardens in America* (London: Herbert Jenkins), 133; Horace D. Crotty, "Obituary of Florence Green Bixby," *California History* 40, no. 4 (December 1961): 365.

29. For HABS drawings of Rancho Los Cerritos, see Sally Woodbridge, *California Architecture: Historic American Buildings Survey* (San Francisco: Chronicle Books, 1988), 34.

30. Robert Glass Cleland, *El Molino Viejo: Spanish California's First Grist Mill* (Los Angeles: Ward Ritchie Press, 1950; rev. ed., San Francisco: California Historical Society, 1971).

31. Lockwood, *Gardens of Colony and State,* 2:400. Saunders's interview with Señora del Valle is in the Charles Francis Saunders Collection, Huntington Library, San Marino, California.

32. Rexford Newcomb, "Architecture of the California Missions," *Publications of the Historical Society of Southern California* 9, no. 3 (1914): 225–35; Rexford Newcomb, *The Old Mission Churches and Historic Houses of California: Their History, Architecture, Art and Lore* (Philadelphia: J. B. Lippincott, 1925), v–vi.

33. Florence Atheron Eyre, *Reminiscences of Peninsula Gardens* (San Francisco: San Francisco Garden Club, 1933); Helen Weber Kennedy and Veronica K. Kinzi, *Vignettes of the Gardens of San José de Guadalupe* (San Francisco: San Francisco Garden Club, 1938); Bell M. McGee, *Reminiscences of East Bay Gardens from 1860–1890* (San Francisco: San Francisco Garden Club, 1933); Mrs. Silas Palmer, *Vignettes of Early San Francisco Homes and Gardens* (San Francisco: San Francisco Garden Club, 1933).

34. Stella Haverland Rouse, *Santa Barbara's Spanish Renaissance and Old Spanish Days Fiesta* (Santa Barbara: Schauer Printing Studio, 1974), 53.

35. Carol Greentree, "Hazel Wood Waterman, 1865–1948," in *Pioneers of American Landscape Design,* ed. Birnbaum and Karson (New York: McGraw Hill, 2000), 431–34. See also Sally Bullard Thornton, "Hazel Wood Waterman," in Winter, *Arts and Crafts Architects,* 219–28.

36. Hazel Waterman, "The Restoration of a Landmark" (typescript, San Diego Historical Society Library, San Diego), 1–2, 4. Kirker refers to her restoration as a "questionable reconstruction," in *California's Architectural Frontier,* 8.

37. Hazel Waterman, "Part of Specifications Used on Restoration of Old Adobe Building at Old Town" (typescript, San Diego Historical Society Library, San Diego); D. E. Kessler, "The Restoration of Ramona's Marriage Place," *Pacific Monthly* 23 (June 1910): 585–88.

38. Kirker, *Old Forms,* 82–84.

39. Rouse, *Santa Barbara's Spanish Renaissance,* 26, 42.

40. Ibid., 30; Hunt, *Glimpses of California,* 98.

41. Pearl Chase, "Bernhard Hoffmann," *Noticias* 5 (1959): 15–23.

42. See Winsor Soule, "The New Santa Barbara," *American Architect* 130 (July 5, 1926): 1–10. Photographs showing the transformation of Casa de la Guerra can be found in Newcomb, *Old Mission Churches,* 323–24; plan drawings are in Clarence Cullimore, *Santa Barbara Adobes* (Santa Barbara: Santa Barbara Book Publishing, 1948), 21.

43. Newcomb, *Old Mission Churches,* 328; Sharon Crawford, *Gardens of Santa Barbara* (Santa Barbara: Easton Gallery, 2000), 70–71.

44. Emerson Knight, *Preliminary Report Concerning the Master Plan for Historic Monterey, California Project for Protection and Treatment of the Beach,* National Park

Service Region IV, Los Angeles, February 11, 1938, Emerson Knight Collection, Correspondence and Reports, 1936–38, box 1, folder 1, Environmental Design Archives, University of California, Berkeley, submitted by the Planning Commission in collaboration with Emerson Knight, city planning adviser, May 24, 1939; Newcomb, *Old Mission Churches,* 334–43.

45. Van Slyck, "Racial Stereotypes," 98–100; Charles Fletcher Lummis, "Carpet of God's Country," *Out West* 22, no. 5 (May 1905): 307–17; Eugene O. Murmann, *California Gardens* (Los Angeles: E. O. Murmann, 1915).

46. Victoria Padilla, *Southern California Gardens: An Illustrated History* (Berkeley and Los Angeles: University of California Press, 1961), 165.

47. Ibid., 165–67. See also David E. Myrick, *Montecito and Santa Barbara,* vol. 2: *The Days of the Great Estates* (Glendale, CA: Trans-Anglo Books, 1991), 360, 362.

48. Padilla, *Southern California Gardens,* 166.

49. Diane Kostial McGuire, "Beatrix Farrand's Contribution to the Art of Landscape Architecture," in *Beatrix Jones Farrand: Fifty Years of American Landscape Architecture,* ed. Diane Kostial McGuire and Lois Fern (Washington, DC: Dumbarton Oaks, 1982), 48–49.

50. E. P Meinecke, "Reduction of Visitors on Point Lobos, Where the Trees Grow May Save Monterey Cypress," *Carmel Pine Cone,* July 29, 1927; Frederick Law Olmsted [Jr.] to Duncan McDuffie, April 15, 1927; Frederick Law Olmsted [Jr.] to Dr. John C. Merriam, April 18, 1932; Frederick Law Olmsted [Jr.] to Newton Drury, March 10, 1932; all in box 2, Olmsted Brothers Papers, Frederick Law Olmsted National Historic Site, Brookline, Massachusetts.

51. Frederick Law Olmsted [Jr.], "Memorandum as to Investigations and studies for the landscape treatment," July 12, 1934, box 2, Olmsted Papers.

52. Frederick Law Olmsted [Jr.], "Notes and Comments by F. L. Olmsted, January 1935: Intended Primarily for Consideration of Scientific Sub-Committee"; Olmsted Brothers, "Point Lobos Reserve: Contributions toward a Master Plan; II: Reviews of Observations on Esthetically Significant Features in the Scenery of the Point Lobos Reserve; III: Specific Recommendations for Preservation and Utilization," November 1935; both in box 2, Olmsted Papers.

53. Frederick Law Olmsted [Jr.] to Duncan McDuffie, March 20, 1933, box 2, Olmsted Papers.

54. Frederick Law Olmsted [Jr.] to George B. Vaughan, July 17, 1935, box 2, Olmsted Papers.

55. Pitt, *Decline of the Californios,* 290.

Frederick Law Olmsted Jr.

History, Preservation, and the Planning Process

CYNTHIA ZAITZEVSKY

Frederick Law Olmsted Jr. (1870–1957) had a distinguished career as a planner, related to but distinct from his career as a landscape architect. With Arthur Shurcliff and John Nolen, he was a pioneer in what was then the emerging field of city planning. By himself or in collaboration with others, Olmsted wrote more than a dozen city plans and reports between 1905 and 1940. He made recommendations for large industrial cities such as Detroit, Pittsburgh, and Cleveland; for small cities, such as Springfield and Holyoke (Massachusetts), Rochester (New York), and Boulder (Colorado); he also advised on the development of Toronto's waterfront. In addition, he delivered an address on some aspect of city planning at nearly all the annual National Conferences on City Planning held by the American Civic Association in the first three decades of the twentieth century. He also advised on the acquisition of municipal, state, and national parks and occasionally on the landscape rehabilitation of historic properties.

As early as 1913, Olmsted produced the "Report to the Newport Improvement Association," which was remarkably forward looking in the importance he placed on what today would be called the vernacular landscape of the town. Olmsted identified two different kinds of scenery in Newport. One was "the larger kind of scenery . . . of distant views and of the shores of open water . . . a natural asset due to the topography of the island." He recommended that the Ocean Drive, the Cliff Walk, and Easton's Beach should be conveniently accessible. The second kind of scenery, he observed, is that "which the people of the city have made in adapting their environment to their own uses. It is the scenery of the streets and of the houses and gardens and other things along the streets. It is the dominant visual aspect of Newport."[1]

The two reports discussed in this essay offer a glimpse of Olmsted's extensive interests and activities in planning and resource protection. In the 1929 "Report to the California State Park Commission," his main concern was the preservation of the many types of extraordinary natural scenery—seacoast scenery, redwood forests, mountains and buttes—found within the wide geographical and climatic boundaries of the state. He also recommended the preservation of some of California's historic sites.

Olmsted's 1935 report to Franklin Delano Roosevelt, "Improvements and Policy of Maintenance for the Executive Mansion Grounds," stressed practical solutions to the problems of one of the country's most revered national sites and took into consideration both the needs of the first family and the wishes of United States citizens and foreign visitors who, then as now, loved to view the grounds from without. A remarkable aspect of the Olmsted report on the White House grounds was that it included a systematic study of the history of the grounds from their beginnings, written by Morley Jeffers Williams. Williams's pioneering role in the field of landscape preservation is discussed in another essay in this collection by Thomas E. Beaman.

BIOGRAPHY

Frederick Law Olmsted Jr., born when his father was nearly fifty years old, was the son of Frederick Law Olmsted Sr. and Mary Cleveland Perkins Olmsted. He was known to family and friends as Rick to distinguish him from his father. Olmsted graduated from Harvard College magna cum laude in 1894. In 1893, during a college vacation, he apprenticed with his father at the Chicago World's Fair and, in 1894, spent a summer with the United States Coast and Geodetic Survey. He also periodically assisted at the George Washington Vanderbilt property, Biltmore, in Asheville, North Carolina,

Frederick Law Olmsted Jr., c. 1925, in Palos Verdes, California. (Courtesy of the National Park Service, Frederick Law Olmsted National Historic Site)

where his father was developing a huge country place for Vanderbilt. Frederick Law Olmsted Jr. did not, however, come into the Olmsted firm, then called Olmsted, Olmsted and Eliot, as a paid member until September 1895, when his father retired due to ill health. Thus, he did not have the advantage of the long professional association with his father that his half brother, John Charles Olmsted, had enjoyed. In 1897, after the unexpected death of partner Charles Eliot, the firm became first F. L. and J. C. Olmsted and then Olmsted Brothers, a name that was retained even after the death of John Charles Olmsted in 1920.[2]

Although he went into landscape architecture only after much persuasion by his father, Frederick Law Olmsted Jr. made his mark early in the profession. Before 1900, there was no systematic course of study in landscape architecture available anywhere in the country. In 1900, Charles W. Eliot, president of Harvard University and father of the landscape architect who had been a partner in the Olmsted firm, asked Frederick Law Olmsted Jr., then in practice for only three years, to initiate a course in landscape architecture similar to that already established at Harvard in architecture. In 1901, Olmsted was appointed by President Theodore Roosevelt to be a member of the Senate Park Commission, which produced what became known as the McMillan Plan for the parks of Washington, D.C.[3]

It was his experience on the Senate Park Commission that led Frederick Law Olmsted Jr., in later life, to devote great attention to public and semipublic service, both for the District of Columbia and for the nation as a whole. Between 1910 and 1918, Olmsted was a member of the Commission of Fine Arts. Later he served on the National Capital Park and Planning Commission. After the United States entered World War I, he became manager of the Landscape Architecture Division of the United States Housing Corporation, which built housing and new towns for workers in war-related industries. Between 1928 and 1956, he served as a member of a Committee of Experts that advised on plans and policies concerning Yosemite National Park.

REPORT OF THE STATE SURVEY OF CALIFORNIA, 1929

Olmsted undertook the 1929 "Report to the California State Park Commission" as a survey of all existing and potential sites for state parks so that recommendations could be made for the allocation of a six-million-dollar bond issue. Given the size of the state of California, its almost one thousand miles of coastline, its mountain ranges, its forests and specimen trees, it is remarkable that a study such as the 1929 survey could be undertaken at all. Needless to say, Olmsted did not accomplish the survey alone. He had the assistance of a technical staff as well as input from volunteers appointed by the commission from the twelve districts into which the state was divided for the purpose of the survey. Several of the advisers and regional reporters were selected for their historical expertise.[4] In another essay in this volume, Ethan Carr discusses the role played by Daniel Hull in the California Survey as well as the tremendous impact it had as a prototype for the National Park Service through the agency's chief planner, Thomas Vint.

In the report, Olmsted recommended the preservation of eight his-

Old mining town of Columbia, Tuolumne County, from the Report of the State Park Survey of California, *1929. (Courtesy of the Frances Loeb Library, Harvard Design School)*

toric sites. These included the missions of Santa Barbara County, which he observed were rapidly falling into decay and would soon disappear; the old mining town of Columbia; Mark Twain's cabin; and General Guadalupe Vallejo's home in Sonoma.[5]

Olmsted considered the value of scenic prospects for a variety of purposes: automobile pleasure trips and tours; boating, hiking, and horseback riding; supporting commercial hotels, camps, and so on; and private vacation homes. He stressed that it was necessary to teach the public how to develop such scenic and recreational values without destroying natural assets and also to curb the activities of exploiters of the landscape who wanted only a quick profit.[6]

Numerous state park projects were recommended to the commission, with seacoast projects being the most numerous. In discussing these projects, Olmsted was particularly concerned with protecting the view of the coast from buildings on private properties and also with providing temporary stopping places "in the form of turn-outs, short spurs, or loops for the enjoyment of views in quiet, or for picnics."[7] The completion of Scenic

Point Lobos, Monterey County, from the Report of the State Park Survey of California, *1929. (Courtesy of the Frances Loeb Library, Harvard Design School)*

Highway 1 along most of the coast from Malibu to Carmel in 1937 secured stunning views on this long stretch and also provided turnouts, although rarely large enough for picnics.

Two special seacoast projects were Point Lobos, four miles south of Carmel, which Olmsted deemed "the most outstanding example on the Coast of California of picturesque rock and surf scenery in combination with unique vegetation, including typical Monterey cypresses." Point Lobos, now a California state reserve, was photographed extensively by Edward Weston and others and was also the subject of numerous poems by Robinson Jeffers, a resident of the area. Olmsted called Santa Cruz Island off Santa Barbara "the most notable of the islands off the coast of Southern California in respect to vegetation, scenery, sea-caves and running water."[8]

Olmsted also singled out the coastline of Del Norte County, Bodega Bay in Sonoma County, and Morro Bay in San Luis Obispo County. He praised Point Reyes Peninsula in Marin County as "hilly, forested, mesa, canyon, beach and bluff lands fronting on Drake's Bay, Pacific Ocean and Tomales Bay. Scenically fine. High recreational potential."[9] In 1962, Congress endorsed Olmsted's assessment by designating the peninsula as Point Reyes National Seashore.

The Redwood Forest projects included the completion of Humboldt

State Redwood Park, additions to the California Redwood Park in Santa Cruz County and the Redwood Canyon in Big Sur, Monterey County. Other "big trees" projects included the Calaveras Grove in Calaveras County and Castle Crags in Shasta County. An important lake project was Lake Tahoe on the Nevada border in northern California. Mountain and butte projects included Mount Diablo in Contra Costa County, and desert projects included the Victorville Joshua Trees.[10]

Since the completion of Olmsted's report, most of the sites that he recommended as California state parks appear to be protected. Although it is unclear whether this happened as a direct result of the report, this fact demonstrates Olmsted's abilities and foresight as a land planner on a very large scale, integrating cultural, natural, and scenic resources into a comprehensive conservation plan.

REPORT ON IMPROVEMENTS FOR THE EXECUTIVE MANSION GROUNDS, 1935

On a smaller scale, Olmsted guided the development of the White House grounds. Between 1929 and 1948, the primary design influence on President's Park (which includes Lafayette Park, the grounds of the White House, the Ellipse, and the grounds of the Treasury Building and the Old Executive Office Building) was Olmsted's 1935 plan for the White House grounds. By this time, however, Olmsted had been involved peripherally with plans for the White House grounds for over thirty years. In 1903, while designing the new West Wing of the White House, Charles F. McKim asked Olmsted informally for advice on the White House gardens and north drives and paths. McKim and Olmsted each produced a drawing, but the architectural and structural problems of the White House were so massive that little attention could be given at that time to the grounds.[11] During the administration of President Calvin Coolidge, Olmsted was again asked to consult on the White House grounds. On January 24, 1928, he wrote a letter to Colonel Ulysses S. Grant III of the Army Corps of Engineers, which was then administering President's Park, and thoroughly discussed the issues of the landscape. Although Charles Moore, then chairman of the Commission of Fine

Arts, tried to move the study forward during the Hoover administration, little was done at this time. On March 4, 1933, Franklin Delano Roosevelt was inaugurated president. As part of Roosevelt's reorganization of government agencies, the Department of the Interior assumed control of the President's Park from the Army Corps of Engineers.[12]

Early in 1934, a determined Charles Moore took Olmsted's 1928 report to Eleanor Roosevelt, who promptly brought it to her husband's attention.[13] Some time in the last week of April, the president and Olmsted met, and Roosevelt, himself an inveterate amateur architect, instructed the landscape architect to prepare detailed recommendations for improvements to the White House grounds. At this point Olmsted began the study, but his first step was to request a full account of the practical requirements that affected the grounds.[14] On May 12, Olmsted returned with the firm's plant specialist, Hans Koehler, to examine the grounds further.[15]

The first correspondence from the Olmsted firm regarding the White House grounds was a letter from Olmsted to Col. Grant on January 24, 1928. This early document provides insights into Olmsted's assessment of the major issues that needed to be addressed. Olmsted made the following general observation:

> While the general effect is distinctly "respectable" . . . and while the general plan, as regards the form of the ground and the disposition of the tree-masses and means of communication and their relation to the building and to the exterior surroundings is emphatically good, it would be fair to say that almost anyone of cultivated taste and a fairly broad and appreciative acquaintance with fine examples of the landscape surroundings of great mansions, both private and official, in this country and elsewhere, would have to rate the White House grounds as distinctly disappointing.[16]

Olmsted criticized the lack of residential character in the grounds, feeling that there was little that distinguished the White House landscape from the grounds of a public institution or that indicated that a family lived there. However, he considered that there was ample opportunity to develop parts of the grounds for domestic uses. For example, he felt that there was considerable space on either side of the south vista for secluded spaces that could be allocated for the personal and social needs of the first family.[17]

Six years later, Olmsted Brothers was fully engaged with the White House grounds. But it was a somewhat frustrating situation for the firm, which was not really in charge of the project in the usual professional manner. Olmsted and other members of the firm made recommendations, either in the form of letters and memos or in the final report itself, and they also made sketches. From these recommendations and sketches, National Park Service landscape architects prepared construction drawings and sometimes also estimates. The Olmsted firm did not supervise construction, although it was usually informed of what was going on, and occasionally Olmsted's opinion was asked.[18]

By June 1934, Olmsted had obtained the services of Professor Morley Jeffers Williams of Harvard's Department of Landscape Architecture to do the historical research necessary for the White House project. Williams had already carried out similar research on the history of the Mount Vernon grounds and was stationed at Mount Vernon that summer.[19] Williams located and analyzed all the plans and views that were available to him at the time. He studied everything from the Pierre L'Enfant plan of 1791 to many later plans. His research on the "The Historical Background of the Design of the White House Grounds," consisted of a twenty-five-page narrative and fifty annotated historic plans, maps, and views. Williams was apparently the first person to attempt a thorough study of the history of the grounds, and much of his research is still valid today.[20] Williams followed what is today the basic methodology of the research and documentation phase of a cultural landscape report. Given the amount of space in the 1935 report devoted to Williams's research, it was evidently highly valued by Olmsted, although he never stated how, specifically, the historian's work influenced his own thinking or shaped his recommendations.

By September 1934, the firm had prepared an early draft of their report. Olmsted visited the White House grounds on September 28–29, studied certain aspects of them with Clarence E. Howard, another landscape architect from the Olmsted firm, and made revisions to the draft report.[21] On October 9, 1934, President Roosevelt toured the grounds with Olmsted,

Moore, members of the White House staff, including Lieutenant Lock, and a Mr. Peterson, an architect at the National Park Service.[22] Several important decisions were made at this site visit and are worth quoting from Moore's account:

> It was the consensus of opinion that: The inner one of two driveways south of the White House may be eliminated. . . . That the south vista be opened in the grounds by the elimination of now obstructing trees. That the vista open to the public be enlarged to approximately 150 feet, giving the finest possible view of the White House. . . . That those trees which have outlived their beauty and usefulness be replaced by trees preferably those keeping their greenness through the winter. The tulip poplar, the magnolia and certain varieties of pine were favored. The President drew on his experience at his estate of Hyde Park on the Hudson, and his love and knowledge of trees. Apparently the expedition was successful in bringing about complete agreement between the President and Mr. Olmsted as to the general features of the restoration, with the approval of the other participants.[23]

Before Roosevelt came out on the grounds, Olmsted spent considerable time discussing the grading around the West Wing with architect Eric Gugler.[24] On October 16, 1934, Olmsted submitted a thirteen-page report on the White House grounds, with additional explanatory notes and a map. The substance of the report had already been discussed with the president in the site visit a week earlier. The final version of the report, which was submitted in October 1935, was an expanded version of the 1934 draft. Additions to the 1935 report included plans, discussion of the plans, and the historical section by Morley Jeffers Williams.

Olmsted had wanted to produce an official government document, but the Secret Service adhered to the policy of not allowing publication of accurate official maps of either the grounds or the interior of the White House. It was decided that there would be only a few copies of the final report, but they would be very attractively presented. Two of them—

Roosevelt's personal copy and that for the White House Library—would be elegantly bound.[25] In June 1935, the Olmsted Brothers' "General Survey of the Executive Mansion Grounds" was completed and was incorporated into the report.

At the beginning of the report, Olmsted described certain defects in utilitarian features of the White House grounds, such as the limitation of office space, inadequate space for cars to load and unload visitors at the East Entrance, inadequate service yard space, and defects of the road system south of the White House. The last problem was the most serious. As Olmsted noted:

> The present system of roads within the White House Grounds south of the building is the result of numerous past changes of a rather patchwork sort, adapting very different earlier plans to changing practices in use. . . . The roads produce unpleasant landscape effects, they are not entirely convenient for the vehicular uses to which they are now put. . . . Unpleasant landscape effects of the present road system are (1) the interruption of the axial lawn by a conspicuous band of transverse roadway cutting it in two in the middle as seen from the White House, (2) the duplication of the lateral roads on each side of the axis, and (3) certain details of crowning, guttering and surface material.[26]

Olmsted next addressed what he described as general landscape defects, especially lack of privacy. Most areas of the grounds were not screened sufficiently from the outside. He criticized the existing privet hedge, which was both too low and too "diaphanous." On the other hand, the one place where the public should be allowed to look in, at the end of the south axis, was blocked by inappropriate plantings. He also recommended planting a few long-lived trees to replace those existing ones that were nearing the end of their life spans but cautioned that their exact demise could not be accurately predicted.[27]

Another tree planting proposal by Roosevelt was endorsed by Olmsted in the report but not carried out until 1939. This was "a sylvan feature suggested by the President, and rightly noted by him as both pleasing in

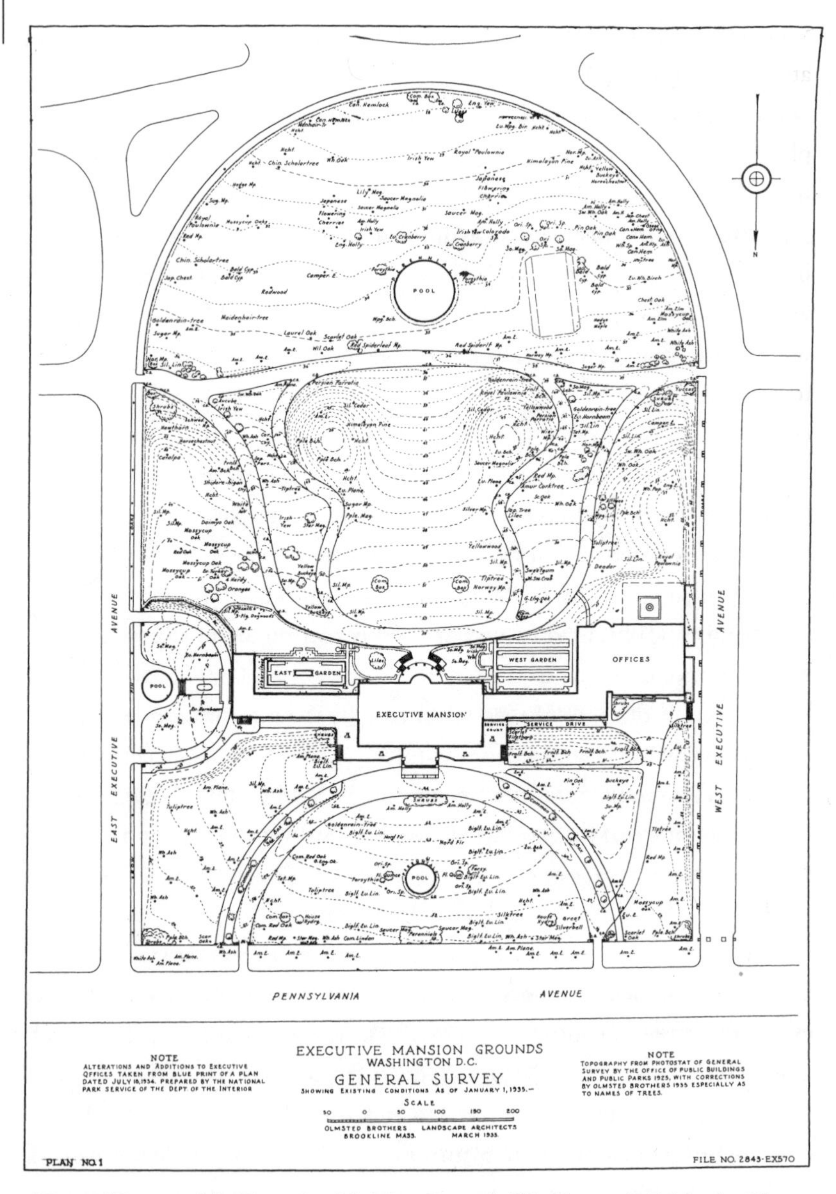

"General Survey of the Executive Mansion Grounds, Washington DC," by the Olmsted Brothers, Landscape Architects, March 1935. (Courtesy of the National Park Service, Frederick Law Olmsted National Historic Site)

itself, highly characteristic of the region surrounding Washington, and relatively durable. This is a dense pure stand of nearly even-aged tulip-poplars, with columnar aspiring trunks and high foliage canopy, which would completely fill this ineffective gap within the surrounding stand of more spreading and wide-spaced trees."[28]

Roosevelt implemented a number of Olmsted's recommendations immediately upon completion of the report. In March 1937, specifications were written for the revision of the roads south of the White House and were sent to Olmsted Brothers for review.[29] Olmsted wired back: "For historic and aesthetic reasons gravelled surface of private roads south of White House should preferably adjoin turf without any intervening border of other material. I concurred for ease of maintenance in Park Service suggestion of metal edging so thin and low as to be unnoticeable but consider concrete curb as specified very undesirable."[30]

Roosevelt took part enthusiastically in the plans for new trees and shrubs on the White House grounds, especially the hemlocks by the west gate and lilacs in the northeast grounds. A linden still on the grounds may be one of two *Tilia cordata europaea* planted in honor of the 1939 visit of King George VI and Queen Elizabeth of England to the White House.[31]

In 1939, Roosevelt initiated another commemorative tree planting, this one a memorial to Thomas Jefferson. In answer to an inquiry by Roosevelt, Captain Howard Ker, Corps of Engineers, suggested planting a *Sophora japonica* within the White House grounds, but the president felt very strongly that Jefferson's memorial should be a native American tree. He also wanted something more impressive than a single tree and favored a planting that would connect the White House symbolically and, to a certain extent, physically with the Jefferson Memorial. Roosevelt revived his earlier idea of a grove of tulip poplar trees *(Liriodendron tulipifera),* found in the Olmsted Brothers 1935 report. In April 1939, two groves of ten tulip poplars each were planted on either side of the south grounds of the White House not far from the east and west boundaries. These tulip poplar trees were extant until at least 1947, although they cannot be seen in any photographs located thus far. (An undated plan showing the location of the tulip tree groves on the south lawn of the White House is in the collections of the Franklin Delano Roosevelt Library, Hyde Park, New York.) In 1971, a for-

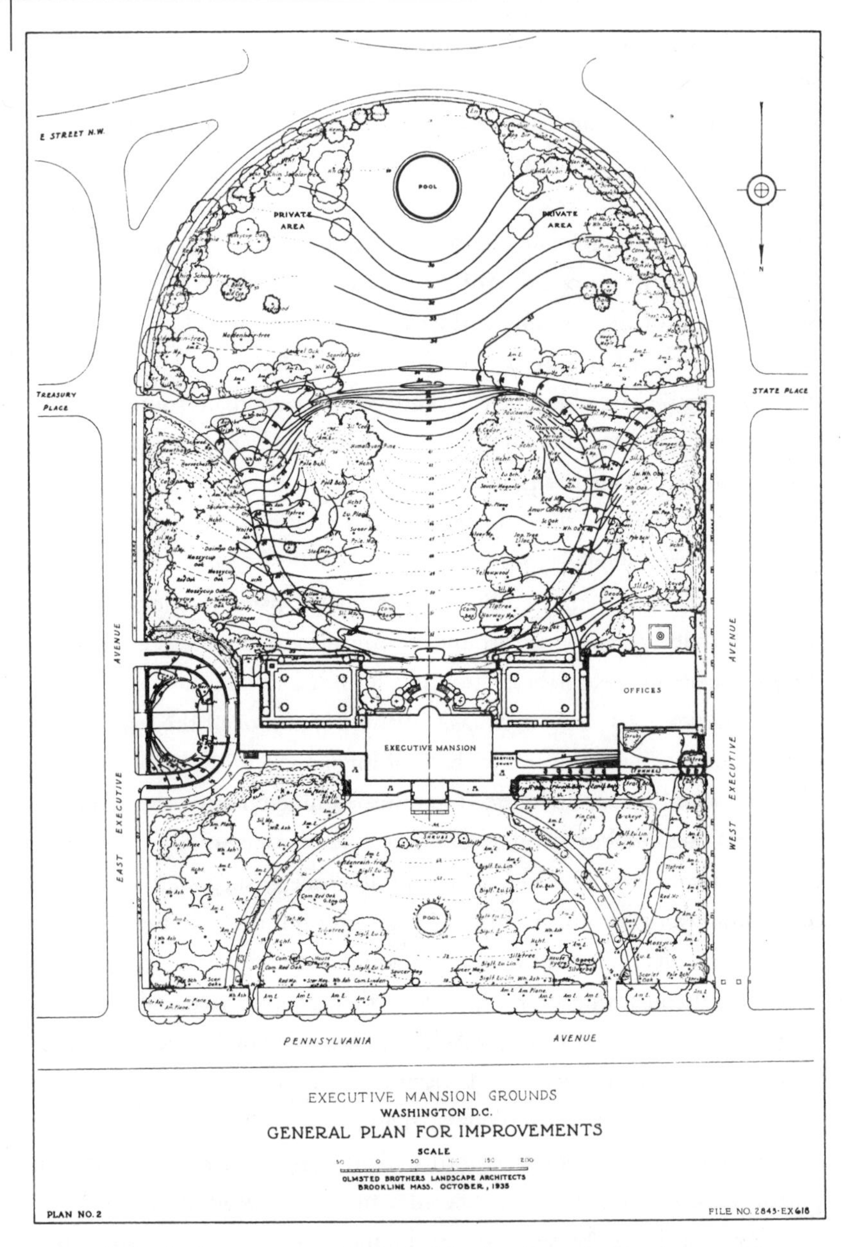

General Plan for Improvements, Executive Mansion Grounds, October 1935. (Courtesy of the National Park Service, Frederick Law Olmsted National Historic Site)

mer White House gardener, Robert Redmond, remembered President Roosevelt inspecting the new tulip poplar plantations in a jeep.[32] The White House–Jefferson Memorial tulip poplars were undoubtedly intended to form a link with the existing "Jefferson Memorial Vista" of tulip poplars.[33]

Within days of the Japanese attack on Pearl Harbor, casual visitors were barred from the White House grounds, where they had once strolled freely in the north grounds and sometimes in the south grounds as well.[34] World War II put a damper on landscape activities at the White House. On April 12, 1945, Franklin Delano Roosevelt died of a stroke only a few months into his fourth term, and little more implementation of Olmsted's recommendations was undertaken by the new president, Harry S. Truman.

In general, Olmsted took a very pragmatic approach to improving the grounds of the White House. He was very aware of historical precedent but was no slave to "sacred cows." He wished to keep the north/south vista of the south lawn open, and to this end several poorly placed or unhealthy trees were removed. At the same time, the east and west boundaries north of the transverse road were more thickly planted, since more seclusion for the first family was desired. In addition, two "private areas" were reserved near the approximate spots where Roosevelt's tulip trees were planted and may have been sheltered by them. Furthermore, the road system in the south grounds was rationalized. In fact, of all the changes recommended in the report, only the extreme simplification of the east and west gardens did not occur at the time, although these Wilson-era gardens were obliterated and then redesigned during the massive rebuilding of the White House under the Truman administration.

If the Olmsted Brothers' 1935 plan for the White House grounds is compared with other residential or public projects by the firm at the time, many unusual aspects of this project are immediately apparent. First, probably at Roosevelt's request, a study of the history of the landscape was a major part of the project from the beginning. Second, in the 1935 Olmsted Brothers report, the emphasis was always on preserving the historic aspects of the landscape while at the same time making it work for present-day needs. This is a strikingly modern approach—neither an antiquarian restoration/reconstruction as at Colonial Williamsburg nor a complete overhaul of the existing design. Today this approach would be classified under the Secretary of the Interior's Standards as an example of "rehabilitation." Third, because of the Depression, the project started small and stayed small, a positive effect in many ways, since it prevented the more radical changes that might have been made in a more prosperous time.

CONCLUSION

The two reports discussed above—one a survey of state park sites in California and the other a plan for improving the White House grounds—were prepared by Frederick Law Olmsted Jr. at the height of his career and clearly demonstrate his contribution to the fields of planning and design. They also illustrate his awareness of historic precedent, which consistently guided him when suggesting improvements to the state park system of California or the nationally revered grounds of the White House. As such, they offer a mere glimpse of Olmsted's tremendous contributions to the field of planning, a cause to which he gave many hours of volunteer service on influential boards and commissions as well as working as a paid consultant. In all these activities, he promoted an integrated approach to resource preservation, blending cultural, natural, and scenic values with aesthetic and functional concerns. His work served as an influential model for future practitioners in two distinct ways: directly, he was a pioneering educator who shaped the curriculum and directed the nation's first professional program in landscape architecture at Harvard, and indirectly, he was a gifted planner whose body of work, produced over his half-century career, provided an invaluable guide for later generations of park planners.

NOTES

1. Frederick Law Olmsted, *Proposed Improvements for Newport: A Report Prepared for the Newport Improvement Association* (Cambridge, MA: University Press, 1913), 3, 5.
2. Edward Clark Whiting and William Lyman Phillips, "Frederick Law Olmsted—1870–1957: An Appreciation of the Man and His Achievements," *Landscape*

Architecture 48, no. 3 (April 1958): 144; Susan L. Klaus, *A Modern Arcadia: Frederick Law Olmsted Jr. and the Plan for Forest Hills Gardens* (Amherst and Boston: University of Massachusetts Press in association with the Library of American Landscape History, 2002), 13–26.

3. Klaus, *Modern Arcadia,* 26–29.

4. Frederick Law Olmsted, *Report of State Park Survey of California Prepared for the California State Park Commission* (Sacramento: California State Printing Office, 1929), 4, 7–12.

5. Ibid., 66. Except for Columbia Town, these eight sites are merely listed and not discussed in detail.

6. Ibid., 15–17.

7. Ibid., 32–33.

8. Ibid., 57.

9. Ibid., 59.

10. Ibid., 60–65, 69.

11. EDAW, Inc., Land and Community Associates, Cynthia Zaitzevsky Associates, and John Milner Associates, *President's Park Cultural Landscape Report: Site History, Existing Conditions, Analysis and Evaluation,* prepared for the National Park Service, Denver Service Center, May 1995, 5-10–5-17. The drawings referred to are at the Frederick Law Olmsted National Historic Site, Brookline, Massachusetts, under job number 2845.

12. Ibid., chapter 6. By 1933, the annual reports that had been produced since 1818, first by the commissioner of public buildings and then by the chief of engineers, ceased publication. From this point on, the historical record consists of the body of letters, reports, memos, plans, photographs, etc., produced by the National Park Service relating to the various sites within the National Capital Region, including President's Park.

13. Commission of Fine Arts, minutes of meeting held October 19, 1934, Report of Mr. Moore on the Landscape Plan, White House Grounds, National Archives, Record Group 66, Project Files, box 206.

14. A. P. Cammerer, secretary, Commission of Fine Arts, to Frederick Law Olmsted Jr., April 18, 1934; Frederick Law Olmsted Jr. to the Honorable Marvin H. McIntyre, secretary to the president, May 4, 1934; all from the Olmsted Associates Records, B-files, Manuscript Division, Library of Congress, hereafter cited as Olmsted Associates Records.

15. Report of Mr. Olmsted's visit to White House, May 11 and 12, 1934, Olmsted Associates Records. Olmsted said that he obtained the photostat of the topographical map "from Finnan's office." C. Marshall Finnan was then superintendent of the National Capital Parks. Hans Koehler, who lived in Marlboro, Massachusetts, was employed by the Olmsted firm between 1890 and 1941 and was its chief horticultural specialist for most of that time. Koehler's presence on the White House job undoubtedly indicates that Olmsted considered horticulture to be one of the most important issues of this project.

16. Frederick Law Olmsted Jr. to Col. U. W. Grant III, January 24, 1928, Olmsted Associates Records.

17. Ibid.

18. The plan index cards for the White House project located at the Olmsted National Historic Site in Brookline, Massachusetts, number 40 cards. Of these, 26 were received from the National Park Service, and only 14 were generated by the Olmsted firm. Seventeen of the cards are marked "destroyed," which could mean either that they were destroyed by accident, as when the firm's plans vault was flooded, or that they were "weeded" by the Olmsted firm's plans clerk, Harry Perkins, as was the case with plans for many projects.

19. Frederick Law Olmsted Jr. to Marvin H. McIntyre, assistant secretary to the president, June 12, 1934; Frederick Law Olmsted Jr. to Professor Morley Jeffers Williams, June 12th, 1934; Frederick Law Olmsted Jr. to Mr. C. Marshall Finnan, superintendent, National Capital Parks, June 12, 1934; all in the Olmsted Associates Records.

20. Olmsted Brothers Landscape Architects, "Report to the President of the United States on Improvements and Policy of Maintenance for the Executive Mansion Grounds" (Brookline, MA, October 1935), 56–81, plus illustrations. The original "master" of this report is at the Olmsted National Historic Site. There are copies in the Olmsted Associates Records at the Library of Congress; at the Office of the Curator, the White House; and at the White House Liaison Office, Support Facility.

21. "The White House, Visit by F. L. Olmsted, Sept. 28–29, 1934," Olmsted Associates Records.

22. This was probably Charles E. Peterson, FAIA, who, in 1933, began the Historic American Buildings Survey (HABS), and whose archive is now in the University Libraries, University of Maryland, College Park, MD.

23. Commission of Fine Arts, minutes of meeting held October 19, 1934, Landscape Plan, White House Grounds, Mr. Moore's report regarding an inspection of the White House grounds on October 9, 1934, National Archives, Record Group 66, Project Files, box 206.

24. "White House Grounds. Visit, Oct. 9, 1934. F. L. O.," Olmsted Associates Records. This is a handwritten and fragmentary Report of Visit.

25. Frederick Law Olmsted Jr. to Partners from La Junta, Colorado, October 25, 1934, Olmsted Associates Records.

26. Olmsted Brothers, "Report on Improvements for the Executive Mansion Grounds," 2–6.

27. Ibid., 7–10.

28. Ibid., 12–13.

29. United States Department of the Interior, National Park Service, Prepared by the United States Department of Agriculture, Bureau of Public Roads, "Bid, Bid Bond, and Supplemental Specifications, Project 10A1, National Capital Parks, Roads

in White House Grounds," March 1937; Thomas C. Vint to Frederick Law Olmsted, April 24, 1937; both in Olmsted Associates Records.

30. Telegram, Frederick Law Olmsted to Thomas C. Vint, chief architect, April 29, 1937, Olmsted Associates Records.

31. Harry T. Thompson, acting superintendent, to Miss Marjorie B. Gratiot, September 19, 1947; Map of the Commemorative Trees, Various Trees and Plantings at the Executive Mansion Grounds, April 1956; both at the National Park Service, Office of White House Liaison, Executive Support Facility. "The White House Gardens and Grounds" (undated pamphlet [Clinton Administration], map).

32. Howard Ker to Mr. Hassett, January 10, 1939; Franklin D. Roosevelt, memorandum to Captain Ker, January 10, 1939; Howard Ker to Mr. Gartside, March 4, 1939; Howard Ker to President Roosevelt, March 27, 1939; Howard Ker to Mr. Hassett, April 12, 1939; all in Franklin Delano Roosevelt Library, Hyde Park, New York; copies also in the Papers of Harry S. Truman, Post-Presidential Files, Harry S. Truman Library, Independence, Missouri. Harry T. Thompson, acting superintendent, National Park Service, to Miss Marjorie B. Gratiot, *Richmond News Leader,* September 19, 1947, National Park Service, Office of White House Liaison, Executive Support Facility.

33. The Jefferson Memorial Vista, which consisted of pairs of tulip poplars, extended on a north/south axis from the southern part of the Ellipse across the Washington Monument grounds. It can be seen on aerial photographs as early as the 1920s. (The Jefferson Memorial had not yet been built but had been planned for many years.) The tulip poplar vista was probably removed some time in the Truman administration, when the trees had grown very large and were blocking the east/west vista.

34. Doris Kearns Goodwin, *No Ordinary Time: Franklin and Eleanor Roosevelt: The Home Front in World War II* (New York: Simon and Schuster, 1994), 298–99.

The "Noblest Landscape Problem"

Thomas C. Vint and Landscape Preservation

ETHAN CARR

Thomas C. Vint is best known as the landscape architect who, more than any other individual, guided landscape planning and design at the National Park Service (NPS) during its early years. Vint developed a specialized design discipline in the 1920s that addressed the modernization of the national parks at a time when large numbers of automotive tourists were overwhelming facilities built for a pre-automobile era. Under NPS directors Stephen T. Mather and Horace M. Albright, Vint devised sensitive approaches to road construction, "park village" design, and "rustic" architecture that aesthetically "harmonized" park development with landscape scenery. The scope of Vint's practice ranged from individual landmarks of what came to be called Park Service rustic style, such as the 1929 Grand Canyon Second Administration Building, to the establishment of park service "master planning" procedures that standardized the planning approach for every park and historic site in the national park system.[1]

What is less appreciated regarding Vint's contributions in the field of national park planning and design is the degree to which his approach to park making shaped historic preservation theory and practice at a critical time. Between the late 1920s and the early 1930s, the NPS went from having very limited responsibilities in the management of historic sites to becoming the leading national institution in the field of historic preservation. By the end of 1933, the agency managed dozens of historic sites, many of

Tom Vint at work in the 1930s. (Courtesy of the Historic Photographic Collections, NPS Harpers Ferry Center)

which were experiencing unprecedented levels of public interest and visitation. This sudden expansion of the national park system (and of the professional capabilities within the NPS) was brought about directly by FDR and the New Deal. The success of this expansion, however, depended on the adaptation of Vint's landscape planning and design techniques from the context of western scenic reservations to that of eastern "historical parks." This adaptation of national park planning influenced the practice of American historic preservation through the rest of the century.

Tom Vint was born in Salt Lake City in 1894 and grew up in Los Angeles. In 1914, he went to work as a draftsman and subsequently enrolled in the landscape architecture program of the University of California, Berkeley. In the fall of 1922 Vint moved to Yosemite National Park to take the job of "assistant landscape engineer" with the National Park Service. At Yosemite, Vint worked under landscape architect Daniel R. Hull, drafting both architectural and landscape plans.[2] At the time, Hull was designing the Grand Canyon and Yosemite park villages, as well as the first of the Arts and Crafts–inspired residential and administrative buildings now known as Park Service rustic architecture.

Vint and Hull made up the entire planning and design staff of the NPS, although they were working closely with consulting architect Gilbert Stanley Underwood. Hull and Underwood were close friends and collaborators; in 1923 Hull relocated the NPS design office to Los Angeles, where he and Vint shared office space with Underwood.[3] Although Daniel Hull was a federal employee at this time, in some ways he conducted himself more as a consultant. Tom Vint, on the other hand, concentrated on developing his government position, although a career as a public employee (rather than as a professional consultant) was a somewhat new kind of design practice. When Vint applied to become a member of the American Society of Landscape Architects (ASLA) in 1930, Frederick Law Olmsted Jr. (who knew Vint well through their work together at Yosemite) supported not only Vint the individual but also the professional practice that he had established as a government employee. "It is the very essence of most landscape architecture," Olmsted wrote, "that it involves . . . the arrangement and management of land on a large scale, often under different administrative and personal conditions." If Vint's qualifications were notably different from those of other applicants (mainly because he lacked private sector commissions for garden

Second Administration Building at Grand Canyon National Park; Thomas C. Vint, architect, 1929. Photograph by author.

and subdivision designs), Olmsted felt his association with the ASLA would "strengthen the slowly growing public recognition of the part our profession can wisely be called on to take in public affairs."[4]

In 1927 Vint replaced Daniel Hull as the agency's chief landscape architect and began expanding the "landscape division." He hired recently graduated landscape architects as well as engineers and other professionals, all of whom adapted to become part of a multidisciplinary park planning office. "The work of the landscape division is that of a professional advisor to the service in matters pertaining to the field of landscape architecture," Vint reported in 1929; "its primary purpose is to obtain a logical, well-studied general development plan for each park, which includes a control of the location, type of architecture, planting, grading, etc. in connection with any construction project within the parks."[5] By 1930 Vint had helped establish what would now be described as a "public practice" of landscape architecture.

The greatest achievement of this practice was the park "general development plan," which by 1931 was known as the "master plan."[6] The goal of producing rational, comprehensive plans that would coordinate and control all aspects of park development had been put forward for decades; but the reality was that hotels, roads, and other facilities had usually been built on an ad hoc basis. Lack of sewers and permanent campgrounds, in particular, caused severe damage to parks as well as unpleasant experiences for tourists. This was the situation the NPS had been created in 1916 to correct, and the implementation of a successful master planning process was at the heart of the new agency's mandate.

In the late 1920s, however, Vint still had to struggle within the agency to assure that master planning would indeed be enforced as a prerequisite to any construction activity in the parks. In a 1929 appeal to Director Horace Albright, he made a strong case for the primacy of landscape planning in park management. Vint argued that landscape architecture was a profession that attempted to offer "a practical solution to the problem at hand," but that also considered "the element of beauty." And the element of beauty could be attained in park development, he observed, only when the "congruity of parts gives harmonious form to the whole. . . . The first work of the National Park Service is the protection and preservation of these landscapes. Its second work is to make these areas accessible to the people that they might be used and enjoyed. What is the work of the Park Service but landscape work? What organization was ever given a nobler landscape problem?"[7]

The "landscape problem" Vint described was essentially that of landscape preservation, specifically preservation as achieved through public park development. Preserving places by making them into scenic reservations entailed a conceptual and physical transformation. As roads, trails, and other facilities were developed, growing numbers of (mostly automotive) tourists were able to appreciate scenery and other resources, camp, hike, and, in general, "enjoy" the parks. In the process land became landscape; the place became a park. As Vint passionately argued, this transformation needed to be controlled by a unified aesthetic conception (the master plan), which limited the development of roads and other facilities, enhanced a consistent sense of place, and protected scenery from encroachments.

The master plans Tom Vint and his staff devised beginning in the late 1920s reflected a twentieth-century adaptation of a long tradition of American landscape park development. In the nineteenth century, many large parks (or "landscape parks") were planned and developed by municipalities in order to provide a plan and framework for the construction of new residential neighborhoods around industrializing cities. Municipal park development often involved extensive grading and planting, as well as the construction of roads and trails.

The preservation of existing landscape character, however, was another intended result of such park development. Parks were laid out in advance of urbanization to preserve areas of existing natural beauty. By developing them judiciously, and "interfering with" their natural character as little as possible (as the elder Olmsted and his partner Calvert Vaux put it) areas such as the wooded north end of New York's Central Park or the pasture land of Boston's Franklin Park were preserved—if transformed—as park landscapes.[8] By the 1890s, regional park systems were being developed in relatively distant suburbs under basically the same assumption that scenic places could be best preserved from other forms of development by developing them as public parks. Landscape preservation in this sense, however, was never a passive act: limited management of vegetation and other landscape features, the construction of roads and other facilities, and increased accessibility for the public were all part of the transformation.

Master plans for national parks were based on the same assumption that preservation was not a passive act but required a limited amount of physical site development and public access in order to be successful. A park (or an area of a park) that went unvisited by the public also often went unappreciated by Congress. Politicians might therefore allow mining, grazing, or reservoir construction in parks, as they did when they allowed the damming of the Hetch Hetchy Valley of Yosemite National Park in 1913.

For Vint, whose master plans implemented the policies of Mather and Albright, the waves of automotive tourists in the 1920s were seen as the means of park preservation; tourists would be the strongest possible assurance of protection and expansion of the national park system. Their presence in the parks did not preclude preservation, as long as facilities were properly structured and planned with adequate respect for the awesome natural scenes that surrounded them.

But even in the 1920s, some critics insisted that achieving preservation through park development was a paradox; that developing an area for public use was just another utilitarian form of exploitation only marginally better than extractive industries or dam construction. By the 1930s, early "wilderness" advocates increasingly considered any sign of human presence, particularly roads and overnight accommodations, to be inconsistent with what they hoped "preservation" would mean in national parks. By the end of the 1930s a growing number of preservationists believed that the National Park Service had failed to protect wilderness aggressively enough and had not met its mandate to preserve natural areas "unimpaired."

But if they were a growing force in the 1930s, advocates for such total wilderness preservation would become a dominant influence in national park management only during the post–World War II environmental movement. In the meantime, NPS landscape architects continued to put forward what they considered appropriate and constructive management: master plans that strictly limited development to certain areas, while promising to proscribe any development for the vast majority of the park.

Vint established planning procedures that accommodated public access (especially by automobile) but also prevented more intrusive, ad hoc development proposals. Vint's master plans for parks reflected an ideal of a sustainable society in which people got along with one another and with their environment. In the context of vast federal reservations, park planners were able to implement some of the ideas of the leading regional planners of the period, such as Warren H. Manning, Raymond Unwin, and Thomas Adams. Regional zoning control could be absolute within a large national park, for example. Designated land uses, from backcountry "wilderness" to front country "developed areas," could be realized in a way that would be impossible outside park boundaries, where private ownership and local governments prevented the implementation of such plans. Within the park, road systems were not engineered independently by a highway authority, as they were in surrounding areas, but were planned with full awareness of their effects on land use. Park villages (large developed areas) employed unified architectural idioms, central civic plazas, and separated residential, public, and utility zones. National parks were developed as ideal landscapes, indicating how society could more successfully exist in the larger environment through planning and creative design. Preservation, in this sense, was the product of landscape design and planning; it was not a denial or rejection of progress, but its most enlightened manifestation.

This more active definition of preservation soon took on great significance in the field of historic preservation, as well as scenic preservation. The master planning procedures Vint had pioneered were applied in the management of historic landscapes beginning with the George Washington Birthplace National Monument and Colonial National Monument (later National Historical Park) in 1930. In 1933 Roosevelt transferred some forty battlefields and other historic sites and monuments from the War Department and other agencies to the National Park Service.[9]

Horace Albright, who succeeded Steven Mather as director of the National Park Service in 1929, had personally sought to acquire eastern sites that related to European American history. For Albright, this was a means of giving the park system regional balance and giving the NPS a dominant role in interpreting the nation's most significant sites of shared memory and patriotic identity. Albright had two great ambitions during his four-year leadership of the NPS: expanding into the field of historic preservation (more specifically into the development of national historical parks) and enforcing the park master planning procedure as the basis of park management.[10] These two goals were actually closely related. The success of Albright's new historical park depended on applying park master planning to preserve history, just as it had been used to preserve scenery.

In this sense, there was a shared meaning of the word *preservation.* Whether used in connection with scenic or historic landscapes, preservation in National Parks was, in fact, oriented toward preserving *landscapes.* And preserving historic landscapes would also mean transforming them in an essential way, just as preserving scenic landscapes had required active intervention by designers. Historic landscapes would become public parks, in other words, conceived and developed under Vint's supervision through the master planning process.

In this regard, Olmstedian theory continued to influence Vint and other officials during this important transition. Frederick Law Olmsted Jr. had many contacts with the NPS, partly through his membership on the Commission of Fine Arts, a group established in 1910 that often gave advice on the management of federal parks and historic sites. In 1928, he served as the first chair of the Yosemite National Park Board of Expert Advisors, a position in which he worked closely with Vint to resolve a number of contentious issues affecting that park.[11] Olmsted also published a portion of his father's papers in 1928, which, as noted above, clearly affected Vint's own attitudes toward park planning at that time.

But it was the younger Olmsted's 1929 state park plan for California that may have been the most direct influence on both Vint and Albright. As described by Cynthia Zaitzevsky elsewhere in this volume, the *State Park Survey of California* involved an organized and ambitious survey of both scenic and historic resources.[12] Olmsted Jr. was hired to begin the California plan in 1927 and consulted with several California landscape architects over the next two years, including Daniel Hull, who had only recently ended his relationship with the NPS. They began by regionalizing the project into twelve districts. Parks were selected to be geographically distributed and to preserve characteristic forests, beaches, and mountains and "areas of special interest, historic, scientific, and otherwise." This methodology became a procedural blueprint for scientific and comprehensive state park planning and served as an important model of a "comprehensive" park system that included the preservation of cultural heritage along with scenic landscapes.[13]

Horace Albright's appointment as NPS director in 1929 assured that his vision of an equally comprehensive *national* park system would also be implemented. There are many reasons why the NPS emerged as the leading national historic preservation organization in the early 1930s. Charles Hosmer, for example, suggests that it was simply because of "the size of its program and the quality of its professional staff," especially historians and restoration architects, who were hired through the New Deal.[14]

More to the point, however, the rise of the NPS as a historic preservation agency was linked to the development of the historical park. As chief of planning and design, Tom Vint oversaw the development of new historical parks, such as Colonial (Virginia), Salem Maritime (Massachusetts), and Hopewell Village (Pennsylvania). Up until this point, the "house museum" had been the most typical means of preserving history in the United States. In the late 1920s, the Williamsburg Restoration became the ultimate house museum, in the sense that the project emphasized individual house restorations and garden reconstructions. Many of these gardens, such as the grounds of the Governor's Palace, were designed by Arthur A. Shurcliff, a preeminent historical landscape architect of his day, who typified the academic interest in colonial garden research and design.[15]

But it was the neighboring Colonial National Historical Park, rather than the houses and gardens of Williamsburg, that better illustrated how Albright, Vint, Charles E. Peterson, and other Park Service staff now adapted their process of national park master planning to preserving history. This historical park, for example, was in fact a parkway connecting Yorktown, Williamsburg, and Jamestown across the peninsula between the York and James Rivers in Virginia, a distance of over twenty miles. While numerous historians, restoration architects, and other officials contributed to the overall concept of the park, it was the landscape design itself—a parkway—that provided the physical context and continuity between the three historic sites that spanned two hundred years of American colonial history.

As stated in the "Outline of Development" (master plan) of 1933, the parkway would make the park a "single, coherent" entity and would "transcend mere considerations of transportation . . . [and] contribute to the commemorative purposes of the monument."[16] The resulting landscape was in no sense a reconstruction of a colonial-era road corridor (although apparently some of the historians and restoration architects involved favored such an approach); landscape architects and engineers designed a modern automotive parkway, very much in the manner Gilmore D. Clarke and other landscape designers had developed since World War I in Westchester County and elsewhere. As at the Mount Vernon Memorial Parkway, which was also underway in 1928, the Colonial project combined advanced roadway design with "appropriate" design details, such as brick veneers over the concrete of the overpass bridges and culvert headwalls.[17] The result was an entirely contemporary landscape that combined the design features of a parkway with the historic house reconstructions, archaeological excavations, and other "restorations" taking place at various sites along the corridor.

As described by Ian Firth in another essay in this volume, the Blue Ridge Parkway became the ultimate scenic and historical park project in the 1930s by showcasing preserved scenes of agricultural landscapes and vernacular architecture along a four-hundred-mile route through Virginia and North Carolina. One of the great works of twentieth-century landscape architecture, it is also one of the most massive historic preservation projects ever undertaken. This process owed more to traditional NPS techniques of scenic preservation (park making) than to historic house restoration or garden reconstruction. The historical park of the 1930s might feature a landscape restoration, or a house museum, or a commemorative battlefield; but it did so in the context of an overall new landscape design calculated to present what Vint described as historic "scenes."

For Tom Vint, there was total conceptual unity in planning for the preservation of either scenery or history. "National parks and monuments fall into two groups," he explained in 1946, "natural and historical. In one, the primary purpose is to preserve and protect one of the great works of nature. . . . In the other, to preserve and protect the scene at one of the great moments of our national history—to stop the clock and hold the scene of the moment in history that makes the area important." Whether in the case of scenic or historic preservation, he continued, preservation coexisted with provisions for public access and enjoyment: "The development scheme

View of vernacular landscape along the Blue Ridge Parkway. Photograph by author.

[master plan] has to do with providing the facilities to permit the people to see and enjoy these areas. It is constantly working on the compromise that determines how far these facilities will intrude into the scenes that are to be preserved, as nearly as possible, as nature or history has left them to us."[18]

For Vint, the historic scene could be best preserved by "stopping the clock" at a particular date of maximum significance. Although the problems with this approach to cultural landscape management surfaced almost immediately, the idea of "freezing" a landscape in a particular era continues to appeal to park managers even now. But just as early wilderness advocates questioned national park development in the 1930s, at least some historians wondered whether the new historical parks of that era did not restrict the educational usefulness of historic sites.[19] More recently, critics have pointed out that freezing a landscape is not only a practical impossibility, but it serves as a justification for the removal of later, often significant, landscape features and limits the interpretive potential of a site often to a single narrative directly associated with the chosen scene or historical moment.[20] The idea of freezing a landscape to reflect a historic scene, however, retains a powerful appeal.

There is an interesting parallel between the persistence of the desire to re-create a historic scene and what Richard Sellars describes as "façade

Hopewell Village Visitor Center, Hopewell Furnace National Historic Site, c. 1958. (Courtesy of the National Park Service History Collection, NPS Harpers Ferry Center)

management" in the realm of natural resource management. Sellars describes an unfortunate tendency for park managers to be more concerned with the appearance of a park than the true, biological condition of its ecosystems. This concern for the aesthetic over the biological is also traced back to the influence of Vint and other professional landscape architects within the agency, who since the 1920s had indeed been concerned with the visual "harmony" of tourist facilities in the preparation of park plans.[21] In both cases, perhaps, critics have found reason to deplore the emphasis on "scenery" in national parks over other purposes and truths, as defined mainly by scientists and historians, based in postmodern theory and attitudes.

Tom Vint's influence in historic preservation was not limited to the prewar park master plan. Vint was also responsible for administering other historic preservation programs in his division, such as the Historic American Building Survey (HABS), which was initiated by his close friend and protégé, Charles Peterson.[22] Vint's interest in historic preservation only increased later in his career, and although this volume of essays is concerned primarily with prewar preservation, it is worth noting some of Vint's postwar activities. In the 1950s, for example, it was Vint who assured the reactivation of HABS by funding the program as part of the "Mission 66" park development program. NPS director Conrad L. Wirth invented the Mission 66 program in 1955 to convince Congress to fund an extensive modernization and expansion of the park system in time for the fiftieth anniversary of the NPS in 1966. Mission 66 budget increases provided for the construction of "visitor centers," park housing, park roads, and other basic park facilities. Influenced by contemporary modernist architectural and planning trends, the program perhaps diverged from earlier "rustic" design tradition. But Mission 66 also perpetuated some of the park planning and landscape preservation theory that Vint had established before World War II.

Vint continued in his role as chief of planning and design during the Mission 66 period, and he also sat on the steering committee that oversaw all Mission 66 development proposals. Conrad Wirth was also a landscape architect, and in the 1930s he had been in charge of the NPS state park program, which was responsible for the development of dozens of state park systems. Mission 66, in other words, was planned and implemented by the same cadre of park managers and planners who had been responsible for the "rustic" era of national and state park development in the 1920s and 1930s. Some aspects of the Mission 66 program were quite new. The "visitor cen-

Tom Vint (front right) and the Mission 66 steering committee in 1958. (Courtesy of the Historic Photographic Collections, NPS Harpers Ferry Center)

ter," for example, was an enlarged building type that unified park museum, administration, and visitor service functions. But in other ways, Mission 66 continued some basic premises of NPS design and development that had evolved since the early 1920s.

In the field of historic preservation, there was evident continuity between earlier historical park development and the postwar concern for "heritage," a term used by Mission 66 planners to refer to both the history and the scenery of the national park system. Mission 66 eventually funded dozens of historical park developments of increased variety and scope. Independence National Historical Park in Philadelphia was one of the most significant and controversial national park planning projects of the early 1950s and became a showcase of the Mission 66 approach to historic preservation. The brochure introducing Mission 66 to the public, in fact, was entitled simply "Our Heritage" and featured a "typical" American family superimposed over an image of the Liberty Bell, the centerpiece of the new Philadelphia historical park.

During the course of developing the master plan for Independence, important debates about historic preservation in the postwar era were undertaken, if not resolved. The Independence park project had been initiated by local civic leaders, not as a national historical park, but as a civic improvement project or, more accurately, an urban renewal project. The NPS became involved immediately after World War II. The park planners assigned to the job, especially Charles Peterson, soon discovered that "the period of significance," or the moment of the historic scene, needed to be reconsidered. The park's purpose had been defined as interpreting and preserving buildings associated with eighteenth-century American history.

But the park's nineteenth-century buildings included extremely significant works of American architecture in the heart of downtown Philadelphia. Freezing the colonial historic scene suggested that the nineteenth-century buildings should be removed, and this is exactly what the 1957 master plan approved by Tom Vint recommended, over Peterson's vigorous protests. But Vint and others felt demolition was consistent with the preservation of the historic scene, frozen in time during the period of greatest significance. As a result, many beautiful and important nineteenth-century buildings were destroyed to create today's historical park.[23]

Cover of 1956 brochure introducing Mission 66 to the public. (Courtesy of the National Park Service History Collection, NPS Harpers Ferry Center)

Such a policy would probably not be approved today, although plans for some Civil War battlefield parks have suggested a similar approach, ironically by proposing the demolition of Mission 66–era improvements. But for most cultural resource managers, the long-standing NPS policy of attempting to freeze a landscape, or aggressively restore it to create a limited historic scene, has been discredited. Nevertheless, historic preservation was an important and successful dimension of the Mission 66 program. Dozens of national monuments and historic sites, many of which had been acquired during the New Deal, finally received funding in the 1950s and 1960s. Civil War battlefields were of particular interest during Mission 66, in part because of the events and commemorations being planned for centennial celebrations. At many battlefields, the basic development and interpretation of the landscape had not changed significantly since the late nineteenth century; Wirth and his Mission 66 planners intended to have every site ready for the increased attention and visitation they could expect in the coming decade. Planned improvements often included the acquisition of abutting land, as well as the construction of new visitor centers, roads, and other facilities. There were other reasons, perhaps, that commemorative battlefields commanded particular attention. A former general was in the White House (and he happened to own a house in Gettysburg as well), and the commemoration of the nation's greatest conflict fit the national mood during the Cold War era.[24]

There were other historic preservation components of the Mission 66 program. While Vint reactivated HABS with Mission 66 funds, chief historian Ronald F. Lee reinvigorated the Historic Sites Survey, which later evolved into the National Historic Landmarks Program.[25] Ronald Lee, in fact, became one of the principal planners of Mission 66, in part because of the emphasis on historical parks and "heritage" in the program. The historic preservation activities of Mission 66, which were national in scope, prefigured aspects of the National Historic Preservation Act of 1966.

Tom Vint retired in 1961 after thirty-nine years with the NPS, thirty-four of which he spent as the overall chief of planning and design. He died six years later. Because of the role of the master planning process in the development of both national parks and national historical parks, Vint had helped shape federal policy for the preservation of both scenery and history for over three decades. Although Vint expressed certain policies that few preservationists would agree with today (such as "stopping the clock" on the historic scene), his ideas influenced the preservation of scores of historic sites, not only during the New Deal years but in the postwar era as well.

If Vint's master planning process amounted to a twentieth-century adaptation of municipal park planning, his concept of historic preservation similarly was based in nineteenth-century precedents of historic landscape preservation. Landscape and history were, in fact, inseparable. The preservation of the "scene," whether described as a historic or scenic landscape, demanded the same planning process—the master plan—based in a comprehensive and unified aesthetic approach. The successful preservation of nature, or history, required the creation of a work of public art: the public park. Not only was preservation not a passive act, it was an expressly creative one, requiring planning, design, and construction.

The shortcomings of the practice of preservation through park making, as employed by Tom Vint and the NPS from the 1920s through the 1960s, have been well documented in important histories of both natural and cultural resource management in the national parks.[26] But it may be time to reconsider, as well, the persistent appeal of seeing land as landscape—of appreciating natural and historic "scenery"—as a basis for public appreciation and emotional connection to the natural and cultural heritage. The popularity of neo-rustic architecture in national parks, for example, makes it clear that most people still judge the appropriateness of park development mostly in aesthetic terms. Neo-rustic style may be described as "sustainable" architecture today (and may feature improvements in energy efficiency), but the real source of its appeal goes back to a rustic tradition of landscape imagery that was so effectively exploited by Tom Vint to create a systemwide identity for national parks in the 1920s.

The public stubbornly persists, as one historian puts it, in "outmoded perceptions" of the parks that hinder "the realization of sound ecological management."[27] Indeed, a recalcitrant public clearly continues to indulge in an emotional communion with landscape scenery, even as the NPS now interprets the significance of that scenery almost entirely in biological terms. But recognizing the emotional appeal of scenery—and the importance of aesthetics in park design and management—would not require a return to "façade management." And the intense communion of millions of park visitors with scenic beauty should not be dismissed as a purely superficial, or even irrelevant, consideration in landscape management.

The public remains equally insistent on discovering and perceiving the historic "scene" when visiting historical parks. These parks are often cultural landscapes of great complexity and layering, and most managers would not advocate attempting to freeze them by removing later, historically significant features to create landscapes of limited interpretive potential. But recognizing the power in the public's perception of a historic scene does not require the erasure of other layers and narratives in the landscape. It does require, perhaps, a less dogmatic approach to historic preservation as a creative process.

New, contemporary landscape design must be better incorporated into preservation, for example. In certain cases, the removal of newer (even significant) landscape features, when necessary and desirable, should be a possibility. Reconstructions, as well, should not be held to standards for authenticity that make them an impossible option. Prewar historical parks such as the Colonial and Blue Ridge Parkways, even if they would never be developed in the same manner today, remain examples of how landscape architecture was used as a powerful means of connecting the American public to a constructed past of enormous appeal. Current preservation practice tends to deny that landscape preservation succeeds, ultimately, through a creative transformation of a place into a new work of landscape art. But the construction of historical narratives and "heritage" through landscape design is not in itself deplorable; it is, in fact, inevitable in managing historic landscapes. However such constructions of the past are devised, a frank acknowledgment of this fact should be a first step in the process.

National historical parks of the Vint era continue to hold our attention, in part because of the power of landscape design that enhanced the power of existing landscapes to evoke historical associations. National park making, at its best, exploited this power of design to connect the public to history, and to nature as well. But postmodern critique and theory require us to discover new ways of addressing the preservation of places as a creative process. We should not return to the creation of frozen scenes or one-dimensional historical narratives in cultural landscape management, nor are we likely to undertake new Colonial or Blue Ridge Parkways. But we can more frankly accept the reality that preservation is a creative transformation of place, like another work of design. New landscape preservation can build on old theory, in this sense, but only after reconsidering the role of new design in the process, both in the past and present.

NOTES

1. For information on Vint's life and career, see William G. Carnes, "Tom Vint," *National Park Service Courier* (August 1980); Linda Flint McClelland, "Vint, Thomas Chalmers," in *Pioneers of American Landscape Design,* ed. Charles A. Birnbaum and Robin Karson (New York: McGraw Hill, 2000), 413–16; Ethan Carr, *Wilderness by Design: Landscape Architecture and the National Park Service* (Lincoln: University of Nebraska Press, 1998), 190–95.

2. Thomas C. Vint, Personnel Information Sheet, United States Civil Service Commission, July 1, 1940, Papers of Charles E. Peterson; Carnes, "Tom Vint."

3. Department of the Interior, National Park Service, *1924 Annual Report,* 151–52. Architect Myron Hunt also collaborated with Hull and Vint at this time. See "Daniel Ray Hull," Mather Collection, entry 135, RG 79, National Archives, Washington, D.C.; Carol Roland, "Hull, Daniel Ray," in Birnbaum and Karson, *Pioneers,* 180–84.

4. Frederick Law Olmsted to Alfred Geiffert, February 7, 1930, Papers of Charles E. Peterson.

5. Department of the Interior, National Park Service, *1929 Annual Report,* 163–65.

6. See Thomas C. Vint, "National Park Service Master Plans," *Planning and Civic Comment,* April 1946; Conrad L. Wirth, *Parks, Politics, and the People* (Norman: University of Oklahoma Press, 1980), 59–61.

7. Thomas Vint to Horace Albright, May 22, 1929, Papers of Horace M. Albright, entry 17, RG 79, National Archives, Washington, D.C. In this appeal for applying Olmstedian theory in the management of national parks, Vint drew on the elder Frederick Law Olmsted's description of Central Park as a "single work of art . . . framed on a single, noble motive, to which the design of all its parts, in some more or less subtle way, shall be confluent and helpful." Vint was no doubt aided by the publication in 1928 of the first significant volume of the elder Olmsted's writings, edited by Frederick L. Olmsted Jr. and Theodora Kimball.

8. Frederick Law Olmsted and Calvert Vaux, "Description of a Plan for the Improvement of Central Park, 'Greensward,'" in *Creating Central Park, 1857–1861,* vol. 3 of *The Papers of Frederick Law Olmsted,* ed. Charles E. Beveridge and David Schuyler (Baltimore: Johns Hopkins University Press, 1983), 119.

9. See Ronald A. Foresta, *America's National Parks and Their Keepers* (Washington, DC: Resources for the Future, 1984), 129–45; Barry Mackintosh, *The National Parks: Shaping the System* (Washington, DC: Government Printing Office, 1991), 24–43.

10. See Horace M. Albright, *The Birth of the National Park Service: The Founding Years* (Salt Lake City: Howe Brothers, 1985), 285–97.

11. Olmsted Jr. had first suggested the establishment of such a group for Yosemite in 1911, in an open letter to the national parks conference of that year.

Department of the Interior, *Proceedings of the National Park Conference Held at Yellowstone National Park, September 11 and 12, 1911* (Washington, DC: Government Printing Office, 1911), 20–21.

12. Frederick Law Olmsted Jr., *Report of State Park Survey of California Prepared for the California State Park Commission* (Sacramento: California State Printing Office, 1929).

13. Olmsted, *State Park Survey,* 9, 39–53; Joseph H. Engbeck Jr., *State Parks of California: 1864 to the Present* (Portland, OR: Graphic Arts Center, 1980), 47–56; Norman T. Newton, *Design on the Land: The Development of Landscape Architecture* (Cambridge, MA: Belknap Press of Harvard University Press, 1971), 572–75.

14. Charles B. Hosmer Jr., *Preservation Comes of Age: From Williamsburg to the National Trust, 1926–1949* (Charlottesville: Published for the Preservation Press, National Trust for Historic Preservation in the United States by the University Press of Virginia, 1981), 1005.

15. Elizabeth Hope Cushing, "Shurcliff, Arthur Asahel" (Shurtleff until 1930), in Birnbaum and Karson, *Pioneers,* 351–56. Shurcliff also studied colonial era town planning as a context for his garden restorations.

16. Quoted in Historic American Engineering Record, "Colonial National Historical Park Roads and Bridges, HAER no. VA-115," Michael G. Bennett, project historian (unpublished government report, 1995), 21.

17. Charles Peterson and Edward Zimmer were two of the Park Service designers responsible for the parkway design. Peterson reported directly to Tom Vint in Washington, D.C. HAER, "Colonial National Historical Park," 22, 26. Also see LANDSCAPES, Inc., *Colonial Parkway Context* (unpublished government report, National Park Service, Philadelphia, 1998).

18. Thomas C. Vint, "National Park Service Master Plans," *Planning and Civic Comment,* April 1946.

19. See Foresta, *America's National Parks,* 130.

20. This has been particularly true in battlefield parks, such as Antietam. See Martha Temkin, "Freeze-Frame, September 17, 1862: A Preservation Battle at Antietam National Battlefield Park," in *Myth, Memory, and the American Landscape,* ed. Paul A. Shackel (Gainesville: University Press of Florida, 2001), 123–40.

21. See Richard West Sellars, *Preserving Nature in the National Parks: A History* (New Haven: Yale University Press, 1997).

22. Vint was cited for three achievements when he received the Department of the Interior Distinguished Service Award in 1952: coauthoring the "inter-bureau agreement" with the Bureau of Public Roads in 1925, developing the "master plan idea" in the late 1920s, and organizing the Historic American Building Survey in the 1930s and again in the 1950s. Oscar L. Chapman, "Citation for Distinguished Service, Thomas C. Vint," Papers of Charles E. Peterson.

23. See Hosmer, *Preservation Comes of Age,* 767–79; Constance M. Greiff, *Independence: The Creation of a National Park* (Philadelphia: University of Pennsylvania Press, 1987).

24. Wirth, *Parks, Politics, and the People,* 268–76; Sarah Allaback, *Mission 66 Visitor Centers: The History of a Building Type* (Washington, DC: Government Printing Office, 2000), 95–143.

25. Barry Mackintosh, "The Historic Sites Survey and the National Historic Landmarks Program: A History" (unpublished government report, National Park Service, Washington, DC, 1985).

26. See, for example, Sellars, *Preserving Nature;* Shackel, *Myth, Memory, and the American Landscape.*

27. See Alfred Runte, *National Parks and the American Experience,* 2nd ed. (Lincoln: University of Nebraska Press, 1987), xx–xxi, 1–5, 11–32.

The Blue Ridge Parkway

Road to the Modern Preservation Movement

IAN FIRTH

The preservation of vernacular rural landscapes and the communities that have created them and continue to live within them is one of the most important challenges facing the modern preservation movement. The Blue Ridge Parkway was the first project of the National Park Service (NPS) that addressed this challenge in a constructive way. Its history provides several lessons, some cautionary and some inspirational.

The Blue Ridge Parkway runs between the Shenandoah and Great Smoky Mountains National Parks, a distance of 469 miles, following for much of its length the Blue Ridge of the Southern Appalachians. The parkway was initiated in 1933 as a means of relieving unemployment and stimulating the regional economy during the Great Depression. It stands as one of the great achievements of Franklin Delano Roosevelt's New Deal, but its construction extended well beyond Roosevelt's time. Construction began in 1935, and two-thirds of the road was built over the next seven years. Construction was suspended in 1942 with America's entry into the Second World War. When work resumed after the war, it proceeded at a much slower pace. By 1967 the parkway was complete except for a short section around Grandfather Mountain in North Carolina. Work on the final section was delayed for many years, and the parkway was not finished until 1987.

An enormous undertaking, the Blue Ridge Parkway was the product of many people's efforts: in the Roosevelt administration, in Congress, in

Stanley Abbott. Date and photographer unrecorded. (From the Historic Photograph Collection, Blue Ridge Parkway Archives, Asheville, North Carolina)

the governments of Virginia and North Carolina, and in the many federal and state agencies involved. In the context of landscape preservation, it is appropriate to focus on the role of Stanley W. Abbott, the parkway's first resident landscape architect and acting superintendent.[1] Abbott saw preservation of vernacular rural landscapes in the mountains as a thread that could draw together the various aspects of the planning, design, and construction of the parkway. He provided a coherent and original vision for the entire project.

Abbott was appointed in 1933 as a result of a recommendation by Jay Downer and Gilmore Clarke, pioneers in parkway design, who had been engaged as consultants by the NPS. Abbott had graduated from Cornell with a BA in landscape architecture in 1930. Shortly thereafter, he had gone to work as part of the team that Downer assembled to design parkways in Westchester County, New York. He was only twenty-five years of age when he left Westchester to join the NPS. Downer's and Clarke's expectation seems to have been that Abbott would serve as their representative on site, but their consultancy terminated abruptly after a disagreement over fees with Harold Ickes, the secretary of the interior. With their departure, Abbott became his own man, and his responsibilities increased as his superiors in the NPS, notably Arthur Demaray and Thomas Vint, gained confidence in his abilities. He was given two roles, first as resident landscape architect and then acting superintendent; in this dual capacity he was able to address the full range of planning, design, and management issues. He was regarded by those who worked with him as an intellectual, a visionary, fond of literary quotations, and somewhat absentminded. One of his colleagues remembers him as follows: "Stanley Abbott was the most amazing man I ever knew in my life. In little practical things he was a dunce almost. He'd say, 'Do you have a cigarette?' Yeah, you'd hand him a cigarette and he'd fool around with it a little while and light it and stick it in his pocket and walk off. But when it came to being a brilliant thinker, and a writer, oh gosh, he would sit down and dictate most anything beautifully."[2]

The growth of Abbott's ideas is the subject of this essay. The process is recorded in his writings, most importantly in his monthly and annual reports to his superiors in the NPS.[3] His experience working on the Westchester parkways was useful, of course, but the Blue Ridge Parkway presented challenges that earlier parkway designers had not faced.

EARLIER PARKWAYS

The idea of a scenic road in the Southern Appalachians had been discussed for at least twenty years before the Blue Ridge Parkway was authorized. But the early proposals were for a conventional road rather than a parkway. The recommendation that the road be designed as a parkway has been attributed to Thomas H. McDonald of the Bureau of Public Roads.[4]

Frederick Law Olmsted Sr. and Calvert Vaux had used the term "parkways" to refer to a "series of ways designed with express reference to the pleasure with which they may be used for walking, riding, and driving of carriages, for rest, recreation, refreshment and social intercourse."[5] In 1868 the partners had proposed parkways in Brooklyn, Buffalo, and Chicago. By the end of the nineteenth century the term was in widespread use, and parkways were regarded as hybrids, exhibiting some of the characteristics of both roads and parks. They were advocated to link conventional urban parks into citywide networks, protecting and rehabilitating natural areas within city regions by incorporating them into wide rights-of-way.

The advent of the automobile produced demands for new types of roads, and suburban parkways were built for recreational motoring.[6] The first public parkway designed for automobiles was the Bronx River Parkway in New York, begun in 1916 and completed in 1925. Jay Downer was the chief engineer, and Gilmore Clarke served as superintendent of landscape construction. It provided a model for later parkways with its curvilinear alignment, limited points of access, with bridges carrying other roads across it, and a wide, landscaped right-of-way. Enthusiasm for this parkway led to the establishment of the Westchester County Park Commission in 1922, and over the next ten years a network of parks and parkways was built north of New York City.

Meanwhile, inspired by the ideals of the City Beautiful Movement, parkways were being planned in other cities including the nation's capital. The McMillan Plan of 1902 for Washington, D.C., had called for the creation of several parkways to link major parks and bridges within the city and to connect the city with Great Falls upstream and Mount Vernon downriver. So the federal government became a player, and several federal agencies, including the Bureau of Public Roads, began to share responsibility for the design and construction of these federal parkways.

The NPS became involved in the planning and design of parkways in 1930 with the authorization of the Colonial National Monument in Virginia. The Colonial Parkway was to be an integral part of this park, connecting Jamestown, Williamsburg, and Yorktown. The NPS had already established a partnership with the Bureau of Public Roads to set standards for the design of roads within national parks.[7] Close cooperation between bureau engineers and NPS landscape architects was encouraged to ensure park roads gracefully fit their environments. This partnership provided the frame for McDonald's recommendation that the Blue Ridge Parkway become the responsibility of the NPS.

So by 1933, when the Blue Ridge Parkway was authorized, existing parkways provided excellent examples of how to design a modern road for recreational motoring and how to use a wide right-of-way to protect and enhance landscapes seen from the road. At a length of hundreds of miles, the Blue Ridge Parkway was far more ambitious in scale than any of its predecessors. Indeed, it was the longest road ever planned as a single unit up to that time in America. Moreover, it was distant from all major cities, and it was to pass through the most mountainous terrain east of the Mississippi. Therefore, its length and location challenged its designers to think afresh about the potential of parkways.

THE ROUTE

In June 1934, Stanley Abbott produced a report evaluating three alternative routes through the mountains between the Shenandoah and Great Smoky Mountains National Parks. The main question was whether the southern half of the route should follow an eastern line through North Carolina, a western line through Tennessee, or wind between the two. In Abbott's opinion the third alternative offered the best combination of scenery, reasonable construction costs, and good direction. However, he was prepared to dismiss all three mountain routes in favor of an "all year parkway, with a high standard of alignment and grade, located in the broad valleys, with spur roads to scenic and recreational areas in the mountains."[8] Clearly, in those early days, he was considering the parkway as essentially a park-to-park connection, rather than a recreational attraction in its own right.

However, the advice of Abbott and others in the NPS and Bureau of Public Roads was overshadowed by a political fight between representatives of North Carolina and Tennessee. This vigorously partisan debate took nearly a year to resolve and involved figures at the highest levels of the federal and state governments.[9] In November 1934, Secretary Ickes decided in favor of a Virginia–North Carolina mountain route. In doing so, he was influenced by the economic, scenic, land acquisition, and topographic arguments advanced by the representatives of North Carolina, and also by the fact that federal funds were already being channeled to Tennessee by the Tennessee Valley Authority.

This decision still left the exact line of the road to be located by the landscape architects in the NPS and engineers in the Bureau of Public Roads:

> The detailed locating procedure was to reconnoiter the country over a considerable distance—30 to 100 miles or more and establish major controls, generally gaps, and from these work down to lesser control points and then finally establish a tentative flagged location on the ground which would satisfy alignment and grade standards. This was then reviewed by both landscape architects and engineers, and if approved, the State would be authorized to proceed with their topographic surveys, which covered a strip two to several hundred feet wide following the flagged line.[10]

Abbott's counterpart in the bureau was William M. Austin, resident engineer in the bureau's Roanoke office. Austin had supervised construction of the General's Highway in Sequoia National Park and was now responsible for the construction of Skyline Drive in Shenandoah National Park. He had a clear understanding of the importance of fitting roads into their landscapes, and he had a good working relationship with Abbott.

The Blue Ridge Parkway was to start at the southern end of the Skyline Drive. The idea of a mountaintop drive accessible to city dwellers of the Northeast had been a key element in proposals to establish Shenandoah National Park. When construction began in 1931, the design had been based on experience in Western parks. Nearly all evidence of human settlement was removed from the mountains in the park so that motorists would look out across an apparent wilderness. Abbott and Austin agreed the design of the Blue Ridge Parkway should be very different. Since this parkway was to be several hundred miles long, it was imperative that it pass through a wide variety of scenery. It should, therefore, depart from the crests of the mountains to avoid the monotony of long passages through mountain forests broken only by occasional panoramic views into blue distances: "We and the engineers together just drilled and drilled, all of us, on the business of following a mountain stream for a while, then climbing up on the slope of a hill pasture then dipping down into the open bottom land and back into the woodlands."[11] This routing distinguished the design of this parkway from that of previous parkways, or indeed existing park roads, and it called for still more innovative thinking on the part of Abbott and his colleagues.

LAND ACQUISITION

Passing through settled areas complicated the process of land acquisition, which was the responsibility of the states. State officials had hoped that some mountain people would donate land to secure the benefits of a highway, but these hopes were based on a misunderstanding of the nature of the proposed parkway. The NPS had considerable difficulty in selling the idea of a limited-access road within a wide right-of-way to these officials, particularly those in Virginia. Acquisition was generally by agreement. The states were reluctant to condemn land, and the NPS recognized a need to foster good relations with landowners who would adjoin the parkway, as Abbott describes:

> Studies by the Service call for a taking which varies in width from 200 to 1,200 feet, and the requirements must be judged as much for effect upon the residual property as for control of the roadside picture. Private and public roads, cattle crossings, water rights, and phone and power lines seriously involve the entire economy of many larger mountain properties. Relocation of these facilities must be arranged or the entire holdings purchased outright. Those considerations and the natural tendency of many mountain people to hold to the homes of their forefathers combine to make a more than usually difficult problem of acquisition, especially if condemnation is to be avoided.[12]

However, difficulties in acquiring the right-of-way did not deter Abbott from advocating the acquisition of additional land for a series of recreational areas along the parkway. These wayside parks were referred to by Abbott as "beads on a string, the rare gems in the necklace" and more prosaically by Thomas Vint as "bulges in the right-of-way."[13] The master plan for the parkway, which was approved in 1936, proposed nineteen such areas. The acquisition of these additions was not the responsibility of the states. Some of them were already in federal ownership as national forest lands, but elsewhere Abbott realized the Federal Resettlement Administration's submarginal lands program might be used. The first five areas to be acquired with these funds were Pine Spur, Smart View, and Rocky Knob in Virginia, and Cumberland Knob and The Bluff in North Carolina. In these areas abandoned woodlots, old fields, and overgrazed pastures acquired new lives as recreational spaces.

The acquisition of land for both the right-of-way and recreation areas caused less disruption to mountain communities than the acquisition of lands for the Shenandoah and Great Smoky Mountains National Parks. Nevertheless, a number of communities were affected, and a few, such as the one at Peaks of Otter in Virginia, were to be completely removed. Naturally, this caused resentments that added to many mountaineers' suspicion of outsiders and doubts about the promised benefits of the parkway. It was against this background that Abbott sought to devise ways to become a good neighbor to the mountain farmers, but at first his attention had to be focused on the design and construction of the road.

THE ROAD

The location of the parkway in the mountains presented a challenge for the designers of the road. They were determined to fit a modern highway into the rugged terrain. The engineers and landscape architects cooperated well, but there were also significant differences in priorities. In general, the engineers were trying to build a modern highway with standards for grade and curvature that would provide for speed and safety, while the landscape architects were concerned about fitting the road into the terrain in ways

The Blue Ridge Parkway at Buck Creek Gap in North Carolina, 1942. Photograph by E. H. Abbuehl. (From the Historic Photograph Collection, Blue Ridge Parkway Archives, Asheville, North Carolina)

that would minimize construction scars and provide the most interesting views. In the end they agreed that the road was intended to be a recreational highway, and it should not be a high-speed or high-capacity road. A design speed of thirty-five miles per hour was selected, the width was restricted to two lanes, and the maximum grade was to be 8 percent.

The designers followed the examples of earlier park roads and the Westchester parkways by featuring rustic stonework in many of the bridges, retaining walls, and drainage structures. The stone in each section of the road was obtained from local quarries, and the details of the stonework varied accordingly. The intent was to give each structure an appearance of permanence and of belonging to its site. But this elaborate use of stone was alien to the region, and the contractors had to rely on immigrant stonemasons, many of them from Italy, Spain, or South America.

The first contract for construction was let in August 1935, for section 2A in North Carolina. (The road was divided into sections, each about twelve miles long, numbered from 1A to 1W in Virginia and from 2A to 2Z in North Carolina.) Actual work began in September. Within six months over two thousand men were employed on the road; by the end of 1936, over 133 miles were under construction.

While the bureau's engineers were supervising road construction, the Park Service's landscape architects were developing plans for improving the roadside landscapes. Once construction contracts were completed on each section, work began to fine-grade side slopes and replant native vegetation. This labor-intensive landscape work was made possible by the cooperation of emergency work agencies. Men from various Works Progress Administration (WPA) projects were assigned to the parkway, and four Civilian Conservation Corps (CCC) camps were built beside the road. The objective of the landscape improvements was not only to heal construction scars but also to frame a sequence of views to be enjoyed from the road and from overlooks that were strategically placed about every two miles. Eventually a series of plans called PLUMS (Parkway Land Use Plans) were produced, recording every improvement and land use along the right-of-way. Drawn at a scale of one inch equaling one hundred feet, more than six hundred drawings were required to illustrate the entire parkway.

The design and construction of the road illustrates the state of the art in the 1930s. Downer and Clarke made a tour of inspection in 1940 and gave the road high praise: "The location, alignment and gradient of the drive, and the attention to the policy of utilizing the most modern practices give to this great parkway a distinction unequalled by any other project of its character in the world."[14]

The gracefully curving line of the road, built to consistent standards of alignment and grade, provides a design unity throughout the 469 miles of the parkway. This is reinforced by the repeated use of masonry in the structures that support the road and the consistent use of native vegetation on the slopes beside the road. Abbott realized it was essential to balance this unity with a variety of scenery, so as construction proceeded he turned his attention to the management of countryside visible from the road.

LANDSCAPE MANAGEMENT

In 1937 Abbott initiated a program to lease parkway land back to the former owners or to neighboring farmers. He summarized the advantages of this plan: "The wide interest shown by the farmer in this program has demonstrated, in our opinion, its value to the parkway in two important phases; (1) It will maintain the open character of the country where this is desirable without any considerable maintenance cost to the Federal Government and (2) it will build up the friendly feeling of the farmer toward the parkway."[15]

However, much of the land required remedial work before it could be leased back. Large areas of mountain farmland were in poor condition in the 1930s. The parkway crossed some valleys where fertile soils sustained fine crops and cattle, but for much of its length it ran through mountain areas where families struggled to draw a meager subsistence from the steep slopes. A system of shifting cultivation had been widely practiced in the mountains. Farmers cleared the land by girdling trees to "deaden" them. After a number of years, as the soil was depleted and crop yields declined, the worn-out land would be retired to pasture or allowed to revert to forest, and a new area would be cleared. This system worked as long as virgin forest was available to be cleared, and sufficient time could be allowed for exhausted land to recover. But by the early years of the twentieth century, the pressure of population on the land was causing farmers to continue to work exhausted areas. The average size of a farm along the Blue Ridge in Virginia and North Carolina had shrunk from 154 acres in 1880 to 89 acres in 1920. On a few farms steep slopes were terraced and soils retained by stonewalls, but such soil conservation was not common. Thus, within the parkway right-of-way the National Park Service acquired long stretches of badly eroded land. Programs were needed to reforest land that was too steep to cultivate, and to rehabilitate land that could be returned to agriculture.

Forests and woodlands also needed remedial work. Many had suffered years of exploitation by both mountain farmers and commercial logging companies. The Southern Appalachian timber boom in the first two decades of the twentieth century had left few areas untouched. Many areas had been cut over one or more times and left in a condition that made them highly susceptible to burning. The establishment of national forests in the region had called a halt to the most destructive practices within their boundaries, but elsewhere some destructive cutting continued beside the future line of the parkway. In addition to the damage caused by logging, many acres of the mountains had been affected by the chestnut blight, which left large areas of dead trees. Accordingly, a silvicultural program was needed to remove the unsightly evidence of logging and to encourage regeneration.

The landscape development program that had been initiated to heal construction scars beside the road was expanded to undertake this remedial work on agricultural and forested lands. Steep slopes that should never have been cleared were reforested. This was done by planting and seeding, or by allowing natural regeneration in some areas that were to be maintained as wildflower meadows and game-food areas. Areas intended for agriculture were first improved. This involved correcting any drainage and runoff problems and then preparing a seed bed, liming, fertilizing, seeding, and mulching. The condition of streams that ran through the fields was improved by these measures to reduce soil erosion. In addition, some stream banks were regraded, seeded, and planted, and the velocity of certain stretches was reduced by building log or boulder dams.

In 1938, the NPS started "cleaning up" forests and woods. Abbott reported enthusiastically on the effects of remedial cutting:

> This first work in many respects is one of the most spectacular parts of the whole program. Comparisons before and after the work show how much of the natural beauty of the woods and fields have formerly been hidden by the debris, the slash and especially the sucker or stump growth resulting from careless forestry in the past. Beautiful vistas to the distance, glimpses into the woods and specimen laurel, rhododendron and azalea in the backgrounds are often revealed by a slight cutting under judicious supervision.[16]

However, after criticisms of the effects on wildlife habitat, the program was modified. Cutting became more selective, hollow trees and stumps were left, and operations were limited beyond the areas visible from the road.

When land was leased back to neighboring farmers, the agreements were designed to ensure good land management. The terms of the agreements specified such measures as crop rotations, limits on the density of grazing animals, use of cover crops in the fall, liming, fertilizing, reseeding, and fencing. Fences were not constructed between the right-of-way and

Split-rail fences along the Blue Ridge Parkway in Virginia, 1942. Photograph by E. H. Abbuehl. (From the Historic Photograph Collection, Blue Ridge Parkway Archives, Asheville, North Carolina)

adjacent land to avoid the appearance of traveling within a restricted corridor. The logical outcome of this policy was to extend soil and moisture conservation programs beyond parkway boundaries. Several state and federal agencies, including the newly established Soil Conservation Service (SCS), cooperated in this effort, which also required the support of individual farmers. Here Abbott's skill in communicating ideas was a valuable asset. In 1937 he began to distribute the *Blue Ridge Parkway News* to help explain NPS ideas and actions. In 1940 an agronomist, Daniel Levandowsky, was assigned to the parkway by the NPS regional office, and this boosted what Abbott called "missionary work." Reporting on the establishment of a number of soil conservation demonstration farms visible from the parkway, he commented: "It is hoped that this missionary work will over a period of time bring about improved understanding and use of mountain farm lands in a wide region, and it is believed that many Parkway visitors from other states will profit likewise from the demonstration."[17]

The resulting landscapes along the parkway were different from the ragged fields of the early 1930s. In place of eroded gullies there were stands of white pine, and where there had been sheet erosion there were permanent pastures, or strips of corn, hay, and grains arranged along the contours.

Traditional farming practices being continued alongside the parkway. Date and photographer unrecorded. (From the Historic Photograph Collection, Blue Ridge Parkway Archives, Asheville, North Carolina)

At the same time, the NPS made efforts to preserve certain traditional features of highland farms valued for their picturesque qualities. The NPS constructed miles of split-rail fences around pastures, much of the material coming from forest improvement projects. Some farmers were persuaded to continue to grow crops of pumpkins, buckwheat, and linen flax to enrich the scenery close to the parkway.

RECREATION AREAS AND HISTORICAL EXHIBITS

The chief provision for recreation along the parkway was the road itself, which provided a new opportunity for long-distance recreational motoring. The recreation areas planned along the route were intended to complement this experience by providing opportunities for rest, refreshment, and healthy outdoor activities. Perhaps influenced by his experience with the Westchester County parkways, Abbott wanted to include a wide range of activities and structures in these areas. But his superiors restricted recreational developments in the early years to facilities for hiking, camping, and picnicking.

Abbott and his team of designers followed the precepts of "rustic architecture" in designing the various park structures.[18] They designed each structure to fit into the landscape through the use of natural materials, regional building forms, and pioneer construction techniques. Although they were clearly influenced by the rustic structures found in other national parks, Abbott's team sought to develop a vocabulary of forms and materials appropriate to the Southern Appalachians:

> This office feels that on the Blue Ridge Parkway we have made a start toward developing a unique and very fitting architectural style in the public buildings which have been constructed and in the plans which have been projected. It is simply an adaptation of the general forms, lines and materials of the local sheds, barns, and dwellings, which adapt remarkably well to Parkway needs. This office feels that the recall of pioneer building methods in the Parkway structures is one of the principal opportunities that we have to preserve something of the backwoods feeling that otherwise may disappear from the mountains.[19]

The most elaborate building completed in the prewar period was a combined picnic shelter, sandwich shop, and comfort station at Cumberland Knob. Like most of the prewar buildings, it was built by WPA crews.

Cumberland Knob, combined picnic shelter, sandwich shop, and comfort station. Date and photographer unrecorded. (From the Historic Photograph Collection, Blue Ridge Parkway Archives, Asheville, North Carolina)

Rocky Knob, trail lodge cabins under construction by the Civilian Conservation Corps (CCC) in 1941. Photograph by K. C. McCarter. (From the Historic Photograph Collection, Blue Ridge Parkway Archives, Asheville, North Carolina)

It is an L-shaped structure with an enclosed kitchen and sandwich shop at the junction of the two parts. The design features heavy timber construction and stone fireplace walls in the picnic shelter, while using a simple frame structure clad in boards and battens for the comfort station.

The largest group of prewar buildings, the trail lodge cabins at Rocky Knob, were built by CCC enrollees using pioneer building techniques and low-cost materials: walls of squared logs with half-dovetail notches at the corners and V notches at the junction of interior partitions with outside walls. The larger cabins had rubble stone chimneys. All floors were concrete, though there was flagstone on porch floors. Built in 1941, the cabins were intended to be a camp for youth groups, but the idea was never fully realized because of the war.

This study of vernacular architecture led to plans for a series of historical exhibits along the parkway featuring the "simple homestead culture of the mountains," in Abbott's words. A picture of the region as an enclave of pioneer America had long been promulgated and accepted in the rest of the nation. Vivid accounts by "local color" writers had appeared in national magazines such as *Harper's* and the *Atlantic* since the 1870s. To many outsiders, the log cabin symbolized this pioneer way of life. So in 1940, work began on the restoration of three log cabins, the Trail and Puckett cabins in Virginia and the Brinegar cabin in North Carolina, plus the picturesque Mabry Mill in Virginia. As Abbott reported: "Emergency programs have provided a suitable means of undertaking the work as native craftsmen who have built in this manner through a lifetime may be employed under skilled labor allotments and have been found among enrollees. For instance a near neighbor of Mabry Mill who is the last hand known to have operated it was

Mabry Mill during restoration of the wheel in 1942. Photograph by K. C. McCarter. (From the Historic Photograph Collection, Blue Ridge Parkway Archives, Asheville, North Carolina)

employed to repair the mill machinery contrived with such incredible ingenuity as would have defied faithful repair by one less familiar with it."[20]

While authenticity was a concern in the treatment of the structures, the settings were treated like the rest of the parkway landscape and altered to frame picturesque views. At Mabry Mill, for example, a pond was dredged below the waterwheel to create what is probably the most photographed scene along the parkway.

These exhibits were intended to educate passing motorists about mountain customs, and signs were erected that dwelled on the hardiness and resourcefulness of mountaineers. But Abbott also saw the exhibits as a means of preserving something of the old way of life, giving local artisans employment demonstrating traditional handicrafts and manufacturing articles for sale. In addition to promoting handicrafts, Abbott proposed that the parkway should provide an outlet for other products of mountain farms:

> There are several respects in which the Blue Ridge Parkway might innovate a distinctive trade. A large part of the Parkway traverses a cultivated or farmed countryside wherein hillculture methods of agriculture are practiced in an almost unique fashion. Many of the products of these farms and of the hills themselves are saleable. Some of them are considered delicacies and bring large prices in metropolitan areas. They might easily be popularized in Parkway gift shops. Among these items we would include sorghum molasses, sourwood honey and other preserves, mountain blueberries, chinquapins, and various aromatic and medicinal herbs.[21]

SYNTHESIS

The idea that historical exhibits could both record the life of past generations and offer employment to the present one was typical of Abbott's thinking. He had a mind that saw connections between diverse things. He was able to respond to the multifarious challenges posed by the parkway project and make of it an organic whole. Since he was involved in all aspects of the project, he was able to articulate the connections between large-scale planning decisions, such as route selection and land acquisition; design issues, such as development of appropriate forms of rustic architecture and healing construction scars; and management concerns, such as leasing of farmland and provision of outlets for farm products. The Blue Ridge Parkway marks the entry of the NPS, which had hitherto focused on the preservation of spectacular natural scenery, into the field of rural preservation and utilitarian conservation. In 1943, Abbott explained this to a skeptical regional director in the following words:

> Because of the variety of scenes that it has set about to preserve as a first and primary function its conservation policy has necessarily been a many-sided one. Through much of its length, the Parkway goes through a "managed" landscape and I think it has been pretty clear and relatively unquestioned within the Service that the problem was to marry ourselves to the managed landscape. This has required a feeling for the rail fence, the old barn, and the farm field. It has been successful, even practical, due to the arrangements for the nearby farmer to maintain that picture without cost to the Service but under its watchful eye. . . . To a very real extent the parkway is inextricably bound up with its community. I think that this should be looked upon as an opportunity to accomplish by means of the parkway idea a new sort of conservation in which the national parkway becomes a museum of managed American countryside.[22]

In several ways Abbott's thinking reflects the ideals and attitudes of the New Deal, in particular the idealization of America's rural past and a belief that a return to the land was central to the economic and social recovery of the nation from the Great Depression. This return meant providing new opportunities for work and recreation in the countryside, and it also required an end to the abusive land management practices that had undermined the economies of rural communities. The Blue Ridge Parkway began as a road-building project, but it had evolved into a program of rural preservation and conservation intended to set an example to farmers throughout its region and to educate passing motorists. It became part of the Roosevelt administration's national exercise in morale building. In Phoebe Cutler's words: "A cohesive, integrated society was sought in which land patterns would promote a wholesome combination of work, play, and education. In the 1930s Americans still viewed the landscape, along with church and family, as a force in character formation. Recreation enjoyed the moral hegemony that conservation still retains. This idealism imbued the landscape."[23]

POSTWAR DEVELOPMENTS

The construction of the parkway came to a halt in 1942, at which time about two-thirds of the road had been built and five recreation areas established. After the war construction was resumed under different leadership. Abbott had been called into the army and was succeeded as acting superintendent by Samuel P. Weems in 1944. Weems had become associated with the parkway in 1935, when he was sent by the Resettlement Administration to appraise the lands to be acquired for recreation areas. He had stayed on as project manager for the development of these areas. Now as superintendent he worked tirelessly for the completion of the parkway.

Abbott returned to the parkway briefly after the war as resident landscape architect but was soon transferred to other duties. In 1949, he was involved in the survey for the proposed Mississippi River Parkway. As regional landscape architect for Region One, the parks east of the Mississippi, he continued his interest in preservation issues. In 1953, he was appointed superintendent of Colonial National Historical Park in Virginia. There he oversaw the completion of the twenty-three-mile Colonial Parkway begun in 1930. This parkway is a processional link between historic sites in the Tidewater area and is very different in character from the Blue Ridge Parkway. Abbott's main contribution was to ensure completion in time for the observance in 1957 of the 350th anniversary of the settlement of Jamestown.[24]

Along the Blue Ridge Parkway, Abbott's ideas continued to guide developments during Weems's tenure as superintendent. Additional recreational areas and historical exhibits were added, and another agronomist,

William Hooper, continued the work with neighboring farmers. Weems retired in 1966 when the parkway road was virtually completed. But at this time the experiment in integrating rural preservation and conservation was beginning to unravel. Although the historical exhibits were retained and even expanded, the missionary work among the farming population was largely abandoned, and Hooper had been assigned to other duties. In part this was a response to changes in the farming population and in mountain agriculture. Farming was becoming a part-time occupation as pastures for beef cattle replaced the earlier mix of tilled land, hay meadows, and pastures for sheep and dairy cows. But the failure to continue the experiment also reflected a shift of focus within the NPS to the protection of natural areas in the mountains. In settled areas, limiting the impacts of suburban developments alongside the parkway was becoming the main concern.

CONCLUSION

In 1950, an essay by Stanley Abbott appeared in *Landscape Architecture Magazine* entitled "Perpetuation of Scenes Where History Becomes Real." In this article, Abbott discussed the problems associated with "stopping time" at historic places. The more extensive and varied the landscape, the more necessary it is to accept the inevitability of some changes. Nowhere is this truer than in the case of rural vernacular landscapes, which are the type of landscapes closest to Abbott's heart. He concluded by confessing "a certain tenderness for the unimportant things of history" and gives the example of the Caudill Cabin along the Blue Ridge Parkway as a type of landscape embodying American democracy. "Great History? It doesn't matter as long as we keep alive the appreciation, which is an American thing, of the folklore and legend of our provincial countryside, which is an American thing."[25]

The conservation and preservation programs initiated by Abbott along the Blue Ridge Parkway in the 1930s remain relevant today. In the 1980s the NPS rediscovered its rural historic districts and began to search for ways to manage them by retaining rather than displacing their farming populations.[26] A number of interesting experiments have been started, of which the management of the Boxley Valley, in the Buffalo National River unit in Arkansas, is probably the best known. These new experiments should be welcomed, but we should also take advantage of the experience gained along the Blue Ridge Parkway, for it has lessons both cautionary and encouraging for those interested in preserving rural vernacular landscapes.

In the cautionary category, it should be acknowledged that the parkway came to present in its historical exhibits a very selective view of mountain life. Nostalgia for a pioneer period created a picture that focused on isolated subsistence farms and ignored the real social and economic diversity of the mountains. In some cases too much attention was paid to the picturesque and not enough to authenticity. It should also be admitted that the conservation and other programs intended to support the continuance of traditional farm life were quite inadequate to deal with the strong economic and social pressures that transformed the region after World War II. Abbott and his colleagues knew they were dealing with a region in transition, but they could not foresee the scale or nature of the changes. Some of the scenic variety that Abbott loved and hoped to preserve was doomed, and there was probably no way to save it.

At the same time, twenty-first-century readers should take encouragement from what was accomplished and inspiration for the way it was achieved. The Blue Ridge Parkway was an enormously ambitious, multifaceted project that was made possible through a remarkable cooperative effort. Abbott and his colleagues in the NPS recognized a need to build alliances with an extraordinary range of people, including the inhabitants of the landscapes crossed by the parkway. They tried to find a balance between preserving elements of historic scenes and improving the economic base for the society that had created those scenes. These alliances were based not only on recognition of multiple interests but also on a shared idealism. The spirit of the times and Abbott's ability to see and articulate connections between the many facets of the project were responsible for this unity of purpose. In recent years the NPS has returned to this idea of building alliances that reach beyond conventional park boundaries in its support for heritage areas and through a variety of partnership programs. The pace of change affecting society has not slowed; indeed it seems to be accelerating. Such alliances may be the best, and perhaps the only, hope of retaining more than scattered fragments of treasured rural countryside.

NOTES

This essay is based on a Blue Ridge Parkway Historic Resource Study (Draft) in 1992 prepared for the NPS Southeast Regional Office by this author. For that study many of the sources are unpublished government documents located in the collections of the Blue Ridge Parkway in Asheville, NC; the Federal Highway Administration in Sterling, VA; and the National Archives in Washington, DC, and Philadelphia.

1. For biographical information see Nancy Robinson and Ian Firth, "Abbott, Stanley William," in *Pioneers of American Landscape Design,* ed. Charles A. Birnbaum and Robin Karson (New York: McGraw Hill, 2000), 1–3.

2. William Hooper, oral history interview by Richard Westmacott and Nancy Robinson, 1991 (transcript, University of Georgia, School of Environmental Design, Athens, GA), 4.

3. Abbott wrote annual reports to the director of the NPS from 1937 to 1943, and his successor as superintendent, Samuel P. Weems, continued the practice into the 1950s. These reports are the best source for the ideas behind the development of the parkway. Abbott later recalled his role in an interview with S. Herbert Evison in 1958, which is in a collection of oral histories at NPS Harpers Ferry Center, Harpers Ferry, WV.

4. Harley E. Jolley, *The Blue Ridge Parkway* (Knoxville: University of Tennessee Press, 1969).

5. Albert Fein, *Landscape into Cityscape: Frederick Law Olmsted's Plans for a Greater New York City* (Ithaca, NY: Cornell University Press, 1967), 126.

6. For a history of parkways, see Christian Zapatka, "The American Parkways, Origins and Evolution of the Park-Road," *Lotus International* 56 (1987): 97–127.

7. The history of park roads is discussed in Linda Flint McClelland, *Presenting Nature: The Historic Landscape Design of the National Park Service, 1916 to 1942* (Washington, DC: USDI, NPS, Interagency Resources Division, National Register of Historic Places, 1993); and in Ethan Carr, *Wilderness by Design: Landscape Architecture and the National Park Service* (Lincoln: University of Nebraska Press, 1998).

8. S. W. Abbott, "Proposed Locations Shenandoah–Great Smoky Mountains National Parkway," report to chief landscape architect, NPS, June 8, 1934, National Archives, Washington, DC, Record Group 79, box 2736, file no. 601.

9. A blow-by-blow account of this conflict between North Carolina and Tennessee is given in Jolley, *Blue Ridge Parkway.*

10. Edward H. Abbuehl, "History of the Blue Ridge Parkway," paper prepared for a rangers conference, 1948 (Blue Ridge Parkway Archives).

11. S. W. Abbott, oral history interview by Herbert Evison, 1958, tape no. 55 (transcript), NPS, Harpers Ferry Center, WV, 13.

12. S. W. Abbott, "The Blue Ridge Parkway," *Regional Review* 3, no. 1 (NPS Region One, Richmond, VA, 1939): 4.

13. Abbott, oral history interview, 1958, 2.

14. Jay Downer and Gilmore D. Clarke, "Notes on Shenandoah–Blue Ridge–Great Smoky Mountain Parkway," August 27, 1940, Blue Ridge Parkway Archives, 8.

15. S. W. Abbott, "Annual Report of the Blue Ridge Parkway, Roanoke, VA, to the Director, National Park Service," January 8, 1938, Blue Ridge Parkway Archives, 5.

16. S. W. Abbott, "Annual Report of the Blue Ridge Parkway, Roanoke, VA, to the Director, National Park Service," June 30, 1938, Blue Ridge Parkway Archives, 15.

17. Abbott, "Annual Report" June 30, 1940, Blue Ridge Parkway Archives, 10–11.

18. For a discussion of rustic architecture in national parks, see McClelland, *Presenting Nature.*

19. Abbott, "Annual Report," December 3, 1943, Blue Ridge Parkway Archives, 10–11.

20. Abbott, "Annual Report," June 30, 1942, Blue Ridge Parkway Archives, 16.

21. S. W. Abbott, "Memorandum for the Superintendent, Instructions to Park Operators, Blue Ridge Parkway, re: Merchandise Authorized for Sale in Gift Shops," February 20, 1946, National Archives, Philadelphia, 2.

22. S. W. Abbott, "Confidential Memorandum for Regional Director Taylor, Region One," December 3, 1943, Blue Ridge Parkway Archives.

23. Phoebe Cutler, *The Public Landscapes of the New Deal* (New Haven: Yale University Press, 1985), 4.

24. LANDSCAPES, *Cultural Landscape Report for Colonial Parkway, Colonial National Historical Park: Park One, Site History, Existing Conditions and Analysis* (Charlotte, VT: LANDSCAPES, 1997), 210–13.

25. S. W. Abbott, "Historic Preservation, Perpetuation of Scenes Where History Becomes Real," *Landscape Architecture* 40, no. 4, 1950, 153–57.

26. Linda Flint McClelland with J. Timothy Keller, P. Genevieve Keller, and Robert Z. Melnick, *National Register Bulletin 30: Guidelines for Evaluating and Documenting Rural Historic Districts* (Washington, DC: U.S. Department of the Interior, 1990).

Contributors

Phyllis Andersen is Fellow for Cultural Landscape Studies at the Landscape Institute of the Arnold Arboretum of Harvard University where she is also an instructor. She was formerly director of the arboretum's Institute for Cultural Landscape Studies. She has been a consultant on landscape preservation and urban landscape issues for a number of government agencies and has taught at the Boston Architectural Center and in the Yale College Seminar Program. She has published on both urban and historic landscape issues and is currently on the editorial board of *ArchitectureBoston.*

Thomas E. Beaman Jr. is an independent researcher in Wilson, North Carolina. To date his career has focused primarily on investigations of archaeological sites and reexamination of excavated material culture in Virginia and North Carolina. His published research interests continue to focus on the history and development of colonial American landscapes and towns, the history of American historical archaeology, and the material culture of colonial period high-status households.

Charles A. Birnbaum, FASLA, is coordinator of the National Park Service Historic Landscape Initiative in Washington, D.C., and the founder of the Cultural Landscape Foundation. He is the coeditor of *Pioneers of American Landscape Design* (2000) and *Preserving Modern Landscape Architecture I* and

II (1999, 2004). Most recently, he served as the Samuel H. Kress Fellow in Historic Preservation and Conservation at the American Academy in Rome.

Ethan Carr is an assistant professor in the Department of Landscape Architecture and Regional Planning, University of Massachusetts, Amherst. He has previously worked for the National Park Service, the New York City Department of Parks, and private design offices. His book *Wilderness by Design: Landscape Architecture and the National Park Service* received an American Society of Landscape Architects honor award in 1998.

Elizabeth Hope Cushing is a practicing landscape historian who writes and lectures on landscape matters. A former editor of the *Journal of the New England Garden History Society,* she is currently a candidate for the PhD in the American and New England Studies Program at Boston University.

Ian Firth, FASLA, is Professor Emeritus at the University of Georgia, where he taught courses in landscape architecture and historic preservation. For over twenty years, he has conducted research in cultural landscapes for the National Park Service in a wide variety of locations, including the Outer Banks of North Carolina, the Southern Appalachians, and the Red River region in Louisiana. He has recently completed a cultural landscape report on Oakland Plantation in the Cane River Creole National Historical Park in Louisiana, and is currently working on a Historic Resource Study and National Historic Landmark Nomination for the Blue Ridge Parkway.

Catherine Howett, FASLA, is Professor Emerita of the College of Environment and Design of the University of Georgia, where she taught in both the Landscape Architecture and Historic Preservation programs. She has served as a contributing editor of *Landscape Architecture* magazine, a fellow of the Bunting Institute of Harvard University, and a senior fellow in the Studies in Landscape Architecture program of Dumbarton Oaks in Washington, D.C. Her essays have principally addressed critical and theoretical issues in American landscape history, cultural landscape preservation, and contemporary public art.

Mary V. Hughes, FASLA, holds the position of University Landscape Architect for the University of Virginia, where she also serves as a lecturer in the Department of Landscape Architecture. In this position, she has responsibility for long-range planning and design oversight for the landscape of the Charlottesville campus, which contains the UNESCO-designated World Heritage Site of Thomas Jefferson's "Academical Village." With Peter Hatch of Monticello, she is also codirector of the Historic Landscape Institute.

David C. Streatfield is Professor of Landscape Architecture, Urban Design and Planning at the University of Washington in Seattle. He has written extensively on western landscapes and garden history and is the author of *California Gardens: Creating a New Eden* (1994).

Cynthia Zaitzevsky, PhD, teaches the history of landscape design at the Landscape Institute, Arnold Arboretum, Harvard University. She is the author of *Frederick Law Olmsted and the Boston Park System* (1982), *Long Island Landscapes and the Women Who Designed Them* (2004), and numerous cultural landscape reports, including those for the Vanderbilt Mansion at Hyde Park, New York, and the Mount, Edith Wharton Restoration, in Lenox, Massachusetts.

Index

Italicized page numbers refer to illustrations